Eric Louis Kohler
Accounting's Man of Principles

William W. Cooper and Yuji Ijiri
Editors

Reston Publishing Company
A Prentice-Hall Company
Reston, Virginia

Library of Congress Cataloging in Publication Data

Main entry under title:

Eric Louis Kohler, accounting's man of principles.

Includes bibliographies.
1. Accounting—United States—History—Addresses,
essays, lectures. 2. Finance, Public—United
States—Accounting—History—Addresses, essays,
lectures. 3. Kohler, Eric Louis, 1892–1976.
4. Accountants—United States—Biography.
I. Kohler, Eric Louis, 1892–1976. II. Cooper,
William W. III. Ijiri, Yuji.
HF5616.U5E73   657'.092'4 [B]   78-18397
ISBN 0-8359-1773-8

10 9 8 7 6 5 4 3 2 1

Printed in the United States of America

Table of Contents

Photograph courtesy of Mr. Jae Yoo, Chicago, Illinois

ERIC LOUIS KOHLER, 1892-1976

The son of F. Edwin and Kate Evelyn Bently Kohler was born on July 9, 1892, in Owosso, Michigan.

He received a bachelor's degree from The University of Michigan (1914) and a master's degree from Northwestern University (1915). He was with Arthur Andersen & Co. from 1915 to 1917 and from 1919 to 1920. From 1922 to 1933 he was with Kohler, Pettengill & Co. (later E. L. Kohler & Co.); he returned to Arthur Andersen & Co. in 1933 until 1937. During the next few years he served the federal government as controller, Tennessee Valley Authority (1938-41); a member of the staff, Office of Emergency Management and War Production Board (1941-42); and executive officer, Petroleum Administration for War (1942-44). During the period 1945 to 1948 he was an accounting consultant. After serving as controller of the Economic Corporation Administration (1948-49), he resumed his consulting. He was certified as a CPA in 1916 (Illinois).

He was active in professional organizations serving for two years as president (1936; 1946) of the AAA. He was editor of *The Accounting Review* (1928-42), and a member of the Illinois State Board of CPA Examiners (1928-31). He served as chairman of the AICPA's Committee on Terminology. He was also affiliated with the NAA and the Illinois Society of CPAs. In 1945 he received the AICPA's highest honor, its Gold Medal; and in 1958 he was the recipient of the Alpha Kappa Psi Foundation Accounting Award.

A professor in the evening school of Northwestern University (1922-28), he was a visiting professor at The Ohio State University (1955-60), University of Minnesota (1955), University of Chicago (1958), and University of Illinois (1966). He wrote more than 100 articles for professional journals. He also authored a number of books including *Accounting Principles Underlying Federal Income Taxes* (1924), *Principles of Auditing* with Paul W. Pettengill (1924), *Principles of Accounting* with Paul L. Morrison (1926), *Accounting for Business Executives* (1927), *Advanced Accounting Problems* and *Solutions to Advanced Accounting Problems* (1939), *Auditing, An Introduction to the Work of the Public Accountant* (1947), *A Dictionary for Accountants* (1952), *Accounting in the Federal Government* with Howard W. Wright (1956), and *Accounting for Management* (1965). His dictionary, a notable achievement, was published in its fifth edition in 1975. He was national president of Beta Alpha Psi (1924-27); he was also a member of Beta Gamma Sigma.

His public service included financial advisor, U.S. Secretary of Agriculture (1946); consultant, U.S. General Accounting Office; and membership on the Advisory Panel, U.S. Comptroller General; and the Excess-Profits Tax Council, U.S. Treasury (1946-47). He served as a member of the U.S. Chamber of Commerce Advisory Panel an Organization of Congress. He was a member of the Board of Trustees (1947-68) and a member of the Advisory Council of the College of Business Administration (1957-71) of Roosevelt University.

He was a life-long bachelor. In his leisure time he enjoyed music, photography, and electronics. He died February 20, 1976.

Reproduced with permission from "The Accounting Hall of Fame" by T. J. Burns and E. N. Coffman, 1976.

"We might add that in his early years, Kohler had studied music composition at advanced levels with Adolph Weidig, a renowned teacher at the Chicago Conservatory of Music, in preparation for a career as a composer and critic. Kohler's interest in music continued throughout his lifetime and it was with considerable satisfaction that he was able to bring his knowledge of accounting to the service of music and the other performing arts as Controller and Adviser to the Auditorium Theater Council of Chicago from 1960 until his death in 1976.

Part I

A Preface and a Memorial

Chapter 1

Eric Louis Kohler—Accounting's Man of Principles*

William W. Cooper and Yuji Ijiri

Introduction

The title of this memorial volume to Eric Louis Kohler was selected after due consideration of a variety of alternatives. The reference to him as "accounting's man of principles" is intended in the two significant senses of the latter term: (1) as a leader in the development of an articulated set of basic accounting principles, and (2) as a highly principled accountant. We shall try to elaborate on both these ideas in a way that will serve to memorialize Eric Kohler. In the process we shall also try to provide a preface to one or more aspects of each of the chapters included in this volume.

First we turn to accounting principles. There is no question of Kohler's role as *a* leader in the development of the document, "A Tentative Statement of Accounting Principles Underlying Corporate Financial Statements," which was issued in 1936 by the Executive Committee of the newly organized American Accounting Association.[1] Hereafter referred to as the "Tentative Statement," this document represented a remarkable achievement. Even now it seems ahead of what has since been accomplished in

---

*The authors gratefully acknowledge the criticism and contributions of Stephen A. Zeff, as well as his willingness to allow us to quote extensively from his notes and writings. Acknowledgment is also due Olivia Reyes for felicitously typing this Preface and other materials in the book it introduces.

[1] This is the title subsequently chosen for the reprints (which were widely distributed), although the original article published in *The Accounting Review* of June 1936 bore the somewhat different title, "A Tentative Statement of Accounting Principles Affecting Corporate Reports."

the form of a comprehensive, yet simple, statement of principles.

The essential point to grasp in understanding the genius of the "Tentative Statement" is that, on the one hand, it was a compact but comprehensive statement of very basic principles, while, on the other hand, it recognized and allowed for the variety and complexity of situations that need to be reflected in financial statements covering the gamut of private enterprise activities. Thus, even while insisting on one cohesive statement of principles, the "Tentative Statement" also allowed for deviations.[2] These deviations were to be specifically noted, however, and *by reference to these same principles* each such deviation was to require separate justification. Presumably, if the exceptions were sufficiently numerous they would become the basis for one or more new principles as well as the revision or abandonment of old ones. Thus, a basis for continued but systematic growth was thereby also to be provided.

This, it will be noted, is quite different from the "common law" approach to establishing accounting principles, which was espoused by George O. May, among others (see Zeff, 1966, pp. 49ff.). Here the term "common law" is better regarded as an issue-oriented sequence of developments rather than as an exact analogue of its legal "case law" counterpart. Reed K. Storey (1966, p. 51) refers to this as the "piecemeal approach," which he contrasts with the American Accounting Association's "conceptual approach." That is, the motivating idea in George O. May's approach was to deal with specific issues and then to formulate statements of principle, basic or not, along with permissible alternatives which were intended to cover all possible situations where these issues might be encountered.[3] Exigencies and pressures, as perceived from the standpoint of practicing professional CPAs, were to provide needed guidance not only for the initial formulations but also for continuing growth and elaborations. In sufficient time, perhaps aided by subsequent codification (Grady, 1965, p. xii), this strategy might result in a comprehensive statement in varying levels of detail such as had been suggested in the prior (and continuing) deliberations.

One may surmise that the "Tentative Statement" issued by American Accounting Association's Executive Committee, together with its successors, did have considerable impact, but one is also bound to note that the "common law" approach is the one that was really followed by the public accounting profession—first in CAP (Committee on Accounting Procedure), then in APB (Accounting Principles Board), and, more recently, FASB (the Financial Accounting Standards Board).

We must sooner or later encounter the second aspect of Eric Kohler as "ac-

---

[2] Although present in the "Tentative Statement," this received clearer expression in subsequent versions as follows: "Any deviation [from basic accounting standards] should be carefully weighed and, if made, disclosed both qualitatively and quantitatively in the financial statements." Compare the recapitulation of earlier statements on pages 1 and 2 of the 1948 revision issued by the Executive Committee of the American Accounting Association under the title "Accounting Concepts and Standards Underlying Corporate Financial Reports."

[3] In other words, something more akin to statutory law has evolved (whether intended or not) without the remedies that equity allows in legal practice.

counting's man of principles," and we might here note it in his early participation in the development of accounting principles. Prior to the issuance of the "Tentative Statement," he had authored a series of editorials[4] in *The Accounting Review* which called for such a formulation of principles. The most notable of these, entitled "A Nervous Profession" (Kohler, 1934), seemed to many persons to be overly strong in its assertions and criticisms of the public accounting profession. In any event, this editorial attracted strong reactions, mainly private and unpublished, only to encounter an unyielding Eric Kohler. His devotion to such an articulated set of principles, one may say, was a bedrock principle of Kohler himself. On such matters of bedrock principle he would not yield, and one may safely say that he would be dissatisfied even today with the state of progress of the accounting profession or even the way it is addressing the issue of principle development.

The matter is well put in the following quotation from Leonard Spacek. Subsequently Managing Partner and Chairman of Arthur Anderson & Co., and, with Kohler, on its staff around 1935, when the matters discussed above were coming to a head, Mr. Spacek writes:

> Since I took over the firm of Arthur Anderson & Co. on January 1947, some 12 years after the above events, I missed being able to put the support behind Kohler that he needed. The whole accounting profession for two generations has followed the course that Kohler had criticized and only now (1977) when public indignation turns toward the profession is it

willing to take some of the positive steps forward that he (among others) had advocated.[5]

Developing Accounting Principles

The history of the differences in approach to the formulation of accounting principles discussed above has been told many times. Some of the best minds in American accounting appeared on both sides, and some were also leaders with a strength of conviction, not only adequate for themselves but also sufficient to influence and sustain others.

The 1935 reorganization of the American Association of University Instructors in Accounting into the American Accounting Association with Eric Kohler as its first president (see Zeff, 1966, pp. 38ff.) provided an opportunity for a major advance. High among its statement of purposes was the following objective:

> To develop accounting principles and standards, and to seek their endorsement or adoption by business enterprises, public and private accountants, and governmental bodies (p. 40).

The crystallization of this purpose was an undertaking to which the newly formed Executive Committee immediately addressed itself. As already noted, that Committee sought a single unified statement rather than a series of separate pronouncements. This did not mean that agreement came easily on this matter, which, after all, was supposed to form the very core of CPA practice and

---

[4]We are presently assembling these editorials and a few other selected writings of Eric Kohler, which we hope to publish in a sequel to the present memorial volume.

[5]Quoted with permission from a letter by Leonard Spacek to the editors dated October 2, 1977.

evaluation. Exchanges and correspondence between the editors and Howard C. Greer (as a leader in these developments) produced the following as an example of what was involved:

After half a dozen sessions of lively debate and repartee Greer was appointed secretary to the group and asked to put all the major points together in publishable form. He remembers his submittal of his first toilsomely developed draft for initial criticism by Eric Kohler and Bill Paton, and their replies.

"Great job, Howard," they declaimed in unison. "I doubted that anyone could so ably summarize our collective views, but you have done so most effectively. I have only a few very minor suggestions, which I have noted on your draft, returned herewith."

Referring, much flattered, to the draft, says Greer, he found (in both cases) that the few "minor suggestions" involved proposed changes in almost every sentence in the entire document: "In all my years as a teacher," he assures us, "I never marked up a Master's thesis as my collaborators had amended mine. Their disagreements were not on what we ought to say, but on how we ought to say it. I happily incorporated their verbiage into the statement, as far as possible, doubltless to its improvement, but I wondered afterward whether I could honestly claim to have had much of a part in its authorship. I still think I could write pretty good, but they thought they could do it better, and I'll have to concede them the laurels.[6]

The fact that such a singular document emerged from these deliberations must be partly attributed to the times, as well as to the talents of its authors.

Some idea of these times and the forces that bore on them, including the newly formed Securities and Exchange Commission, may be found in two chapters herein, one by Carman G. Blough and one by Andrew Barr. Actually, these chapters provide a good deal more than historical background. They provide insight and perspective that can be obtained only from major contributors to the events they describe. The article by Blough provides a rare and needed insight into accounting as it was practiced during the 1920s and then into other developments that Blough himself participated in during his years of service as the first Chief Accountant of the SEC and the first Director of Research of the American Institute of [Certified Public] Accountants.

Barr follows this with a scholarly review of the way in which interactions between the SEC and the accounting profession influenced the development of accounting principles. Reflected in this chapter is the same adherence to historical cost that marks the "Tentative Statement." Although the SEC continued to rely on historical cost during Barr's tenure as its Chief Accountant, it did recognize the need for supplementary information on current costs when, as Barr notes, the latter departs markedly from its historical-cost counterpart.

Ever vigorous in his attempts to develop accounting principles, Kohler was also careful to avoid pushing this activity to possibly absurd limits. As a case in point, we may consider his position on the development of standards for cost accounting. Witness, for instance, his discussion of joint costs (Kohler, 1975):

Dividing and averaging [a total of] joint costs is always arbitrary, because the level of costs of one product depends in a variety of ways on the level of production of the joint commodity, so that averages tend to lose mean-

---

[6]Quoted with permission from a letter by Howard C. Greer to the editors dated January 28, 1977.

ing, except where direct, additional or independent costs for each commodity are involved (p. 278).

See also his discussions of "impute" and "imputed cost" (Kohler, 1975, p. 248). Failing a "solution" of these problems, no comprehensive body of standards is possible as a matter of accounting logic only.

Of course, imputations may be effected by reference to increments of total costs when increments in some of the products may be obtained separately.[7] This does not mean that such allocations of total costs should not be made. It only means that they should be made in response to policy needs, either public or private, rather than proceeding as though some underlying accounting logic justifies these policies—instead of vice versa.

The chapter by Herbert F. Taggart in Part II provides abundant examples of the pitfalls involved. This is accompanied by sage counsel and the insights Taggart gained from his own experience with almost all of the conceivable ways in which costs might be related to public regulatory policies. This includes, for instance, his experience as chief of the Cost Accounting Unit of the National Recovery Administration, where the emphasis was on the use of costs to put a *floor* under prices, as a way of ameliorating the effects of economic depression in the 1930s. It also includes the opposite experience of using costs to put a *ceiling* on prices, to help control inflationary pressures while Taggart was Director of Accounting for the Office of

Price Administration during World War II. Finally, it includes a variety of other uses of cost and costing principles in areas directed to enhancing or ameliorating the effects of competition which Professor Taggart encountered during the years he served as Chairman of the Federal Trade Commission's Advisory Committee on Cost Justification.

Of course, a great deal of reflection as well as other experiences and scholarly research have gone into the writing of the chapters mentioned above. The point we wish to make here, however, is that these persons all had direct experience with the subjects they are addressing. A reference to their vitae, which we have included at the back of the volume, will indicate that these authors have, in fact, been distinguished contributors in their own right to many of the issues and events which they describe and discuss.

The same is also true for the authors in Part III, "The Fruits of Practice," where, again, the chapters are written by distinguished contributors to the topics they address. Before proceeding to that section, however, we might close the present one by calling on Stephen Zeff, the accounting historian, who has probably conducted more extensive research than anyone else in the history of the development of accounting principles. After reading and commenting on an earlier version of this preface, Zeff provided the following succinct summary, which we reproduce here with his permission:

In the mid-1930s, Kohler and a number of other progressive accounting thinkers believed

---

[7]Moreover, alternatives to product costing may be devised, as we shall see when we come to a discussion of "activity accounting" as installed under Kohler's direction at the Tennessee Valley Authority.

that the American Institute of Accountants (as it was then known) was delinquent in not leading a movement to define and elaborate a body of accounting principles. The organization of practitioners had been content to outline a half-dozen fairly broad notions and leave the rest for each practitioner to resolve in his own circumstances. Kohler and others spearheaded a movement within the American Association of University Instructors in Accounting to re-organize the group and clothe it with authority to conduct accounting research and take a leadership role in articulating the corpus of accounting principles. Thus was born the American Accounting Association in January 1936.

Kohler, as the Association's first President, was joined on the executive committee by such respected academicians as William A. Paton, A. C. Littleton, Howard C. Greer, and Russell A. Stevenson. They immediately set about the drafting of a cohesive statement of accounting principles, hoping to launch an intellectual debate among accountants and to goad the AIA into taking constructive action. All the while, Kohler, as editor of *The Accounting Review,* the quarterly journal of the Association, was pricking the thin skins of the Institute with biting editorials. Nor was the proud Institute particularly pleased to see the "teachers organization" become an accounting body of general interest and high ambition, for it was in 1936 that the very Institute had finally concluded negotiations culminating in the absorption of the American Society of Certified Public Accountants, its major competitor on the practicing level. Thus, Kohler, as editor of the *Review* and leader of the upstart AAA, was not a favorite of the Institute leadership. It is perhaps not surprising, therefore, that the Association's "Tentative Statement" was greeted coldly by the Institute. It eventually required the forceful intervention of the SEC to persuade the Institute to involve itself in the setting of accounting principles. But the Insti-

tute's course was deliberately inductive, practitioners not placing an abundance of trust in the process of deductive logic. The Association, led by Kohler, preferred the deductive route.[8]

Even Kohler's monumental *A Dictionary for Accountants* had its origins in this struggle for a statement of principles. Starting as a member of a committee chaired by Arthur Andersen, which had its report on the definition of "earned surplus" rejected by the American Institute of Accountants,[9] Kohler then proceeded to work in the committee on terminology chaired by Robert H. Montgomery from 1931 to 1935. Next he became chairman of the latter committee, from 1935 to 1937, during which time he pushed vigorously ahead. Soliciting definitions and reviews of proposed definitions from the academic world as well as practitioners, the committee under Kohler's chairmanship, was able to develop some 1000 definitions of accounting terms in tentative form as embodied in a report which it submitted to the Council of the AIA in 1936.

Not only did the Council reject the report, it also abolished the committee. Partly on the advice of Montgomery, Kohler then decided "to go it alone" (Nolan, 1972). He thereafter continued to work, sometimes intermittently, on his dictionary, gradually altering its scope until it became a "A Dictionary for Accountants" rather than "A Dictionary of Accounting Terminology."

---

[8]See Zeff (1966, pp. 47–52) for a discussion of Kohler's continuing leadership through the 1941 and 1948 AAA Statements and his own formulation, and 1937 presentation of "Some Tentative Propositions Underlying Consolidated Reports" (Kohler, 1938, pp. 63–73).

[9]Zeff reports to us that the life of the committee on earned surplus was 1924 to 1930, with Kohler serving as a member from 1929 to 1930. We are indebted to Zeff for the information on these dates as well as the ones reported above.

Its publication in 1952 represented a plateau, we would say, which was a pinnacle for one stage of the intellectual developments in accounting and a platform for further takeoffs in the subsequent growth of accounting research as well as practice. In the first aspect, this plateau incorporated a wealth of experience and thought as reflected in the practices of accountants and the teachings of accounting instructors up through the 1940s. By incorporating developments from statistics, economics, mathematics, logic, and computer sciences in a wholly novel way, this plateau served as a staging area for the intellectual growth of accounting (and auditing) theory and practice in the future.

We shall return to the latter in order to examine the future, or at least possible futures, in later portions of this preface. This will be done after we cover in the next section some of the results of Kohler's professional practice activities. Here, however, we should conclude with the remark that Kohler intended his dictionary to be a contribution to the development of accounting principles in both its original and subsequent conceptions. Indeed, Kohler's *A Dictionary for Accountants* speaks to this issue in clear and vigorous terms on almost every page of its text. This has been true in every edition from the original 1952 version up to and including the present (fifth) edition published in 1975. Hopefully this will continue to be true in any future revisions that Prentice-Hall, Inc., the publishers, may agree to for this imposing contribution by Eric Kohler to the intellectual development of accounting (and auditing) theory, practice, and pedagogy.

The TVA, the Marshall Plan, and the GAO

In the preceding sections we have emphasized Kohler's contribution with special reference to the formulation of accounting principles. In parts of the period covered by these activities Kohler was in active practice as a CPA, and in other parts of this period he served as an adviser to various CPA firms. One may believe that his contributions in both capacities were substantial. But, as is common in practice, these contributions are hard to document.

We therefore turn to areas of practice where Kohler's contributions are much easier to identify.[10] This will include his activities as Comptroller of, respectively, the Tennessee Valley Authority and the Marshall Plan. It will also include his relations with the U.S. General Accounting Office, starting with an initial confrontation and continuing through subsequent collaborations.

In each of the above we are again fortunate to have chapters contributed to this memorial volume by persons who were distinguished participants in the events they describe. Thus, the opening chapter in this section is provided by Jerry F. Stone, who served as Assistant Comptroller of the Tennessee Valley

---

[10]We leave aside Kohler's contributions as a teacher and a textbook writer since these are discussed in the chapter by Mautz and Previts. We also say little about Kohler's scholarly writings in various journals and books, since we prefer to discuss these in the context of a second volume, which will contain Kohler's editorials and other writings.

Authority during Kohler's tenure there as Comptroller.

It happens that Stone (working with Kohler) had agreed to prepare a report on "activity accounting" and its relations (or at least some of them) to "responsibility accounting" under a grant from the Arthur Andersen Foundation. It thus became relatively easy to persuade him to undertake the additional effort needed to write the chapter that we have included in this volume. The result comes as close as possible to a report on the times and conditions under which these highly original contributions were developed. In addition, we have an account of extant GAO practices "from the other side," so to speak (i.e., from the side of an auditee) since Jerry Stone was also involved in TVA's dealings with the GAO. Finally, we also have a vivid discussion of Kohler's point of view in "organization costing," as distinguished from product costing, recounted by his immediate collaborator in developing this approach, and we also have Stone's testimony as a direct participant in forming the policy standpoint from which the common cost allocations of TVA were effected.[11]

The depth and continued value of these contributions is perhaps best stated in the following quotation from Willard R. Stinson, the present Comptroller of the TVA, who writes:

Dear Mr. Stone:
Thank you for the opportunity to read the manuscript about Mr. Kohler's years at TVA.

I commend you for the manner in which the mood of the era was described as Mr. Kohler came into the TVA scene.

My comments can be expressed first as appreciation to read from a first-hand source about the implementation of TVA's accounting system and second as confirmation that the basic framework developed by Mr. Kohler is still in place and meeting the tests of time. . . .
Sincerely

WILLARD R. STINSON
Comptroller[12]

Turning from the TVA to the Marshall Plan, we have a report from Samuel Nakasian, who served as chief of the Price Analysis Branch in the Controller's Office of the Economic Cooperation Administration.[13] Thus, again, we have an account from a direct participant in the events described, and, indeed, a little "reading between the lines" should make it clear that Nakasian himself played a very significant role in these developments. This reading will also provide insight into the ways in which "backup from the top" [*viz.*, from Paul Hoffman as ECA (i.e., Marshall Plan) Administrator] entered into the "direction" in which decisions were made.

"One way of influencing Kohler," as Nakasian observes, "was to suggest that your moral position was superior to his." Another, and better, way to phrase this is to say that Kohler was always ready to consider whether the moral values of a pending decision had been completely thought through and evaluated.

In a program with objectives like those of the Marshall Plan, this was an

---

[11] See our discussion of Kohler's position on such matters as joint and common costs, and how they might be allocated to different products, in the preceding section.

[12] Quoted with permission from a letter to Jerry F. Stone dated November 11, 1977.

[13] This is the title of the agency responsible for administering the Economic Recovery Act—popularly known as the Marshall Plan. See the Appendix to Nakasian's chapter.

extremely important consideration. Some idea of what was involved can perhaps be appreciated by reference to the magnitude of the accomplishments and the unblemished record of the Marshall Plan administration in contrast with its immediate predecessors: the United Nations Relief and Rehabilitation Administration and the Greek-Turkish aid program. The latter programs had succumbed to the advice of various "country experts" who were prone to consider only what was workable, for example, in each particular country or culture with, in general, only glancing attention to underlying moral issues. In UNRRA and the Greek-Turkish aid program, as Nakasian observes, this resulted in widespread corrupting influences and a record of inadequate accomplishments.

An injection of moral considerations was, of course, not in itself enough to produce what was needed. Also required was Kohler's wide knowledge of business practice and the habits of thought of businesspeople plus an imaginative perception of how they could be made to respond to the challenges (moral and otherwise) of the times.

Tenacious in his adherence to principled approaches, Kohler was always willing to reconsider both his approaches and his principles, but he would never consider whether other than a principled approach was possible. Versed in the practices of management, he was wont to observe that it was necessary to distinguish between the "practical" (i.e., what is practiced) and the "practicable" (i.e., what is capable of being put into practice). It was to the latter that he liked to turn his considerable talents and energies in any case where an underlying issue of principle was involved.

In the chapter following this preface, Mautz and Previts recount a story about one of Kohler's experiences as a high-level official in yet another federal agency. We set this out in more detail as follows.

Three very powerful U.S. senators requested an allocation of funds from this agency for a study which they believed was justified by its pertinence to the agency's mission, even though it had not been specifically allowed for in the budget. Kohler's required approval for this diversion of funds was not forthcoming, and so the matter was finally "bucked up" to a cabinet officer to whom the agency reported. Arguments such as "this kind of thing is done all the time" being of no avail, the cabinet officer finally *ordered* the requested diversion. Kohler promptly resigned.

The agency head, an experienced high-level executive, followed Kohler back into his office to try to persuade him to withdraw his resignation. Finally, according to Kohler, this man said "Look, Eric, you've been around. You're experienced enough to know that you have to get along with other people." "No, you don't," replied Kohler. "You have to get along with yourself." The agency head stopped. He looked Kohler squarely in the eye for a few moments. Then, as though for the first time appreciating the basic difference in principle that divided them, he dropped his voice and said to Kohler, "OK. I accept your resignation," and left the room. This, at rock bottom, was Kohler in action as well as in thought.

The high ethical and intellectual demands involved in "living with himself" made it necessary for Kohler to assess the world and its possibilities in the same terms. Note, however, that these possibilities included his assessment of how the world might be made to respond to imaginative use of the considerable intellectual and technical capabilities that Kohler possessed. He would have felt it immoral to short-change the latter almost as much as to abandon the former.

This is to say that Kohler's extraordinary capacity for sustained hard work, as remarked upon by several of our authors, also stemmed from his moral convictions. It also colored his attitude toward those who were not sufficiently diligent and demanding of themselves, and it carried over into the advice which Kohler freely gave, often at considerable cost to himself, whenever he sensed an opportunity to advance or improve the practice of accounting along lines that he considered desirable.

The chapter by Cooper and Frese documents some of this in the vivid experiences in which the latter participated during the "Turnaround at the GAO," but, of course, this is only one phase of the remarkable developments which have occurred at that agency. In fact, the three chapters dealing with the GAO constitute an unusually valuable account of what was involved in these developments—not only in the federal government but also in accounting and auditing generally[14]—by persons who, in one way or another, were involved in the events they describe.

The extent of this turnaround may be gauged from the GAO practices described by Jerry Stone, as well as by Kohler's testimony before the Joint House–Senate Committee to Investigate

the TVA, which Joseph Pois cites in his chapter. As documented by Pois, the formation of a Corporation Audits Division within the GAO was crucial for the subsequent reorientation of all its practices away from their previous legalistic emphasis. The organization of this division within the GAO, again as Pois observes, also provided an opportunity for recruiting the kind of professional accounting staff which could supply the competence that would subsequently move the GAO to a position of worldwide eminence and innovative leadership. Thus, it is worth recording that Kohler played a role in persuading M. T. Werner, whom he had known at Arthur Andersen & Co., to leave his position with the Controller's Division at Ford Motor Company in order to spearhead these recruitment efforts for the GAO's newly formed Corporation Audits Division.

The chapter by Cooper and Frese deals with what was involved in effecting GAO's turnaround. It also supplies both documentation and commentary that would be unavailable or difficult to come by for anyone but a direct participant like Frese. This includes a commentary on the role of Lindsey Warren in bringing this turnaround into existence with illumination—such as that supplied in the chapter by Nakasian—on the interactions between an agency head and his staff in establishing new directions. In this case, however, a still better appreciation may be obtained by recalling that Lindsay Warren had been the chief congressional defender of the

---

[14] Including influencing developments in other parts of the world. See, for example, Appendix II in the report by the Independent Review Committee (1975).

old GAO against the Brownlow committee's reorganization plan—sponsored by President Franklin D. Roosevelt. That is, a turnaround in Lindsay Warren's own thinking was also involved.

We add here one additional detail. It appears that books and writings (and even research) can make a difference—as the following story recounted by Kohler himself makes clear. *The Comptroller General,* a book written by Harvey Mansfield (who had been a member of the Brownlow committee's staff), had only just appeared when the following incident occurred. Boarding a streetcar in Washington, D.C., one day, Kohler was surprised to see Lindsay Warren riding in it. He quickly made his way over to Warren and, after introducing himself, he proceeded to engage the newly appointed Comptroller General in conversation about his job as the head of U.S. General Accounting Office. Learning that Warren was not aware of Mansfield's recently released book, Kohler briefed him on it and promised to send Warren a copy.

Kohler reports that within a few days of sending Warren the book, he received a long-distance call in his Chicago office from the Comptroller General. Warren reported that he was very excited about some of the perspectives opened to him by this book and asked Kohler to come to Washington to discuss it with him. Whether the events described by Cooper and Frese would have occurred otherwise will never be known. We like to believe, however, that Mansfield's book was influential. In any event, Kohler reported that he went immediately to Washington and found Lindsay Warren—the man who had just been instrumental in defeating this part of Franklin D.

Roosevelt's reorganization plan—now well informed on the book and eager to discuss it with an open mind.

Although the accomplishments effected under Warren were substantial in their effects on both the magnitude and direction of GAO activities, no account would be complete without acknowledgment of the even more substantial progress that was made after the turnaround that Warren effected. As Karney Brasfield notes, major credit for this progress must be accorded to Elmer Staats, the present Comptroller General, and to Ellsworth Morse, a CPA who came in via the Corporation Audits Division and became Director of the Accounting and Auditing Policy Staff and finally Assistant Comptroller General of the United States while helping to direct this evolution. This evolution (some would call it a revolution) has now proceeded so far that Brasfield finds it worthwhile to examine whether the CPA profession can or should follow in GAO's footsteps. With the issues and attendant problems and difficulties laid bare, Brasfield suggests that a beginning might be made in the form of audits of municipal and local governments by CPA firms.

Jumping over to the concluding chapter by Churchill and Cooper, we may observe (with Brasfield) that leadership in bringing such possibilities into focus has been supplied by staff from the management services divisions in various CPA firms. Kohler, we think, would be restless in his desire to see further development in these directions but he would also be concerned as to the implications for the future of accounting/auditing relations that this new source of leadership might suggest.

The Present and the Future

The Present

The preceding sections have dealt with Eric Kohler in some of his activities and relations with the past. The chapters in those sections were contributed by others who, like Kohler, were major participants in the accounting developments they describe. Now we turn to the present and the future with, necessarily, a different orientation.

The contributors in the sections that follow are also persons who have had some contact with Eric Kohler in one way or another. Being of a different generation, however, these contacts were necessarily more limited, and so is their participation in the developments—many of them yet to come—that are addressed in the chapters that follow. On the other hand, the authors of these chapters have already achieved recognition and are also likely to continue in the forefront as contributors to the topics we shall be examining.

In addition to criteria of quality and relevance, there was a further element of selection in the contributors to this volume. As we have already indicated, Eric Kohler was a broad-gauged leader in accounting who did not hold his basic positions lightly. Hence, in a memorial volume such as this one, it seemed fitting to avoid including material that would have encountered his strong disagreement. This, in turn, made it necessary to turn to other devices in order to reflect, at least to some extent, Kohler's breadth and depth of interest in all phases of accounting.

The main problems in proceeding along these lines were encountered in dealing with the present. This is not wholly surprising. The accounting profession's attention to different issues has varied in response to outside problems and pressures in the past, and so one first needs to position oneself along this spectrum of possibilities for the present. For instance, in his 1964 publication, Reed Storey (1964) observed that

> if the number of books and articles in the literature can be taken as an index ... concern with the formulation and statement of accounting principles has followed a cyclical pattern. ... The peaks have not been of equal height nor have the troughs been of equal depth. In each case, however, the stimulus for increased interest is apparent, and the two declines of interest came because accountants turned their attention to more pressing matters of the time (p. 3).

Particularly appropriate to the present situation are Storey's (1964) remarks about the Korean War and its immediate aftermath:

> The discussions about formulating accounting principles into a generally accepted code stopped abruptly. ... Although the Korean conflict may have been a factor in the decline of interest ... accountants became concerned with a particular reporting problem, namely, accounting under conditions of changing price levels. They turned their attention almost entirely in that direction. The new trough in concern with accounting principles was neither as long nor as deep as the one during the war [i.e., World War II]. A small number of articles on accounting principles appeared during the height of the price-level debate, and attention returned to accounting principles within three or four years (p. 7).

The situation is very much like the present, including the beginning of a return to interest in an articulated statement of accounting principles with attendant attention by various members of the U.S. Congress and extending into standards for product costing by means of the rules and regulations of new agencies such as the Cost Accounting Standards Board. One difference, however, needs to be allowed for in any such comparison. This is the difference in magnitude of almost everything encountered in the post-Vietnam world. That world, which is capable of providing phenomena such as "stagflation," is also capable of heightening almost everything simultaneously—relative to past levels of activity. Thus, we should not be surprised if we encounter *simultaneously* a heightened interest in accounting principles and a heightened interest in issues of accounting valuation. Nevertheless, as a matter of balance, it is fair to say that interest in valuation issues has far outweighed interest in basic accounting principles, at least up to the present.

Doubtless, the cycle will turn again. To draw upon (and contribute to) the present literature, however, it is necessary to direct major attention to the issue of valuation in financial-statement presentation. This is done in "Financial-Statement Principles That Are Useful for Security Analysis" by Myron Gordon, an outstanding contributor to the fields of corporation finance and accounting. Gordon compares and evaluates historical-cost-based financial statements against a variety of alternatives, such as general price-level adjusted cost (GPLAC), statements, and replacement costs (= current costs). Gordon concludes that historical cost is preferred to replacement cost for noninflationary environments but that in inflationary environments these preferences are reversed, with, in general, GPLAC occupying an inferior position in any case. Moreover:

The conclusion . . . is that when there has been considerable inflation and the inflation is expected to continue in the future, there is some advantage in using replacement cost as the basis of income determination and asset valuation. This advantage is eliminated or at least substantially reduced, however, if historical cost statements present as supplementary information the replacement cost of the depreciation charge and net plant account and the amount of inventory profit in earnings.

This permits a final (footnoted) comment in which Gordon positions himself in fairly close alignment with at least some aspects of statements we noted in the chapter by Barr:

Therefore, the United States Securities and Exchange Commission should be commended for requiring the supplementary reporting of replacement cost inventories and plant assets [in its] SEC Amendment to Regulation S-X adopted March 24, 1976.

The Future

Not readily apparent in the present ferment of accounting, perhaps, there is no gainsaying Kohler's impact on the past. The record of these past contributions to accounting also establishes their continuing relevance for the future. This, in any event, is where the remaining chapters are centered.

The issue of accounting and accountability relations was central to Kohler's approach, whether he was dealing with GAAP (generally accepted accounting principles) or whether he was actively pursuing one of the many applications in his accounting career. Hence, we begin with the topic of accounting and accountability relations in the opening chapter of Part V.

We naturally think that Kohler would have approved of this opening selection on "Accounting and Accountability Relations" by Cooper and Ijiri, although, of course, he might have differed with its authors in particular details or depth of perception and discussion. Where he clearly would have differed, of course, is in the language of mathematical modeling which is used to delineate and develop the details in this chapter. Training in that language or in the related languages and concepts of electronic computers formed no part of Kohler's formal education. Indeed, it could not have formed any part of his training, since many of these developments had not been invented at that time. Nevertheless, computer–mathematical modeling languages will probably become more and more common, so we feel justified in their use to clarify pertinent issues within a relatively short span.

Kohler's lack of training in such disciplines as mathematics and computer science may have prevented him from working actively on his own with these tools. It did not prevent him from understanding them or using others skilled in these tools to help him address issues that were of concern to him. As a case in point, we note his collaboration with the logician David Rosenblatt to help him formulate the first attempt at a formal axiomatization of accounting (see Kohler, 1952, pp. 43–44).[15]

The fact that these contributions by Kohler will continue to exercise their influence into the future is amply evidenced in Yuji Ijiri's chapter, "A Structure of Multisector Accounting and Its Applications to National Accounting." Here only three simple axioms (control, quantity, and ‘exchange) are shown to provide a basis not only for national income and corporate accounting but also for their multisector and consolidating counterparts. Furthermore, these axioms suffice for multidimensional–multimetric extensions, which we think will become increasingly important for the roles that accounting can and should play in the future.

The entity concept that Kohler took as a primitive in his axiomatic formulation of 1952 continues to be fundamental. Indeed, it continues in this status even while Ijiri finds it necessary in this 1977 contribution to alter the mathematical–logical concept of a "set" so that the latter is no longer necessarily identified entirely by its elements. The same is not true for Kohler's assumption that all transactions must be reduced to a monetary equivalent for treatment by double-entry accounting.[16] Indeed, as Ijiri shows, a great deal more can be achieved for national-income (multisector) accounting if this assumption is abandoned or, rather, reserved only for special uses. In short, one should be able to execute the necessary entries in order to relate different dimensions to each other in an orderly and systematic way without first requiring the activities in these dimensions to be reduced to a common metric. *A fortiori* this is likely to be a prime requisite for the kinds of national goals accounting systems that

---

[15] See also the discussion of these axioms in the chapter by Churchill and Cooper.

[16] Kohler appears to have confused the accounting identity (where this assumption is required) with the more basic concept of double entry (where this assumption is not required; see, for example, Charnes and Cooper, 1967, pp. 24–52).

are now being studied by various organizations (see Terleckyj, 1975).

In the final chapter of this book, N. C. Churchill and W. W. Cooper turn to an exploration of auditing in its past, present, and future relations with accounting. Here, again, the theme of multidimensional accounting is explored with special reference to corporate (and governmental) social reporting in expanded scope (comprehensive) audits.

How Eric Kohler might view all of this can only be conjectured. One thing that can be said for certain, however, is that he embraced and, in fact, vigorously espoused the idea of audited budgetary disclosures for private corporations. He arrived at this position late in his career, and we have no writing by Kohler on this topic. We therefore rely on conversations with him about some of our own writings (Cooper, Dopuch, and Keller, 1968; and Ijiri, 1968) to indicate some of the possibilities for budgetary disclosure. For some indication of the strength of his convictions on this topic, we might also record that Kohler had begun to press for such disclosures, with accompanying audits, in companies with which he was associated.

The income-statement and balance-sheet projections described by Cooper, Dopuch, and Keller (1968) appear to be what Kohler had in mind. He was more diffident about the projected funds flow statement that these authors suggested. This may have been the result of his belief that the possible uses for such a statement could be better served in other ways (Kohler, 1965, Chap. 14). It may also have been due to other reasons, including a preference for a projected cash-flow analysis, or it may have been due to some pertinence he perceived that this might have for other issues, such as valuation for economic or accounting purposes.

Supposing that the latter was the case, however, one can see how most of the valuation issues can be accommodated without departing from historical cost. Thus, suppose that half of a *projected* 10 percent increase of sales might be attributable to a price rise as calculated, say, from some suitable price index. Note, however, that this index need not be a reflection of the "general purchasing power of money." It would be directed rather to the indicated budgetary projections. Subsequent audits could then evaluate the worth of these index numbers and their associated values by what actually occurred—in the usual historical-cost accounting sense.

Similar remarks would apply to projected purchases. Fixed assets and other kinds of major acquisitions would naturally enter into the projections at current values—exit values would be the applicable concept for sales of such assets and entrance values for acquisitions. On the other hand, *only* those assets projected for sale or acquisition would enter into such valuations. This would avoid the clutter and cost of undertaking current-value studies for assets where no (budgeted) plans for disposition *or* acquisiton were apparent.

The audits of such transactions should, over time, be able to build up experience—including experience in the need and timing of interim audits and disclosure as when, say, changes in plans and/or budgets made this desirable. Accompanied by cash-flow projections, almost all of what is being addressed in the present medley of valuation issues could then be reasonably accommodated on a more selective basis, with historical cost continuing to supply the needed basis for accountability and control as reflected, ultimately, in actually observable transactions.

One additional point should, however, be noted in association with such budgetary audits. The need for explaining discrepancies between actual and budgeted performance would almost irresistibly move in the direction of auditing the president's letter and other parts of the entire corporate report. That is, even the attest audit would be moved in this direction, instead of being confined, as at present, only to the financial-statement components of the total corporate report. From the standpoint of the Churchill–Cooper chapter with which this book concludes, however, this would only be another path toward the expanded-scope (comprehensive) audits and accounting systems which they examine for the possible future evolution of auditing and accounting.

We have already indicated that some of the immediately preceding remarks are based on inference and conjecture. We can also add that we think that Kohler might also have embraced an extension of these ideas to audited accountability statements involving social as well as economic dimensions, as discussed by Churchill and Cooper and/or Cooper and Ijiri. Witness, for example, the following quotation (Nolan, 1972):

Annual corporate reports are ceasing to be only accountings to stockholders; they are beginning to be proud showings of corporate responsibility to the public and are thus well within the range of the public interest. Reports could be rated in some form other than sequentially; criticisms could point to needed improvements in reporting practices. Thereafter managements rejecting well-founded criticisms in developing future reports would do so at their peril. Already the primary function of the reported annual balance sheet, supported by subordinate statements, can best be regarded as a management discipline consonant with the public interest and only secondarily as a reflection of financial condition (p. 22).

Of course, this all supposes that issues of practicability as well as idealism can be resolved. It is unfortunate that we no longer have Kohler's prodigious talents to bring to bear on endeavors like these.

Professional Biography and Recognition

Finally, we come to the problem of portraying Eric Kohler himself. This is done in a perceptive and tasteful manner in the following chapter by Robert Mautz and Gary Previts. Here we might add that this chapter, "Eric Kohler: An Accounting Original," is reproduced with permission from *The Accounting Review,* where it was published in April 1977. One of only three such which we understand to have been authorized—for the American Accounting Association's "Big Three" (Kohler, Littleton, and Paton)—this article provides a sensitive portrayal of the man in his career as an accountant. As such, its reproduction here provides a fitting way to begin this memorial volume.

References

Charnes, A., and W. W. Cooper. 1967. "Some Network Characterizations for Mathematical Programming and Accounting Approaches to Planning and Control." *The Accounting Review,* 42(1), January.

Cooper, W. W., N. Dopuch, and T. Keller. 1968. "Budgetary Disclosure and Other Suggestions for Improving Accounting Reports." *The Accounting Review,* 43(4), October.

Grady, Paul. 1965. *Inventory of Generally Accepted Accounting Principles for Business Enterprises* (Accounting Research Study No. 7). New York: The American Institute of Certified Public Accountants, Inc.

Independent Review Committee. 1975. "Government Auditing in Other Countries." Appendix II in *Report of the Independent Review Committee on the Office of the Auditor General of Canada.* Ottawa.

Ijiri, Y. 1968. "On Budgeting Principles and Budget-Auditing Standards." *The Accounting Review,* 43(4), October.

Kohler, Eric L. 1934. "A Nervous Profession." *The Accounting Review,* 9(4), December.

——. 1938. "Some Tentative Propositions Underlying Consolidated Reports." *The Accounting Review,* 13(1), March.

——. 1965. *Accounting for Executives.* Englewood Cliffs, N.J.: Prentice-Hall, Inc.

——. 1952. *A Dictionary for Accountants.* Englewood Cliffs, N.J.: Prentice-Hall, Inc.

——. 1975. *A Dictionary for Accountants,* 5th ed. Englewood Cliffs, N.J.: Prentice-Hall, Inc.

Nolan, James. 1972. "It's More Than a Dictionary." *The Journal of Accountancy,* May.

Storey, Reed K. 1964. *The Search for Accounting Principles.* New York: The American Institute of Certified Public Accountants, Inc.

Terleckyj, Nestor. 1975. *Improvements in the Quality of Life, Estimates of Possibilities in the United States, 1974-1983.* Washington, D.C.: National Planning Association.

Zeff, Stephen A. 1966. *The American Accounting Association: Its First 50 Years.* New York: The American Accounting Association.

Chapter 2

Eric Kohler: An Accounting Original*

Robert K. Mautz and Gary John Previts

ABSTRACT: A historian's riddle asks, "Do great men make history or does history make great men?" Of course, the riddle is a taunt that defies resolution, and so it should seem to be, but for the fact that men such as Eric Kohler make it diffcult to believe anything but the premise that "Great men do make history." Kohler's influence over the teaching and practice of accounting covered a half century until his death in February 1976. He was the only person to serve two terms as President of the AAA and was editor of The Accounting Review *for fifteen years. His pioneering efforts in the areas of accounting research, principles development and public sector accounting are near legend. The fifth edition of* A Dictionary for Accountants *(1975) affords us a legacy for contemporary contemplation just as his personal achievements and integrity provide us all with a model worthy of emulation.*

Overview

"History is the essence of innumerable biographies. . . ." If the development of a profession is largely the reflection of the important personalities who contributed to the process, we will do well to reflect on the man who is the subject of this brief paper.

Eric Kohler represented the best in accounting strength, independence, integrity, service, and dedication and in its constant search for precision in concept and improvement in practice. Few in-

*First published in the Accounting Review, 52(2), April 1977.

deed worked actively in accounting for so long; fewer still contributed so widely as a scholar and as a practitioner, in public practice, in government service, and in education.

Eric was a very private person. Some of those who knew him best confess they did not know him well. A bachelor, he gave full attention to accounting. His impressive presence discouraged many from initiating a casual conversation, but those who summoned their courage to do so found beyond his craggy exterior a kind and friendly person eager to discuss accounting.

Many current readers of *The Accounting Review* will not even recognize his name; more the pity, because they would understand accounting better if they had known Eric Kohler both as a leader in the profession and as a person. Those who seek out examples of his writing will be the richer for it.

In 1916 when Eric Kohler joined the ranks of the young accounting profession, CPAs were few in number and CPA laws had not yet been enacted in many states. Accounting education at the university level was in its infancy; textbooks were new; and competent full-time instructors were few. The industrialization of America had just begun to provide opportunities for accounting and accountants. Entrants to the profession were faced with challenges to assist in providing accounting education, establishing professional standards, and providing society with reliable financial information that would facilitate the allocation of its resources on an informed basis.

Eric Kohler spent his life and his remarkable energies responding to these challenges. For more than half a century, from 1916 to 1976 (when he died at age 84), Eric Louis Kohler, a native of Owosso, Michigan, contributed to the advancement of accounting in unique and invaluable ways. The impact of his presence and ideas is unmistakable in many major events of this period. Not content merely to theorize, as a government official and a consultant to business he worked to apply and gain acceptance for the theories he espoused. Literally until the day he died, he continued to revise his monumental Dictionary, more for the love of the work than for any other reason.

The Early Years

Born in Michigan in 1892, Kohler went to high school in Ann Arbor. His respected high school principal, Durand W. Springer, had pioneered accounting instruction at the University of Michigan as early as 1901 and was among those with whom Kohler retained a life-long association. Just as Springer's personality and views had a strong influence on the young Kohler, so the mature Kohler was to encourage, stimulate, and influence a number of later accounting leaders.

Kohler graduated from the University of Michigan in 1914 with an A.B. in Economics and in the following year completed a Master's degree in economics at Northwestern. At Northwestern he met Arthur Andersen, the founder of the international firm of accountants that bears his name. Andersen, as a member of the faculty, and Kohler, as a student, became friends. It was in part due to Andersen's urging that Kohler joined the Northwestern faculty, where he taught from 1922 to 1928.

In the period between completing his studies at Northwestern and joining the faculty, Kohler first established an accounting practice in his own name, then worked with the Andersen firm in Chicago and finally spent 2 years as an officer in the Quartermaster Corps during World War I. He maintained an active contact with the practice of accounting even while he was teaching at Northwestern and writing his early textbooks. After he left Arthur Andersen's firm in 1920, he again practiced as a professional accountant in his own name, only to rejoin Andersen for another brief period from 1933 to 1937.

The Academic Years

In 1916 the organization which is now the American Accounting Association was formed. Kohler took an early and active interest in this group, which in those days numbered only a few hundred members who were scattered at points separated by lengthy days of railroad travel.

Perhaps because of an innate sense of precision, or as a reflection of his Teutonic heritage, Kohler took particular interest in terminology and the use of words and sought clearer definitions for accounting terms. No doubt this early work ultimately led him to attempt to create a dictionary for accountants.

Kohler's early books dealt with a variety of subjects, including income taxes (1924), auditing (1924), and principles (1926). He branched out to make his ideas available to business executives in a special volume prepared in 1927.

For the next several years he had little time for textbook writing because he was called to serve as editor of *The Accounting Review,* which he accepted as a major responsibility. In those days, the editor expressed his personal views in editorials, so from 1928 to 1942, with Kohler as editor, *The Accounting Review* became a clear voice for the Association and often chided the practicing profession for its perceived faults and failings.

The following selection gives some of the flavor of Eric's comments:

> For years [the Editor] has assailed the smugness of the profession and its inability to set standards for its own conduct and for the information of the public that relies upon its findings. . . . For years it has failed to see the problem before it: problems for the complexity of which it alone has been responsible. . . . To instructors in accounting, this condition of affairs should offer a challenge. Now, more than ever, the voice of enlightened opinion within the profession is needed. Shall we as accountants recognize that the responsibilities of the profession are large, particularly to third persons? Or shall we drift as we have done in the past, waiting, at first hopefully and now fearfully, for someone else to tell us what to do? Is it impossible for us to take any initial responsibility for defining our accountability to the business and financial world and to the investing public? (Kohler, 1934, p. 334).

The challenge which Kohler leveled in this 1934 editorial was one for which he himself was preparing a response. In 1936, as President of the American Accounting Association, he was the guiding force in the development of a statement of accounting principles, the first such pronouncement issued in this country.[1] This brief 4½-page document

---

[1] Two authoritative pronouncements on auditing procedure had been issued (in 1917 and 1929) by professional associations that were AICPA predecessors.

appeared in the June 1936 issue of *The Accounting Review* under the title "A Tentative Statement of Accounting Principles Affecting Corporate Reports" and was widely distributed in booklet form.

One must try to picture conditions of that day to appreciate the audacity of the undertaking. A small group of academics, strictly on their own authority, moved to state standards which they believed the organized, practicing profession should observe. Publication was in itself a criticism of corporate reporting. By doing so these leaders established a pattern for important American Accounting Association efforts over the next three decades. If any item in accounting literature deserves the designation of "a classic," the 1936 "Tentative Statement" assuredly does. It contains three notable propositions which underlie the theory and practice of accounting to this day:

1. Accounting is essentially a process of cost allocation rather than one of valuation.
2. The all-inclusive concept of income should be applied in financial reporting.
3. A clear distinction should be maintained between paid-in capital and accumulated earnings (Zeff, 1966, p. 45).

After his 1936 term as President, Kohler remained active in the Association and continued to influence the scope of accounting education, remaining as editor of *The Accounting Review* until 1942 and serving a second term as President of the Association in 1946, the only person ever to have done so. Later he returned to campus as a guest professor at Minnesota in 1955, at Chicago in 1958 and at Illinois in 1966. He also spent much time teaching at Ohio State during the 1955 –1960 period. In 1961, he was honored as an inductee into the Ohio State Accounting Hall of Fame.

The Years of Public Service

In public service, Kohler combined his interest in practical application of his ideas with his desire to influence others through the written word. In 1956, he coauthored *Accounting in the Federal Government*. This book displayed the intimate knowledge of government operation which he had acquired and the systematic approaches which he had been instrumental in developing and installing in the various governmental agencies he had served since his term as controller of the newly formed, massive federal utility complex, the Tennessee Valley Authority (TVA) from 1938 to 1941. The establishment of a functioning activity accounting system for the TVA was an accomplishment which exemplifies Kohler's impact in the area of governmental accounting. As one of the originators of this kind of accounting control, he demonstrated the usefulness of the system and paved the way for its acceptance in other agencies and applications.

During World War II, Kohler served as executive officer of the Petroleum Administration for War and also was a member of the Office of Emergency Management and the War Production Board. After the war years, he spent a brief period in his own consulting practice and then accepted an assignment as controller of the Economic Cooperation Administration (ECA), also known as the Marshall Plan, from 1948 to 1949. In the following years, he continued his government service as an advisor to the General Accounting Office (GAO) and other governmental agencies.

The Years in Practice

Even after the many years in association with Arthur Andersen, it seems clear that Eric Kohler so treasured his personal independence that he was more comfortable practicing on his own as a consulting CPA. His individuality and preference for personal freedom of action were not to be surrendered. These traits were also apparent in his relationships with others in practice with regard to matters of professional concern. Over the years of his active involvement in professional associations there were many stormy, though not necessarily hostile, encounters between Kohler and representatives of the American Institute of Accountants. Kohler expected the highest standards in professional practice, not only at the level of personal performance but also for the organized profession in leading the way to adequate corporate financial reporting.

Kohler's impressive height (6'4") and serious demeanor added to the impact of his presence at professional meetings. He was a master in the use of the English language and held fast to his positions during debates in the profession. An idealist, he pressed home his point persistently, displaying a tenacity of opinion which was firm, but not unpleasant, in light of his gentlemanly fashion. With Kohler there was no compromise. This characteristic caused one noted member of the professional circle to quip: "You know Eric; he may be 'wrong' but he is never in doubt."

He was especially critical of loose terms such as "good accounting," "true income," and "best practice," which he contended could convey no clear meaning, being little more than emotional expressions. At one time he urged that adjectives be eliminated from our technical literature, as they are more confusing than helpful.

He constantly was sought after for advice by professors, professionals, businessmen, and bureaucrats alike. In his many years of activity, he traveled extensively in the United States and overseas. He was not the easiest person to satisfy and displayed at times a marked impatience for inefficiency whether in regard to accounting matters or in the handling of his hotel reservations when he attended a conference.

As a critic of the profession and certain of its leaders, Kohler was often at odds with others. The role of critic can be a lonely one. Yet if he was not much loved, he clearly was respected in the manner that strong opponents in point of view respect one another. In recognition of his service to the profession, the American Institute awarded Kohler the Institute's Gold Medal in 1945, the highest honor which it bestows. Combining this with his election to the Accounting Hall of Fame gives him a recognition achieved by only a select few outstanding leaders.

A Man of Principle

For Eric Kohler, part of the appeal of accounting was its identification with high principles—with honesty, integrity, forthrightness, with truth. No one knew better than he that accounting data can be used to confuse, to obfuscate and to mislead. He recognized the handicap unavoidably faced by the layman investor in reading and understanding accounting data, and the advantage this provided an unscrupulous businessman. His sharpest criticism was directed at those who, in whatever capacity, fell short of protecting financial statement readers from those who were content with presentations that did not meet his high standards of objectivity and disclosure.

But Eric Kohler did not reserve his concern for principles to the actions of others. He held himself to standards at least as high as he expected of others and refused to accept assignments in which his principles would be compromised. On one occasion he felt constrained to resign an important post because he could not in good conscience promote a program he felt was not appropriate in the specific circumstances. The decision was a difficult one, requiring him to disagree on a matter of principle with a superior whom he respected and considered a friend. In trying to dissuade Eric from what he considered unduly drastic action, the friend said something like: "But, Eric, you have to be able to live with these people." To which Eric responded: "No. You have to live with yourself." The conviction in his voice was such that further consideration of his resignation was unnecessary.

To Eric, accounting was a matter of truth—of facts about transactions and their effects. The principles for which he stood permitted no bias, no manipulation, no shading of any kind in reporting truth. In a very real way, accounting principles, for Eric Kohler, were inseparable from the principles of integrity that govern every good man's life.

An Advocate of Historical Cost

Kohler early took a firm position in favor of historical cost valuation as evidenced in this consolidated view which he stated in the 1950s to epitomize positions taken in the AAA Executive Committee statements of 1936, 1941, and 1948.

> The fundamental basis of asset-and-expense valuation is price: the amount of money or objectively established money's worth paid in an exchange between independent parties. Arm's length price is the only objective basis of value; being the consequence of actual transactions it is comprehensible to and serves the interests of management, investor and consumer.
>
> Further it is an operable medium for the application of a wide variety of internal and external controls and for portraying the degree of responsibility attained in the discharge of management accountability (Backer, 1955, Chap. 7).

But to Kohler, objectivity and understandability were not mere conveniences for the accountant, they had broad social implications as well. Writing on the development of accounting principles at a later date and addressing the issues involved in controversies about valuation concepts, he argued that historical cost valuation met important social responsibilities.

> Whatever may be the future of accounting concepts of valuation, it is hoped that accountants will have the courage and conscience to make sure that any new tenets they may profess are subordinated to a fundamental structure of responsibility not only to their clients but to the public at large (Backer, 1955, Chap. 7).

This commitment to historical cost continued throughout his career. During the 1950s and again in the 1960s, Kohler wrote on the subject of historical cost basis accounting. A major paper in 1953, "The Development of Accounting Principles by Accounting Societies," summarized and surveyed the issue. That paper should rank among the classic pieces of recapitulative theoretical literature. We commend it to those who find conventional accounting bare of support, lacking in usefulness, and indifferent to the public interest.

As the profession began to reassess its commitment to historical cost in light of both post-World War II inflation and the overhaul of its theoretical structures proposed by Moonitz and Sprouse, Kohler served as the spokesman for the traditional position. For the June 1963 issue of the *Journal of Accountancy* he wrote "Why Not Retain Historical Cost?" in an attempt to objectively debate the merits of current value accounting and Research Studies 1 and 3. It seemed clear that he did not oppose change per se, but in questioning the supporting positions of those who opposed the accepted method, he found a lack of historical and social perspective. He also asserted that the findings of Studies 1 and 3 should be labeled "proposals" and should not be identified by any term which indicated that such notions had achieved general acceptance.

His "Dictionary"—A Personal Expression

For many people, receipt of the Institute gold medal and election to the Accounting Hall of Fame would have signaled a fitting conclusion to a respected career. Yet in one sense, Kohler had only begun to make his mark on the current generation of the profession, for it was not until 1950 that *A Dictionary for Accountants* appeared, the popular and successful reference work which he originated. The Dictionary represented another "first." It responded to a critical

need of the expanding profession—an authoritative source for terminological reference, where concepts could be identified and interrelated within an unspecified, but nevertheless perceivable, logical mold.

An ambitious project for one man, his Dictionary stands as a major contribution to accounting literature but also is an extension of Eric Kohler's personality and interests. Inevitably, his continuing interest in words and their frequent failure for precise communication and his unquenchable urge for improvement would have had to lead him to just such an undertaking.

To many, the Dictionary is more than a word reference source; it is an exposition of the theory and practice of accounting. Kohler intended it to be so. In private conversations he explained that it was a way to express his considered views, to expose and oppose ideas, and to reveal inconsistencies and emphasize similarities. In his last years it constituted his major activity, an intellectual labor of love.

The Dictionary has grown and changed with the times and, now, in its fifth edition, is among the essential elements of the working accountant's library. It was Kohler himself who stressed the theoretical content of his dictionary and also pointed out that it was a Dictionary *for Accountants* not a Dictionary *of Accounting*.

A Career in Summary

How does one capture the spirit of so active and dedicated a professional as Eric L. Kohler? The answer is clear—no summary can do full justice to such a career.

Who else has served two terms as

president of the AAA; edited *The Accounting Review* for 15 years; filled distinguished positions in academia, government service, and the profession; contributed richly to the accounting literature; contested vigorously for his views against all comers; and received the major honors of his profession?

Above all, Eric Kohler was a great and good man, an intense and intelligent human being, and a towering influence among his peers. A life-long bachelor, his first interest was accounting and the people who made up its world. To some he seemed detached and aloof—but these are the few who did not know him well enough to benefit from his patient attention or to have had the benefit of his counsel. A generous man, he shared his experience in the early years of curriculum development, encouraging young faculty at new schools across the nation and providing needed textbooks which blended theory and practical application. As a member of the Executive Committee of the American Accounting Association for many years, he exerted a profound influence over the course selected by that organization during those years when the role of academics and their research responsibilities were first formulated. He supported the right of academic criticism of practice and the need for research long before these were either well established or popular.

As a theoretician, he was instrumental in establishing an historical-cost-based conceptual model for accounting when that represented a degree of discipline not universally welcome, and he provided a continuing stream of books and articles to support this view. His role in installing activity-responsibility account-

ing in government agencies alone represents a major contribution. The fifth edition of *A Dictionary for Accountants* (1975) continues to stimulate the perceptive student as well as to aid the practitioner in answering those day-to-day questions which are common in the accounting profession.

In any biographical undertaking it becomes apparent that great individuals must have influenced others, and to some extent may have aided in their success. Also great individuals, in the pursuit and defense of their ideals, must come in conflict with others who in good faith do not share the same outlook. So it was with Eric Kohler. We have not mentioned his differences in the 1930s and 1940s with George O. May, or his heated exchanged with Howard Ross in the 1960s in the pages of the *Journal of Accountancy* on the matter of current values. Nor have we mentioned the countless classmates, students, professors, and practitioners who shared his years and experienced the benefit of his advice and friendship. His close relationships with these associates evidenced his vital interest in people, their problems and aspirations.

We think all of these, friend and foe alike, will agree that in those years when accounting was establishing itself as a respected and respectable profession there were giants in the land—and such was Eric Kohler.

Many will note his absence at future gatherings but they will not forget him. Each of us in turn can benefit if from this brief tribute we do no more than recognize, and in our own way emulate, his high accomplishment, personal integrity, and dedication to the advancement of accounting.

References

Backer, Morton, ed. 1955. *Handbook of Modern Accounting Theory*. Englewood Cliffs, N.J.: Prentice-Hall, Inc. Quoting from Eric L. Kohler, "The Development of Accounting Principles by Accounting Societies," *Accounting Research*, 4 (1953).

Kohler, Eric L. "A Nervous Profession," Editorial, *The Accounting Review*, 9(4) December 1934.

Zeff, Stephen A. 1966. *The American Accounting Association: Its First 50 Years*. The American Accounting Association.

Part II

The Past

Chapter 3

Early Development of Accounting Standards and Principles

Carman G. Blough

The Dawn

Up to the beginning of the twentieth century, bookkeeping had evolved very slowly and not too far from the days of Pacioli. Public accounting as we know it today was practically nonexistent.

Professional public accounting began in England in the latter part of the nineteenth century. A number of the early American firms were branches or offshoots of English firms. Price Waterhouse & Co.; Peat, Marwick, Mitchell & Co.; and Touche Ross and Co. are three firms well known today whose names reveal their early relationships with English firms. Others with similar relationships have lost their identity through mergers with other firms.

Even through the first three decades of this century, professional public accounting made rather slow progress.

Much of its work was more or less detailed checking for the satisfaction of management, with little attention to the interests of creditors and investors.

However, in that same period, the rapid industrialization of the country and the mergers and consolidations that took place caused large increases in the size of companies, which in turn caused procedures to be materially improved and systems work increasingly important.

During that time, an increasing number of banks and creditors asked for financial statements in questionable situations. More, but still relatively few, wanted them to be "certified" by independent accountants. Even in such cases, the information included was very condensed and the companies were quite careful to see that very few people other than those in top management got to see them.

While teaching corporation finance at the University of Wisconsin, the writer made an effort in 1921 to secure, from some thirty companies which did issue published reports, some rudimentary data, such as depreciation taken, the sales and cost of sales, and the amount of nonoperating income. However, these requests brought very little information. Time dims the memory of the number of replies and the nature of the data. Something in the neighborhood of 40 percent did not answer at all. About another 40 percent replied that the information was confidential and could not be disclosed. The rest gave part of the information asked for, but none gave all of it. Yet the information requested was all such as we now see in every published report. At that time even the information required by the stock exchange was very limited and, if the stockholders received any statements at all, they too were very brief.

Up until 1913, when the income tax law came into effect, the accounting policies of many companies changed from year to year as the management wished. For example, depreciation might be taken or not as suited management. Some companies provided none while others provided none in poor years, then wrote off large amounts when profits were high. Purchases of large pieces of equipment were often expensed. Some companies, which built their own machinery with their regular factory employees, did not capitalize any labor or overhead. Raw materials and parts acquired from other companies were sometimes capitalized and sometimes expensed. Even in the early days of the income tax, when the rates were low and the Bureau of Internal Revenue (now the Internal Revenue Service) was

feeling its way, little change in accounting practices took place.

However, when the surtaxes were added to help pay for World War I, the field audit staff was enlarged and instructions were issued that resulted in a substantial increase in the Bureau's efforts to bring about consistency from year to year in the amounts of deductions taken by the individual company. Depreciation that had been or should have been taken in prior years, or excessive depreciation taken in the years under review, as well as expensed items that should have been capitalized, became prime targets for disallowance by the field auditors.

In judging the motivations of management behind some of the accounting practices we now consider to be reprehensible, it must be remembered that the more conservative a balance sheet was, the better it was. Bankers and creditors paid little attention to the company's income or its prospects for generating income. They relied on what may be called "the pounce theory": that is, what does the company have that we can pounce upon to protect ourselves if the obligation is not paid? Accordingly, the business that submitted a balance sheet reflecting only rock-bottom values in assets and all possible liabilities was the type of customer they considered to be the safest to deal with.

This, together with the human tendency to play one's cards close to one's chest, probably had the most influence in bringing about and continuing the very sketchy types of statements available to corporate stockholders up to the passage of the Securities Act of 1933 and the Securities and Exchange Act of 1934.

Such statements usually consisted of a very condensed balance sheet and sometimes an income statement. Typically the income statement, if any, started with gross income, from which was subtracted selling, general, and administrative expenses in one figure, to get net income before taxes, then subtracted income taxes with the final figure, net income after taxes. Usually, the only other information was a statement of surplus, and sometimes it was missing. Often the information regarding both the income and surplus accounts was shown short on the balance sheet, beginning with the amount of surplus at the beginning of the year, to which was added the net income for the year, after which dividends were subtracted, and the balance was carried out into the liability column.

Fixed assets were often written up to values determined by the Board of Directors, and the appraised surplus was carried directly to a surplus account, which contained earned surplus, appraisal surplus, paid-in surplus, donated surplus, and any other kind of surplus that existed. Dividends were paid out of this common surplus account regardless of its source. It was also common practice to charge depreciation on appreciation directly to the surplus account so that income never bore any of the burden of a write-up. In this way many companies boosted their asset values and their "net worth" but did not suffer any reduction in net income as a result of the restatement. In this way companies were able to give the appearance of prosperity simply by action of the boards on their own accounts.

Furthermore, nobody knew what accounting practices were being followed by more than a relatively few companies. Public accountants and Internal Revenue agents were, of course, the best in-

formed, but even they were knowledgeable with respect to a very limited number of companies. Since neither of them was at liberty to disclose to one company what any others were doing, the forces for uniformity were virtually nonexistent.

Some practicing accountants and a few teachers undertook to write books, but they simply took what they considered the best of what they had learned in practice and combined it with what they thought should be done and what they had seen in others' writings. Some of these authors, whether due to lack of knowledge or intent to improve, often presented procedures they considered ideal and which in fact did not reflect then-current practice. Not surprisingly, these often became models of reform in later years.

The Market Debacle

The event that probably had more to do with the improvement in accounting practices than anything else was the stock market debacle of 1929. Prior to 1920, the ownership of businesses was largely limited to people of substantial wealth. The shares of stock on the principle exchanges were usually kept at values substantially beyond the reach of any but relatively well-to-do persons.

The government's drive during World War I to sell Liberty Bonds in small denominations to the general public was the first significant effort to enlist the savings of small investors to help finance any project. After the war, when these obligations were paid off, businessmen realized that the savings of these people were a possible source of capital for them.

Accordingly, corporate shares were split into values small enough for these small investors to buy. Corporate bonds, instead of being issued primarily in denominations of $10,000, $50,000, and $100,000, were put out in amounts, in some cases, as low as $100. Active efforts were made to sell these securities to the general public, which in turn developed widespread interest in the securities markets, particularly the stock markets.

It is hard to believe the extent to which speculation took place in the late 1920s. The surest tips were given and acted on by all kinds of people, many of whom should have known better. Elevator operators, barbers, cleaning women, mailmen, secretaries, and garage mechanics were typical of the people who had bought stock on a 10% margin (then the going rate) and could tell you what was a good buy that day. But the fever was also caught by brokers, bankers, lawyers, doctors, accountants, business executives, and government employees. You name a category—they had it. Securities were bought only in anticipation of a rise in price. Income was unimportant.

In such a situation it was inevitable, when the general overinflated economy began to sag and the wisest large investors began to sell, that the prices of stock began to fall. When brokers requested more margin to cover the fall, most of these speculative investors could not furnish it and were sold out. Hopefully, the brokers tried to sell before their own 90 percent was touched. But these sales further depressed the market so that more and more people were wiped out and the whole house of cards collapsed. Only the few gained who saw what was coming and added to the debacle by selling short. Everyone else lost.

The major economic depression of the early 1930s followed. Altogether, a great many tragedies resulted. Many with meager savings, as well as many with substantial wealth, lost all they had. People and businesses went bankrupt. One read daily of suicides by those whose losses left them so hopeless they could see no other way out.

What did this tragedy have to do with accounting? The answer seems to be quite logical. It is only human nature for a person who suffers a severe loss to look for someone besides himself who could be blamed for what happened. So it was with a great many people who lost so heavily in the stock market. What better alibi could an investor have for making a bad investment decision than that his information about the company's financial affairs was insufficient or outright misleading?

This speculation fever had become so great by 1928 and the early part of 1929 that it is very questionable whether any amount of information about the financial condition of a corporation (perhaps other than that it was bankrupt) would have affected the way the general public would have bought and sold its stock. Nevertheless, many turned to the inadequacy of the financial data of the issuing companies as a scapegoat on which to blame their losses and to vent their angers and frustrations.

Newspapers and magazines carried criticisms of the financial reporting and those responsible for it. Politicians took up the cry with promises that, if elected, they would take steps to prevent a repetition of the things that had brought about such losses. Corporate managements were the principal targets, but the public accountants did not escape.

Actually, many leading accountants had recognized the need for improvements but had been relatively helpless to make any significant changes. Managements held the upper hand and dictated their own accounting policies. Furthermore, the accounting profession was far from the cohesive and unified group that it is today.

The Institutions

Two organizations, the American Institute of Accountants and the American Society of Certified Public Accountants, divided the profession. Almost equal in membership, with some people belonging to both, they were not too inclined to cooperate. Indeed, there was a considerable amount of belligerent ill-will by some members of each group toward the other. The AIA based membership on the passage of its own examination, whether the applicant was a CPA or not, while the ASCPA required only that the applicant be a CPA. Nevertheless, both organizations felt the sting of the public criticism and their leaders gave considerable thought to the steps that might be taken to improve accounting practices. Interestingly, most of the leaders were members of both groups.

Being the older and more prestigious of the two, the American Institute naturally took the lead. One of its first steps was to enter into a cooperative effort with the Controller's Institute (now the Financial Executives Institute) and the New York Stock Exchange designed to improve financial reporting. Representatives of these three organizations engaged in a series of discussions and exchanges of letters by which they reached a number of important recommendations.

Among other things they agreed on five principles of accounting, which forbade some of the worst common practices previously followed. For example, they forbade such then-current practices as including unrealized income in the income account and using capital surplus of any kind to relieve the income account of present or future years of charges that properly belong to income. It is interesting to note that all five still continue to be recognized as sound and universally accepted principles. They also agreed upon a model of an audit opinion report to be used by the independent auditor.

The significant letters in this correspondence, including the resulting conclusions, were published by the American Institute in 1934 under the title *Audits of Corporate Accounts.* The recommended auditor's report in this correspondence contained the basic elements of the auditor's report as it is widely accepted today. Previously, the standard report had been very brief and was a certificate and not an expression of opinion. Many auditors were still just signing the balance sheet. Others preceded the signature with the words "Certified Correct" or some other brief statement of certification. The new type of report recommended in this 1934 booklet was really an important step. Legally, there is a tremendous difference between a certification and an opinion.

Meanwhile, the public agitation with respect to corporate reporting was producing other, more authoritative results. Congress passed and the President signed the Securities Act of 1933, which required companies wishing to sell securities in interstate commerce or through the mails to file reports with the Federal Trade Commission. It gave that body wide latitude to prescribe rules and regulations governing the disclosure of information significant to investors, including very comprehensive authority over accounting and accounting reports.

Before much was done under the 1933 act, because of the lack of investor interest in new securities, the Securities and Exchange Act of 1934 became law. That act created the Securities and Exchange Commission and transferred the administration of the 1933 act to it. In the transfer the whole Securities Division of the Trade Commission was moved to the SEC.

The new Commission was given, and still has, authority to establish rules and regulations governing the reporting, accounting, and disclosure of information by all companies whose securities were listed on any national securities exchange. Its authority also extended to the operations of the exchanges and to the regulation of brokers and dealers in securities.

The Unification

Under the 1934 act, all listed companies were required to file registration statements, giving substantial amounts of operating and financial detail, on or before July 1, 1935, or their securities would be delisted. Included in the requirements were a balance sheet and income statements for the three preceding fiscal years in detail far greater than practically any company had previously made public.

One can hardly imagine the impact on the financial and accounting world of having previously confidential information on over 2000 companies suddenly thrown open to the public. All information filed with the Commission could be inspected by anyone at the Commission's office or at any securities exchange on which the company's securities were listed. Copies of any or all pages of a registration statement could be obtained for 10 cents a page.

The rules provided for the confidential filing of specific information if the Commission considered the reasons given to be sufficiently meritorious. Over 600 companies tried to file their figures on sales and cost of goods sold confidentially, but all were rejected and the information became public.

With all the information that became available in these filings, the glaring inconsistencies in accounting practice among companies were easily noted by anyone who made comparisons. They were particularly of major concern to the staff of the SEC.

Through the issuance of "letters of deficiency," the commission attempted to bring about the elimination of the most objectionable practices. In the circumstances, it was not possible to reject very many objectionable practices if they were followed by enough companies to give them credibility. Even so, what could be done was a very heavy task. As a result, it still left practices that varied widely between companies in the same field which should have been comparable.

A great deal of thought was given to the question of what procedures should be followed to eliminate the large number of differences that clearly existed both in accounting practices and in the theories back of them. The Commission clearly had the authority to issue comprehensive rules which would have to be followed by all companies subject to the two acts.

However, the Chief Accountant and a majority of the members of the Commission questioned the wisdom of such a move. They recognized the dangers of arbitrary governmental fiat in this field without extended research and a thorough knowledge of the business activities and the reasons back of each controversial practice. For the Commission or its staff to gain such knowledge seemed to be too great a task to sensibly undertake. Furthermore, the representatives of the accounting profession made very strong arguments against such a policy.

Accordingly, two steps were taken that were of considerable significance. The first was an address in 1937 by the Chief Accountant before a large meeting of CPAs in the City of New York. He discussed the many and wide differences in accounting for similar transactions or events, giving numerous specific examples, and stressed the vital need for reducing such areas of differences. He then stated that the Commission would prefer to have the profession itself take the necessary steps to reduce these differences, but if the profession did not do so, the Commission had the authority to do it and would. While similar statements had been made by the chairman and other members of the Commission, this was the first time substantial examples of what concerned it had been given together with a firm warning.

The second step was the SEC's publication in 1938 of Accounting Series Release No. 4, in which it was stated that unless an official rule, regulation, or opinion to the contrary had been issued, any procedure for which there was substantial authoritative support would be accepted. The clear message was that procedures without such support would be rejected.

The Standards

In the meantime there had been considerable activity among both the practitioners and the teachers of accounting. The American Association of University Instructors in Accounting changed its name to The American Accounting Association, broadened its purposes, and invited anyone interested in accounting to join, whether teaching or not.

The Association developed "A Tentative Statement of Accounting Principles Underlying Corporate Reports" and published it in the June 1936 issue of the Association's journal, *The Accounting Review*. The Chief Accountant responded to it with approval in a subsequent issue of the journal.

In the meantime, the American Society of Certified Public Accountants and the American Institute of Accountants merged in 1936, thus bringing together the two competing organizations of practicing CPAs and giving the profession a unified voice. The Institute in 1938 published *A Statement of Accounting Principles,* sponsored by the Haskins & Sells Foundation.

Following the 1937 meeting in New York, at which the Chief Accountant had stated in no uncertain terms the Commission's offer and warning, steps were taken at the very next meeting of the Council of the Institute, which resulted in the creation of the Committee on Accounting Procedure with authority to issue opinions on accounting matters.

This was something new to the profession. While looking for help and guidance in making decisions, many accountants were quite reluctant to accept a committee opinion if it conflicted with their own. In recognition of this attitude, the Committee's opinions, known as Accounting Research Bulletins, were never issued unless at least two-thirds of the committee's twenty-one members voted for it. To make its views less objectionable to those who opposed the whole idea, each bulletin carried the note that its authority was based on its general acceptability. This made it clear that the opinions were advisory and not rules that had to be followed. Only after such a preponderant number of accountants had accepted the opinion and followed it so that it alone had substantial authoritative support could it be considered the equivalent of a rule.

As the profession has moved further and faster in its efforts to reduce the areas of differences, its pronouncements, first through the Committee on Accounting Procedure, later by the Accounting Principles Board, and now by the Financial Accounting Standards Board, have become virtually the equivalent of laws.

The Deliberations

Very few of those for whose benefit these opinions were issued had the slightest comprehension of the amount of thought, time, and effort that have gone into practically every one of these published opinions. Naturally, if there were no material differences of opinion regarding the proper accounting for a given matter, no statements would be necessary. Accordingly, every problem that was dealt with had at least two and probably more solutions in wide usage.

The twenty-one members on the Ac-

counting Procedure Committee and about the same number on its successor, the Accounting Principles Board, were always selected because they were believed to be sound, independent, and well-qualified accountants. In that number there always were persons with widely divergent views on any controversial subject. No opinions were ever issued that had not gone through a long period of argument both at meetings of the group and by correspondence. Draft after draft was the rule.

Probably if the time put on committee work were to be calculated at the usual per diem charged by members to regular clients, not a single bulletin would have cost less than $100,000. It is safe to say that every possible argument for or against any proposed solution to a problem under consideration was discussed. Usually, every reasonable procedure had some following and was supported by several members who had good reasons for considering it preferable.

When two-thirds or more of such a committee finally reached agreement and issued an opinion, it was certain that the decision was one that could not be lightly brushed aside. Persons who did not like the answer sometimes accused the committees of acting without adequate consideration. Such persons might be assured that such had never been the case. Perhaps in some cases the best decision might not have been reached, but it had never been reached without a tremendous amount of thought and argument.

It was not uncommon for a subject to be abandoned, at least for a time, because it was impossible to get two-thirds of a committee to agree. Another impediment to agreement was sometimes the opposition of the SEC to a favored position. In such cases some members of the committee or the Director of Research were delegated to try to convince the commission or its Chief Accountant that the committee's views were sound. Usually, agreement was reached, but if that was impossible and if the committees were convinced they were right, they accepted the responsibility and proceeded with the issuance.

While at times there were cases in which the SEC refused to accept an opinion of the AICPA when it was first expressed, time has usually demonstrated its soundness, so that today it can be said that the Commisssion is a prime enforcer of the Institute's recommendations. Furthermore, the courts have relied more and more on these Institute pronouncements, all of which has added significantly to their authority.

From time to time there was a tendency for the committee to relax its efforts. When this became noticeable or when officials of the SEC thought it was not making enough progress, they repeatedly made it clear that they were quite cognizant of the fact that they had both the responsibility and the authority to move if the profession did not make all reasonable efforts to get the job done. There were usually some members of the Commission and some of the staff who were not entirely pleased to let the profession do the job, so these were no idle threats.

Accordingly, the profession has good reason to be proud that the rule-making activities in accounting have been so successfully maintained in the private sector.

The Future

In looking back into history, the progress the accounting profession has made since the market debacle in 1929 may receive mixed evaluation. Certainly, the progress could have been faster. But one should not forget the fact that every step in the profession's progress was made after due deliberation and reconciliation of different views.

Needless to say, uniformity in its practice is vital to the well-being of the profession. Without it, the profession would not have the standing it has today and might well be little more than it was in the beginning of the century. But if uniformity alone were the objective, it could have been achieved nearly overnight by an edict of an authoritative body such as the SEC. But if that had been done, many financial statements would have little value to either management or investors.

What is missing in autocratic rule making is the breadth of vision that can be brought about only by the thoughtful deliberation of those who are affected by the rule and who understand its implications. Without it, the rule may paralyze the practice.

Most knowledgeable accountants, financial executives, and analysts believe the SEC took the correct step when it decided in its early days to let the private sector handle rule making insofar as accounting principles are concerned.

The accounting profession is again facing a stormy future. Aroused by recent disclosures of wrongdoing, certain elements of the government, the Congress, and the public in general blame the accounting profession for its failure to detect and disclose corporate irregularities, in a manner that resembles the profession's crisis in the early 1930s. Accepting some reform of the profession as inevitable, major accounting firms presented their own ideas at the congressional hearings on how the reform should take place. Even changes in some basic institutional arrangements have been proposed.

Nevertheless, it is uniformly voiced in the profession that the rule-making activities on accounting principles should remain in the private sector. Rule by government fiat could, in the long run, be only destructive of the progress and flexibility in accounting that is so essential in this rapidly changing economy.

Members of the profession must, however, take their responsibilities very seriously not only as a profession to lead the way toward eliminating unnecessary differences but also as individuals to back the leadership even though some might prefer a different approach.

Only by unity and cooperation can the profession survive and prosper. This is clearly demonstrated by its past.

Chapter 4

Relations Between the Development of Accounting Principles and the Activities of the SEC

Andrew Barr

Prelude to the Securities Acts

Fifty years ago, reports to stockholders in corporations and the behavior of the managements of these rapidly expanding companies were being criticized in somewhat the same manner as they are today. Nevertheless, much change for the better has taken place during this period. Some observers of the record have attributed this in part to the interpretation and enforcement of the securities acts by the Securities and Exchange Commission. The purpose of this chapter is to review the record and identify some steps in which the development of accounting principles and actions by the SEC appear to be closely related.

Reed K. Storey ('1964), in his *The Search For Accounting Principles,* opens his chapter "The Foundation" as follows:

The most important single event in the early efforts to formulate principles of accounting was the work of the special committee on co-operation with stock exchanges, with George O. May as chairman. This committee laid the foundation on which subsequent work on accounting principles has been based. Most of the structure of accounting principles is dependent in one way or another on the report of this committee. This report consisted of correspondence between the Institute's special committee and the committee on stock list of the New York Stock Exchange. The major recommendations resulting from this correspondence were contained in a letter dated September 22, 1932 from the Institute committee to the Exchange Committee.

But what prompted this activity? The direct incentive was provided by J. M. B. Hoxsey, executive assistant to the committee on stock list of the New York Stock Exchange, in an address delivered at the annual meeting of the American Institute of Accountants (AIA), Colorado Springs, Colorado, September 17, 1930. Hoxsey (1930), in his address "Accounting for Investors," discussed depreciation, consolidated statements, showing volume of sales or gross revenues, other income, surplus and surplus entries, stock dividends paid, stock dividends received, and overconservatism in accounting. All these topics were to become subjects for discussion between registrants, their independent accountants, and the SEC. It is interesting to note that the same issue of the *Journal of Accountancy* contains a paper entitled "Some Shortcomings in Consolidated Statements." This was read by Percival F. Brundage, identified as with Price Waterhouse & Co., Boston. He will appear herein again as the firm's senior partner. Hoxsey made another significant address on February 23, 1933, when he spoke to the Massachusetts Society of Certified Public Accountants on the subject "Writing Down Assets and Writing Off Losses," a practice which he said had almost reached the proportions of a mass movement.

William Z. Ripley of Harvard University as early as 1926 had criticized corporate reporting, and in 1927 collected his attack in *Main Street and Wall Street.* In a chapter entitled "Light at the Crossways—Stop, Look, Listen," Ripley (1929) compared the need for better financial reporting by public corporations to the need for traffic control on the highways as the volume and speed of vehicles increased. He said the balance sheet and income account were the two essentials of adequate financial statements and anticipated the conclusion of the May correspondence by stating that "of the two, the income account is perhaps more significant, both immediately and prophetically. Yet, of the two, it is

the income statement, as perhaps too informative, that is the more apt to be suppressed. . . ." In his discussion, he criticized accounting for depreciation, maintenance, obsolescence and depletion, goodwill and inventories, improper combination of items, and, with rare exceptions, the wholly inadequate nature of the income accounts.

Another book widely read at the time and clearly prophetic of the securities acts was Berle and Means' *The Modern Corporation and Private Property,* published in 1932, reprinted five times in 1933, twice in 1934, and once in 1935 and 1936. A. A. Berle, Jr., in the preface, thanks, among others, James C. Bonbright of Columbia University, and George O. May, head of Price Waterhouse and Vice-President of the American Economic Association, and concludes by saying that all students of the subject "owe a debt to Professor William Z. Ripley of Harvard University, who must be recognized as having pioneered this area." To complete this background sketch, it may be noted that the *New York Times* of Sunday, July 24, 1932, contained a full-page review of the book by Ripley under the banner headline, "Our 'Corporate Revolution' and Its Perils."

The Securities Acts

John L. Carey (1969, Vol. 1, Chap. 11) discusses the securities acts in a chapter entitled "Government Intervention in Accounting." The pressure for federal legislation did not wait for the slow-moving AIA–NYSE correspondence to stimulate what clearly needed to be done. But after the Securities Act of 1933 became law and the Federal Trade

Commission needed expert help in drafting regulations and registration forms, which included forms of financial statements, required accountants' certificates, and other matters, accountants and other professionals went to work. This was a logical step, as the AIA had assisted the Federal Trade Commission in preparing *Verification of Financial Statements* in 1929 and its earlier versions in 1917 and 1918. This was the prelude to a cooperative relationship which ultimately developed between the SEC and the American Institute of Certified Public Accountants (AICPA), which continues today (SEC, 1939).

In January 1936, a revision of the 1929 version was prepared and published by the AIA under the title *Examination of Financial Statements by Independent Public Accountants.* The first paragraph of the preface to this edition is of interest here:

Developments of accounting practice during recent years have been in the direction of increased emphasis on accounting principles and consistency in their application, and of fuller disclosure of the basis on which the accounts are stated. These developments have been accelerated by the prominence given to such matters in regulations of the Securities and Exchange Commission dealing with financial statements and also in correspondence during the years 1932 to 1934 between the American Institute of Accountants and the Committee on Stock List of the New York Stock Exchange.

This edition was used by the Commission as the basis for taking testimony from expert witnesses, all leaders in the profession, in the McKesson & Robbins, Inc., investigation in 1939. The SEC is generally credited with having had an important and constructive influence on auditing standards, but no further attention to this aspect of professional accounting practice will be made here, as the objective of this chapter is to discuss the development of accounting principles.

The eastern seaboard had no monopoly in its attack on financial reports of corporations and delay in accomplishing improvement. *The Accounting Review,* June 1933, contains three related editorials, presumably by Eric L. Kohler, the editor, although three well-known professors are linked as assistant editors. The first item, entitled "Business Versus the Public," ends with a short paragraph:

Accountants, as impartial judges, stand between business and the public. Can they suggest an end to the conflict without the enactment of legislation which reflects the public's present temper?

It is interesting to note that the Securities Act of 1933 was approved May 27, 1933.

The second item, entitled "Facts and Purposes," severely criticizes a pamphlet of 55 pages published by the American Institute of Accountants. One of the milder comments of the editor is that the pamphlet pictures the Institute as "the survival of another generation—a static, supremely self-satisfied organization, unashamed to tell the world how good it is, and not afraid to stretch and overstress facts in order to prove a point."

However, the editor finds it "somewhat refreshing" to turn from this to his third topic—"Corporate Accounts and Reporting"—and concludes that the proposals made things better as they were then, but asks if disclosure without more than the meager standardization proposed is a sufficient safeguard for the average investor.

Eric Kohler served as editor of *The Accounting Review* from 1928 through

1942. His editorial in December 1934 appeared six months after the first meeting of the five commissioners of the Securities and Exchange Commission created pursuant to section 4 of the Securities Exchange Act of 1934 (SEC, 1935). Under the caption "A Nervous Profession," Kohler observed that professional accountants were exhibiting a bad case of jitters in the face of rumored drastic regulations by the SEC, and concluded that the practitioners were unprepared to cope with the new responsibilities. This, he said, should offer a challenge to instructors in accounting. He said standards must come, but he saw little hope for constructive effort from the AIA's Committee on Development of Accounting Principles, which seemed to recommend a defensive stance in view of the SEC's wide powers to prescribe methods of accounting.

The Editor believes that the American Association of University Instructors in Accounting can and should take the lead in defining accounting standards. He urges them in the forthcoming convention to seize the opportunity that is now at hand, and thereby perform a service that will secure for themselves their proper leadership in professional affairs.

As a result, the redirection of the AAUIA, with a broadened membership and a change in name to American Association of Accountants (AAA), was accomplished at the annual meeting in 1935 as described in Stephen A. Zeff's *The American Accounting Association— Its First 50 Years.* Eric Kohler was elected president for fiscal 1936. The executive committee gave him the job of writing a first draft of a statement of basic propositions in accounting. SEC commissioner George C. Mathews was a guest at the first meeting of the Commit-

tee (Zeff, 1966, p. 43). At that time, the Commissioners were assigned jurisdiction over certain staff activities. The newly created Chief Accountant's office came under Commissioner Mathews.

By the end of 1935, with the addition of administering the Public Utility Holding Company Act of 1935 to its accumulated experience under the Securities Acts of 1933 and 1934, the Commission concluded that it needed a staff coordinator for accounting matters and appointed Carman G. Blough, who had joined the staff in 1934, as Chief Accountant. The role to be played by this official and his staff is so significant in the work of the Commission that the following description of the duties assigned to the office, as published in the Commission's Second Annual Report to Congress for the fiscal year ended June 30, 1936, warrants reproduction here:

The Chief Accountant of the Commission is responsible for the rendering of advisory service to the Commission in connection with accounting matters; for the conduct of studies, investigations, and researches involving accounting theory, policy, and procedure; for the conduct of conferences with accounting authorities and members of the staff regarding matters involved in the drafting and interpretation of accounting rules and regulations; for the supervision of the accounting work of the Commission whenever unusual matters, new procedures, or new policies are concerned; for supervision over the promulgation and administration of rules regarding uniform classification of accounts; for drafting and establishing procedure to be followed in the conduct of audits and accounting investigations; for rendering advisory opinions and instructions to the accountants assigned to various divisions and regional offices of the Commission in connection with the disposition of highly technical auditing and accounting questions; for the preparation of accounting briefs, reports and memoranda regarding accounting matters under the jurisdiction of the Commission in connection with the administration and enforcement of the Securities Act of 1933, the Securities Exchange Act of 1934, and the Public Utility Holding Company Act of 1935.

During the first years of the Commission, Chairman James M. Landis and Commissioner Mathews were the principal spokesmen for the Commission before professional accounting bodies, both state and national, with the Chief Accountant assuming an increasing amount of the burden of this missionary work of explaining the rules, describing incompetent work, and bringing to light improper accounting in the staff review of filings with the Commission under the several acts (Carey, 1969, Vol. 1, 1896–1936, pp.194–202).

The drafting of the American Accounting Association's statement of basic accounting propositions, launched when Commissioner Mathews was a guest, as noted above, is told very well in Zeff's history of the Association. Strong personalities were involved in the work—Paton, Littleton, Kohler, and Greer. The result was first published in *The Accounting Review*, June 1936, with the title *A Tentative Statement of Accounting Principles Underlying Corporate Financial Statements* by the Executive Committee of the American Accounting Association. The AAA also had an Advisory Committee, of which Carman G. Blough, Chief Accountant of the SEC, was a member (and later, under a new policy, was elected the first nonacademic vice-president). Blough (1937) discussed accounting problems encountered at the Commission and said that he read the "Tentative Statement" with a great deal of satisfaction and that the material in it was a real contribution to the accounting profession. Furthermore, he said that

In general, I subscribe to it. Its importance to me is in the fact that it is an expression of opinion on significant accounting principles from a body of men whose word may be taken authoritatively by practicing accountants seeking guidance in the many problems that face them.

Zeff (1972, p. 131) comments that although the statement was welcomed by the SEC, it was officially ignored by the Institute.

Comments on the statement by T. H. Sanders of Harvard, who had been one of the team recruited to draft the first financial statements prescribed under the Securities Acts, were published in *The Accounting Review* of March 1937. The editor's introduction to these comments stated that no serious criticism had been received on the statement except from Sanders. A reply by Howard C. Greer defended the statement. Sanders' objection was to two paragraphs which he believed imposed unnecessarily harsh limitations on charges to surplus. Later these paragraphs would be considered a recommendation for the all-inclusive income statement–clean surplus approach, as opposed to the operating performance style of reporting defended under the "sharpening income" banner. As will be seen, this was the beginning of a campaign in which the SEC supported the AAA policy.

Sanders' attack was launched with the statement that at some point the principles proposed represented radical departures from common practice and that he was one of those who thought that on most points common practice was right and the new recommendations were in error. This is not too surprising as Sanders at the time of writing his criticism was chairman of a committee commissioned in 1935 by the Haskins & Sells Foundation to make an independent and impartial study of accounting principles (Sanders, Hatfield, and Moore, 1938). The committee completed its work in November 1937. This study was a useful inventory of then-current practice but it condoned some financial reporting practices which the SEC was finding unacceptable (Storey, 1964, pp. 28–31; Paton, 1938; and Fiske, Dohr, and Barr, 1938).

The celebration of the fiftieth anniversary of the American Institute of Accountants in October 1937 afforded an excellent opportunity for the SEC's Chief Accountant to reach a large audience of public accountants, including foreign visitors, with an interest in the work of the SEC. As indicated above, speeches by commissioners and the chief accountant had made it quite clear that improvement in professional practice was necessary. A few nuggets from Robert H. Montgomery's presidential address on that occasion will indicate the temper of the times and perhaps suggest that conditions have not changed much in this respect in the succeeding 40 years (AIA), 1937):

> Whether he likes it or not, the professional public accountant frequently is required to appraise the activities, the transactions of others and say what he thinks, let the chips fall where they may (p. 78).
> A decent profit must be the first thought of management, and the management should be all that the word "decent" implies. There must be no unfair competition, dog's wages, long hours and child labor. If the management can't be decent, it must be changed. In many businesses decency has been the controlling factor for as many years as the businesses have existed. The business man or capitalist who wants to fool the public should not be able to retain a reputable accountant (p. 83).

> I say again that our profession cannot exist, much less flourish, under a dictatorship. Perhaps religion may. Time will tell. Enlightened medicine may. Time will tell. But our profession, as I see it, today requires acquiescence, if not actual support, from the government as well as from the public. Accountants as martyrs will not arouse the enthusiasm nor the support of the people. The truth about accountants must be puslished, not suppressed. It is one thing to cry moral truths in the wilderness and another to cry truths about balance sheets. Under a dictatorship we would not lose our courage, but we could not use it (p. 87).
> We must stand like the Rock of Gibraltar on our independence. On this we must hang together, or we will hang separately. Fifty years ago professional accountants did not consult with each other regarding controversial procedure. To a great extent they do today, but not enough. I look on this as a vulnerable element in our position. I think we should strengthen it (p. 90).

The technical sessions afforded Blough an opportunity to participate with leaders in the profession in discussions of development of accounting theory and practice, consistency, degree of disclosure, the form of the standard certificate, and to declare his policies before an important audience. At one of these sessions, Blough commented on the Commission's announcement on April 1, 1937, of "a program of publication, from time to time, of opinions on accounting principles for the purpose of contributing to the development of uniform standards and practice in major accounting questions" (AIA, 1937, pp. 189–190). He stated that he had emphasized numerous times that the policy of the SEC was to encourage the accountants to develop uniformity of procedure themselves and the Commission would follow what was expected to be the better thought in the profession. Only as a last resort would the Commission feel it necessary to step in.

By this time, the commissioners and staff had gained considerable experience in dealing with dubious alternative accounting practices, as well as what appeared to be sincere differences of opinion, reflected in financial statements filed to comply with the three laws then administered by them. The two securities acts were generally referred to as disclosure acts, but the Public Utility Holding Company Act of 1935 provided for the promulgation of uniform systems of accounts for the holding companies and their mutual service companies which clearly required rules with respect to accounting principles to be followed in preparing the accounts. That a difference of opinion existed among the commissioners came to the surface in a public utility company registration under the 1933 act. This company had disposed of unamortized discount on bonds by charging a substantial sum to capital surplus arising from a prior recording of an appraisal. All the commissioners thought this was improper accounting. The details of this episode are available in several places. McCormick (1948, pp. 271–273) discusses this as embodied in the Securities Act of 1933, Release No. 254 (1934), as does Rappaport (1972, pp. 27–28; see also Healey, 1938). The three-to-two decision permitted disclosure of the effect of a change to the favored solution but did not require amendment of the financial statements. Chairman William O. Douglas and Commissioner Robert E. Healy were the minority on this issue. Both thought that the Commission should take the lead in formulating accounting principles as it was authorized to do under the 1933 Act (Douglas, 1974, pp. 274–275).

Where is this power to be found? Section 7 of the Securities Act of 1933 states that a registration statement for a security other than one issued by a foreign government or political subdivision thereof shall contain the information and be accompanied by the documents specified by Schedule A. Items (25) and (26) specify the balance sheets and profit and loss statements to be furnished, and which of these shall be certified by an independent public or certified accountant. What may have been overlooked by some who have doubted the Commission's authority with respect to accounting principles is that the Commission may prescribe certain details as well as the form of these statements. Section 19 grants special powers to the Commission. The portion of paragraph (a) pertinent here is quoted, as it is too compact to paraphrase:

The Commission shall have authority from time to time to make, amend, and rescind such rules and regulations as may be necessary to carry out the provisions of this title, including rules and regulations governing registration statements and prospectuses for various classes of securities and issuers, and defining accounting, technical, and trade terms used in this title. Among other things, the Commission shall have authority, for the purposes of this title, to prescribe the form or forms in which required information shall be set forth, the items or details to be shown in the balance sheet and earning statement, and the methods to be followed in the preparation of accounts, in the appraisal or valuation of assets and liabilities, in the determination of depreciation and depletion, in the differentiation of recurring and nonrecurring income, in the differentiation of investment and operating income, and in the preparation, where the Commission deems it necessary or desirable, of consolidated balance sheets or income accounts of any person directly or indirectly controlling or controlled by the issuer, or any person under direct or indirect common control with the issuer.

Similar authority is found in Sections

3 (b) and 13 of the Securities Exchange Act of 1934. Under Section 14, the Commission's authority has been extended to reports to stockholders.

The debate over disclosure versus correction finally led to a conclusion that accounting deemed to be improper in the financial statements could not be cured by footnote explanations and qualified certificates. This result was expressed in Accounting Series Release No. 4, dated April 25, 1938:

> The Securities and Exchange Commission today issued the following statement of its administrative policy with respect to financial statements:
>
> In cases where financial statements filed with this Commission pursuant to its rules and regulations under the Securities Act of 1933 or the Securities Exchange Act of 1934 are prepared in accordance with accounting principles for which there is no substantial authoritative support, such financial statements will be presumed to be misleading or inaccurate despite disclosures in the certificate of the accountant or in footnotes to the statements provided the matters involved are material. In cases where there is a difference of opinion between the Commission and the registrant as to the proper principles of accounting to be followed, disclosure will be accepted in lieu of correction of the financial statements themselves only if the points involved are such that there is substantial authoritative support for the practices followed

by the registrant and the position of the Commission has not previously been expressed in rules, regulations, or other official releases of the Commission, including the published opinions of its chief accountant.[1]

This policy raises the question of how to determine whether an accounting practice has substantial authoritative support. Paul Grady, in his *Inventory of Generally Accepted Accounting Principles for Business Enterprises,* gave some attention to this point. For the purposes of this paper, the fourth of his six sources of support is pertinent (AICPA, 1965):

> 4. The regulations and accounting opinions of the Securities and Exchange Commission have the controlling authority over the reports filed with the Commission. The Commission and its chief accountants have demonstrated a high degree of objectivity, restraint and expertness in dealing with accounting matters. The regulations and opinions issued to date are entitled to acceptance by their merit as well as on the basis of the statutory authority of the Commission (p. 52).

Generally Accepted Accounting Principles

This is not the place for a recital of the long history of the development of

---

[1] A description of the Commission's reliance on the profession with only limited prescription for disclosure of accounting principles prior to the publication of Accounting Series Release No. 4 is in the Fifth Annual Report of the Commission, pages 117–118. On page 121 in this report, the philosophy of the Commission's present and prospective activities in accounting matters was recapitulated by quoting from a statement issued by Jerome N. Frank when he took office as chairman succeeding William O. Douglas, who resigned April 16, 1939, to accept appointment as Justice of the United States Supreme Court. Chairman Frank's statement read: "One of the most important functions of the Commission is to maintain and improve the standards of accounting practice. Recent events make it clear that we face a pressing problem in this field. Accounting is the language in which the corporation talks to its existing stockholders and to prospective investors. We want to be sure that the public never has reason to lose faith in the reports of public accountants. To this end, the independence of the public accountant must be preserved and strengthened and standards of thoroughness and accuracy protected. I understand that certain groups in the profession are moving ahead in good stride. They will get all the help we can give them so long as they conscientiously attempt that task. That's definite. But if we find that they are unwilling or unable, perhaps, because of the influence of some of their clients, to do the job thoroughly, we won't hesitate to step in to the full extent of our statutory powers."

the accountant's certificate, report, or opinion, but some comment on the insertion of the word "generally" seems in order as an introduction to the involvement of the SEC in the continuing efforts of the profession to reach a common understanding of the term "generally accepted accounting principles." Paul Grady tied the change correctly to the McKesson & Robbins case, but found no indication of the significance to be drawn from this change in the form of certificate recommended in the 1932–1934 correspondence and widely used and accepted by the SEC as meeting its requirements (AICPA, 1965, p. 50).

Accounting Series Release No. 12, published February 21, 1940, announced the adoption of Regulation S-X, which brought together in one place the accounting instructions previously found in the several forms (SEC, 1940, p. 171). This release stated that, although altered and clarified in some respects, the rules governing certification by accountants were not changed pending completion of the proceedings in McKesson and Robbins. The full report on this investigation was published in December 1940 (SEC, 1940b) and a summary of its findings and conclusions was published December 5, 1940, as Accounting Series Release No. 19. Appendix A to the full report describes action taken by professional accounting and other organizations as a result of the McKesson & Robbins disclosures. The chief accountant and the writer working on the investigation attended one of the joint meetings with committees of the New York State Society of Certified Public Accountants and the American Institute of Accountants. The SEC participants suggested the insertion of the word "generally" to convey the idea that more than limited acceptance was intended by the certificate. The resulting report (Extensions of Auditing Procedure) of May 9, 1939, as modified and approved at the annual meeting, September 19, 1939, is included in the full McKesson and Robbins report. Following this publication, Regulation S-X was amended by Accounting Series Release No. 21 on February 5, 1941. No significant change was made in the rules covering the opinion paragraph of the certificate. This, in effect, was endorsement of the AIA revised certificate, which the SEC has interpreted consistently as a single representation of fair presentation in conformity with generally accepted accounting principles.

When the five rules recommended by the AIA to the New York Stock Exchange in 1932 were adopted by the Institute membership in 1934, a sixth rule had been added. This reflected a decision by the SEC in an early case dealing with donated stock by promoters in a mining venture.[2] This could be said to be the beginning of the cooperation between successive committees and the SEC to deal with problems on a case-by-case basis, as contrasted with the tentative statement by the American Accounting Association, which was revised in 1941 and 1948 with little change. The principles expounded here, which met with SEC approval, were the

---

[2] In the matter of the Unity Gold Corporation, 1 SEC 25 (1934). The rule based on this case and the five rules recommended in 1932 were included in Accounting Research Bulletin No. 1 issued by the Committee on Accounting Procedure (1939).

historical cost basis and the all-inclusive income statement.[3]

The debate on the all-inclusive issue had been going on for some time as a principal post-World War II problem. The chief accountant's office at the SEC had made two studies of charges and credits to earned surplus, the latter being published in September 1946 in the *New York Certified Public Accountant.* In addition, the commission sponsored a round-table discussion of the subject attended by representatives of accounting organizations and others interested in the matter. In December 1947, Accounting Research Bulletin No. 32 on Income and Earned Surplus was released. In January 1948, it was published in the *Journal of Accountancy,* along with the committee chairman's comments in defense of the sharpening income approach and a comment letter from Earle C. King, the chief accountant of the SEC, which was approved by the Commission. The letter stated objections and requested publication in the same issue of the *Journal* as ARB 32. The key paragraph following the basis for objection read:

Under these circumstances the Commission has authorized the staff to take exception to financial statements which appear to be misleading, even though they reflect the application of Accounting Research Bulletin No. 32.

This incident is overlooked by those who think the investment credit matter was the first such open difference of opinion.

This seems to be an appropriate place to cite a little-known incident in which the SEC came to the support of an accounting firm that met resistance from a client in accounting for stock dividends. The firm insisted on applying the policy of the New York Stock Exchange, supported by ARB No. 11, of charging ordinary stock dividends to earned surplus at fair value. The client registrant filed its annual report with the dividends charged at par value, which was less than market, to which the accountants took exception. The filing was amended after the staff warned that failure to comply with requests to amend would result in a recommendation to the Commission to authorize that formal action be taken (SEC, 1946, p. 116). In more recent cases, the commission held that payment of ordinary stock dividends in the absence of earned surplus was a manipulative device (SEC 1972a, and cases cited therein).

Soon after the "all-inclusive" debate described above, the first major revision of Regulation S-X was exposed to public comment. The draft included items that had been cited in letters of comment on review of financial statements filed to make the regulation a more complete reflection of the SEC's views. An attempt to incorporate modern terminology in the equity section of the balance sheet was abandoned as too complicated. However, this change was accomplished

[3]SEC (1941, p. 198; 1946, p. 117; 1948, pp. 111–112; 1952, pp. 182–183. American Accounting Association Supplementary Statement No. 2 (1951) dealt with price-level changes and financial statements and recommended supplementary disclosures. The chief accountant of the commission was listed among six consultants who were not necessarily in agreement with the conclusions and assumed no responsibility for them. The 1957 revision of the 1948 statement recommended supplementary disclosure and commented on several methods now under consideration. The American Accounting Association (1966) advocated reporting on the basis of current-cost information to supplement historical-cost statements. None of these pronouncements after 1948 were recognized by the SEC as authoritative support for financial statements required under the securities acts.

in the current edition (SEC, 1972b; see SEC, 1967, for an approving comment on APB. No. 9). Under a general rule, modern terms were optional before. The proposal was attacked with vigor. The American Accounting Association and the Institute met in Boston in 1950. The chief accountant of the Commission and his assistant were invited to attend a meeting of the AIA's Committee on Accounting Procedure to discuss a proposed opinion of the Committee which would provide for a general upward restatement of assets in connection with a quasi-reorganization, a position known to be in conflict with the SEC's support of historical cost. The SEC officials were cross-examined by members of the Committee and then withdrew. Later they were informed that the topic had been dropped from the committee's agenda. Both organizations adopted resolutions addressed to the Commission.[4] The result was that a proposed rule on the historical cost basis for assets and inclusion of the Commission's policy as stated in ASR No. 4 were omitted on the understanding that the AIA would step up the work of the Committee on Accounting Procedure. However, the Commission took an important step at the same time by including a new provision that in effect made the accounting series releases a part of the regulation.

A compromise was reached on the all-inclusive income statement issue (SEC, 1950; Zeff, 1972) which proved to be unsatisfactory but was resolved when the Accounting Principles Board published its Opinion No. 9 in December 1966, and the next revision of Regulation S-X in 1972 adopted the all-inclusive solution.

Concurrent with the work on the 1950 revision of Regulation S-X was the work of the Study Group on Business Income, sponsored by the AIA and partly funded by the Rockefeller Foundation, whose report was published in 1952 under the title *Changing Concepts of Business Income.* Percival F. Brundage was chairman, with George O. May a principal member of the working party. Members of the Study Group included Carman G. Blough, first chief accountant of the SEC and then Director of Research of the AIA; William W. Werntz, second chief accountant of the SEC and a member of the Institute's Committee on Accounting Procedure; Earle C. King, the third and incumbent chief accountant of the SEC; and chief accountants of other federal regulatory agencies. All of them filed dissents to those portions of the report which proposed that independent public accountants take responsibility for supplementary price-level adjusted values for property or departures from historical costs in the primary statements.

The Accounting Principles Board

Dissatisfaction with the work of the Committee on Accounting Procedure started to build up at the close of World War II. The SEC had taken exception to ARB No. 23 issued in December 1944 on accounting for income taxes in its ASR No. 53, published November 16, 1945 (SEC, 1945, p. 88). The issue of

---

[4] See the reports in *The Accounting Review*, April 1951, p. 254, and *The Journal of Accountancy*, November 1950, p. A-20; see also SEC (1951 p. 163).

the balance sheet treatment of the credit equivalent to reduction of income taxes was resolved by the SEC in Accounting Series Releases Nos. 85 and 86 in 1960 after exposure for comment and a public hearing in 1958 and 1959. The chairman of the Institute's committee was William W. Werntz, and Carman G. Blough was research director. Both supported the Commission's position that the credit involved could not be reported as a part of stockholders' equity in the balance sheet (SEC, 1959, pp. 198-200. See also SEC, 1960, pp. 212-214).

It is not necessary to recite here all of the reasons that led to the appointment in late 1957 by Alvin R. Jennings, the newly elected president of the Institute, of a Special Committee on Research Program to study and make recommendations on the Institute's part in developing accounting principles (Zeff, 1972, pp. 169-173). This committee included Carman G. Blough, the Institute's Director of Research and first chief accountant of the SEC; William W. Werntz, by then in public practice and chairman of the committee destined to be superseded by a new organization; and Andrew Barr, the then-current chief accountant of the SEC, who had been authorized to accept the invitation to join in the effort in which the commission had a vital interest. (SEC, 1958, p. 186.)

The special committee's report, adopted unanimously, contemplated a method of operation for the Institute similar to that required of federal government agencies under the Administrative Procedure Act—exposure of proposed opinions to public comment prior to making them effective. This work was to be supported by adequate research conducted by a strengthened staff and by others not on the staff. The committee contemplated three layers of study—basic accounting postulates underlying a statement of broad accounting principles to which solutions to particular problems would be logically related, and two project advisory committeees, one for postulates and one for principles, each of which included some members of the special committee. Carman Blough, Paul Grady, and the chief accountant of the SEC were members of the latter committee. The study on postulates first published came out in 1961 with comment by one advisor that, although it was a useful study for discussion, it could not provide a foundation on which to build a sound framework of accounting theory.

A Tentative Set of Broad Accounting Principles for Business Enterprises, published as research study number 3 in 1962, ran into trouble. Strong differences appeared in the comments of the advisors—mostly adverse, including that of the SEC's representative. The result was publication by the research director, accompanied by a one-page statement by the Accounting Principles Board (1962a), which included this sentence reflecting the view of some of the advisors:[5]

> The Board believes, however, that while these studies are a valuable contribution to accounting thinking, they are too radically different from present generally accepted accounting principles for acceptance at this time.

Here, the new board and the SEC were in agreement. The two advisory groups

---

[5] See the report of the Securities and Exchange Commission (1965) for authority for the chief accountant to continue as an advisor.

were combined to assist Paul Grady in developing Accounting Research Study No. 7, referred to earlier as an inventory of then generally accepted accounting principles.

A circumstance beyond the control of the Accounting Principles Board was legislation creating the "investment credit," a new idea in U.S. tax law. This stirred up considerable difference of opinion in business and professional circles, to put it mildly. In view of this diversity of opinion and finding a lack of authoritative support for only the one method of accounting adopted by the board (APB, 1962b), the commission announced that alternative methods would be accepted in filings with it (SEC, 1963b; see 1963a, pp. 139–140). A significant part of the Commission's release was the citing of "Audits of Corporate Accounts" for its discussion of the meaning of "accounting principles and practices" as used in the accountants' certificate required by the Commission's rules. The Commission also stated that if an accountant's client adopted an alternative accounting not endorsed by APB No. 2 and the accountant felt constrained to qualify his opinion, the SEC would accept it. This situation, and a change in tax law in 1964 clarifying one debatable point, led the APB to issue its Opinion No. 4 in March 1964, amending No. 2 to permit alternative accounting. This episode has been cited by many as the only serious breech, up to that time, between the Commission and the profession, as represented by the AICPA. While, as indicated above, this is not the case, it was an unfortunate event, but one of very

few situations where there has been a failure to reach mutually acceptable solutions to problems.

On the last day of hearings on the amendments to the securities acts (February 10, 1964) by the Subcommittee on Commerce and Finance of the Committee on Interstate and Foreign Commerce of the House of Representatives, the question of alternative accounting practices was raised by Representative Staggers. In response to questions, Chairman Cary and the chief accountant of the Commission stated that there were areas in accounting where alternative practices could produce materially different results under generally accepted accounting principles. Chairman Cary agreed with Mr. Staggers that the SEC had the responsibility to determine "whether the profession had taken appropriate action to determine adequate accounting principles." As requested, a memorandum was furnished for the record in which the Commission's policy of working with the profession was explained and a list of problem areas was included. The conclusion reached in the memorandum was that, "No legislative endorsement of this policy is considered necessary (SEC, 1964).[6] The legislation extended SEC authority over unlisted companies above a certain size with no change in the accounting provisions of the acts.

Whether this incident had anything to do with it, the AICPA, after much debate in Council, published a Special Bulletin in October 1964 to guide its members as to "Disclosure of Departures from Opinions of Accounting Principles

---

[6]For excerpts from the hearing record and the full memorandum, see STATEMENTS IN QUOTES, *The Journal of Accountancy*, June 1964, pp. 56–61.

Board." This required disclosure of such departures and, where practicable, the effect on the financial statements beginning after December 31, 1965. The term "generally accepted accounting principles" was defined as those principles having authoritative support, and "opinions of the Accounting Principles Board constitute substantial authoritative support." An exception noted recognized that such support differing from the opinions might be found to exist. Note here the similarity to the SEC's ASR No. 4, published 28 years before.

Despite all its efforts, criticism of the APB continued to build up, particularly on the grounds that it had failed to develop a statement of basic concepts and accounting principles to which its opinions on current problems could be related. An effort to meet this challenge was the publication of Statement No. 4 in October 1970. It should be noted that drafts of APB opinions and of this statement were exposed to, and in most cases discussed with, the accounting staff of the SEC, and comment letters were written with the Commission's approval. After publication, the SEC, with rare exception, cited the opinions as authoritative support under ASR No. 4 (SEC, 1971, p. 64).

The critics did not relax their attack. The result was the appointment by the AICPA, in early 1971, of two committees to study ways to improve the Institute's role in establishing standards of financial reporting. The first committee, with a deadline to report in one year and chaired by former Commissioner Francis M. Wheat, was directed to study the operations of the APB. The second

committee, with a two-year deadline and chaired by Robert M. Trueblood, was directed to study the objectives of financial statements. The Wheat report, recommending the creation of the Financial Accounting Standards Board, was adopted by Council of the Institute at its May 1972 meeting, after receiving written support from the chairman of the SEC, who asked that public comment be sought on drafts of charter and by-laws and procedures of the new organization.[7] In its report to Congress, the Commission said it "endorsed this new structure, which it feels should provide operational efficiencies and insure an impartial viewpoint in the development of accounting standards on a timely basis" (SEC, 1972c, p. 35).

The propriety of the Commission's policy of supporting the profession in encouraging progress in accounting and financial reporting as described herein has been challenged by some legal critics. This point was discussed by the Wheat Study Group with representatives of the SEC, including Philip A. Loomis, Jr., then general counsel and now a Commissioner. It was Mr. Loomis' opinion that the administration of the disclosure requirements of the Federal Securities Acts with respect to financial statements had not been in conflict with the Federal Administrative Procedure Act on which the critics relied (AICPA, 1972, p. 51).

Subsequently, in Accounting Series Release No. 150, December 20, 1973, the Commission endorsed the FASB and stated that its statements and interpretations would be considered as being substantial authoritative support for an accounting practice or procedure (SEC,

---

[7]See *The Journal of Accountancy,* June 1972, p. 9.

1974, pp. 36–37). The formal action in 1973 should be read in light of Eric Kohler's editorial in *The Accounting Review* of 40 years before in which he proposed a revision of Section 11 of the Securities Act of 1933 to include a somewhat similar relationship between the SEC and "any national body representing the profession (Kohler, 1933, pp. 339–341).[8]

A number of important issues emerged after early in 1972 to test the strength of this working arrangement between the SEC and the profession. The issue, which has become international in character, is the survival of historical cost as the basis for financial reporting. The Securities Acts, as we have seen, were the answer to a record of optimistic appraisals in the 1920s followed by drastic write-downs in the 1930s, many with no regard to continuing values. The record since then reveals a shifting from an index-number approach to some form of current-value accounting as supplementary disclosure or substitution for historical cost.

The issue was joined with the publication by the SEC on August 21, 1975, of a proposed amendment to Regulation S-X which would require footnote disclosure of certain replacement costs and ASR 190 on March 23, 1976, adopted the amendments. At the time the FASB had under consideration a discussion memorandum published February 15, 1974, under the title "An Analysis of the Issues Related to Reporting the Effects of General Price-Level Changes in Financial Statements." In ASR 190 the SEC stated that "it did not and does not view its proposal as competitive with that of the FASB." The FASB an-

nounced on June 3, 1976, that the Board had decided to defer further consideration at that time pending results of field tests then underway and experience to be gained from implementation of ASR 190 (FASB, 1976b, 1976c). An independent comment on this situation is that of Peterson and Lemon (1976):

Regrettably the SEC intervention through the specification of replacement cost data in financial disclosures represents something quite different from support of the FASB with deliberations on a conceptual basis for financial reporting underway, and with the GPLR [general price level restatement] issue before the FASB, the timing of the release of ASR 190 will very likely have a significant impact on standards which will subsequently be adopted. It seems reasonable to conclude through an examination of the events of 1975 and early 1976 that the SEC has decided to play a much more active role in this area than it has in the past.

See also Lemon and Peterson (1976).

As noted above, chief accountants of several federal regulatory agencies were among the dissenters to the *Report of Study Group on Business Income*. More current criticism of replacement cost accounting and price-level restatement is found in articles by Alfred M. King, Vice-President Finance of American Appraisal Associates, Inc. (King, 1976a, 1976b). King cites many problems in complying with ASR 190, which the SEC admits in the release is experimental. Staff Accounting Bulletins Nos. 7, 9, 10, and 11 have dealt with questions raised. Because of the problems involved, an Advisory Committee on Replacement Cost Implementation was established to assist the Commission's staff. Meetings

[8]For current work of the FASB, see reports of the Financial Accounting Board (1976a).

are open to the public. This is a good example of professional and public cooperation in solving practical problems.

The flavor of King's second article can be gained from the following paragraph (King, 1976b):

If, during periods of inflation, we see a problem in measuring management's ability to structure properly the company's financial position relative to debt/equity or working capital, then trying to solve this through a "purchasing power gain or loss" is hardly the answer. In fact as many critics have pointed out, under the FASB proposal, Penn Central and W. T. Grant would have been reporting very nice price level adjusted incomes just prior to declaring bankruptcy. And a conservatively financed company, such as IBM, might be severely penalized for having substantial cash and marketable securities on its balance sheet (p.18).

King seems to be saying that it is management's judgment that dictates when assets are to be acquired and the time and manner of their disposition; when liabilities are to be incurred and manner of liquidation; and the method of equity financing. These *are* basic business judgments and of necessity involve a projection into the future resting on the best available evidence. So costs are incurred which must then be related to revenue produced to determine the success of the enterprise—the matching principle emerges. Current-value methods of measuring the state of affairs by comparison with prior determinations of progress introduces a "what if" element in accounting which may be interpreted as a challenge of management's judgment at the time the costs were incurred—a test by "hindsight." Such a test may be useful in judging the quality of management decisions but does not serve to expunge the record of the past. Reduced to

simplest terms, the management that consistently buys low and sells high must be successful, while buying high and selling low reflects a serious lack of vision and leads to disaster.

During the period covered by this chapter, the SEC has supported historical cost, the matching principle, consistency and a reasonable degree of comparability, and the restraints of materiality when applied by a going concern as the basic elements of generally accepted accounting principles. To these must be added adequate disclosure fitted to the various circumstances in which financial statements are used. Here the Commission, from time to time, has perceived a need of investors for current values supplementing historical-cost-based statements. An example of a situation where such information was necessary for the investor's decision was expressed in the Memorandum of the Securities and Exchange Commission, Amicus Curiae, in Gustave Gerstle, et al., Plaintiffs, against Gamble—Skogmo, Inc., Defendants, United States District Court, Eastern District of New York, 64 Civ. 1253 (December 1968). In this case, proxy material failed to disclose that the acquiring company in an exchange offer intended to dispose of the acquired company's real estate at a substantial profit immediately after completion of the merger. The Commission's brief supported the following propositions:

I. IN FINANCIAL STATEMENTS FILED WITH THE COMMISSION FIXED ASSETS SHOULD BE CARRIED AT HISTORICAL COST (LESS ANY DEPRECIATION) IN THE ABSENCE OF ANY STATUTE, RULE OR SPECIFIC COMMISSION AUTHORIZATION TO THE CONTRARY.

II. THE NARRATIVE OR TEXTUAL PORTION OF A PROXY STATEMENT MUST

CONTAIN WHAT EVER ADDITIONAL MATERIAL INFORMATION IS NECESSARY UNDER THE CIRCUMSTANCES IN ORDER TO MAKE THE PROXY STATEMENT NOT MISLEADING.

III. WHEN A BALANCE SHEET IN A PROXY STATEMENT FOR A MERGER REFLECTS ASSETS AT AN AMOUNT THAT IS SUBSTANTIALLY LOWER THAN THEIR CURRENT LIQUIDATING VALUE AND LIQUIDATION OF THOSE ASSETS IS INTENDED OR CAN REASONABLY BE ANTICIPATED THE TEXTUAL OR NARRA-TIVE PORTION OF THE PROXY STATE-MENT MUST CONTAIN WHATEVER AVAILABLE MATERIAL INFORMATION ABOUT THEIR CURRENT LIQUIDATING VALUE IS NECESSARY TO MAKE THE PROXY STATEMENT NOT MISLEADING.

Note that the additional information was to be placed in the narrative or textual portions of the proxy statement and not in footnotes as required by ASR 190. The brief contains a comprehensive table of citations on the subject.

References

Accounting Principles Board. 1962a. Statement. New York: The American Institute of Certified Public Accountants, Inc.

——. 1962b. *Accounting Principles Board Opinion No. 2.* New York: The American Institute of Certified Public Accountants, Inc.

American Accounting Association. 1951. Supplementary Statement No. 2. *The Accounting Review.* October.

——. 1966. *A Statement of Basic Accounting Theory.* Evanston, Illinois: The American Accounting Association.

American Institute of Accountants. 1937. Fiftieth Anniversary Celebration. New York:

——. 1947. *Accounting Research Bulletin No. 32.* Income and Earned Surplus. New York.

American Institute of Certified Public Accountants. 1965. Accounting Research Study No. 7. New York: The American Institute of Certified Public Accountants, Inc.

——. 1972. *Establishing Financial Accounting Standards, Report of the Study on Establishment of Accounting Principles.* New York: The American Institute of Certified Public Accountants, Inc.

Berle, Adolph A. and Means, Gardiner C. 1933. *The Modern Corporation and Private Property.* New York: Macmillan Publishing Co., Inc.

Blough, Carman G. 1937. "The Need for Accounting Principles." *The Accounting Review.*

Carey, John L. 1969. *The Rise of the Accounting Profession.* New York: *The American* Institute of Certified Public Accountants, Inc.

Committee on Accounting Procedure. 1939. *Research Bulletin No. 1.* General Introduction and Rules Formerly Adopted. New York: The American Insitute of Accountants.

Douglas, William O. 1974. *Go East Young Man.* New York: Random House, Inc.

Financial Accounting Standards Board. 1976a. *Annual Report 1975, 1976, 1977.* Stamford, Conn.

——. 1976b. News release, June 3.

——. 1976c. *Status Report No. 37,* June 4.

Fiske, Wyman P., James L. Dohr, and Andrew Barr. 1938. *The Journal of Accountancy.* April.

Healey, Robert E. 1938. "The Next Step in Accounting." *The Accounting Review,* March.

Hoxsey, J. M. B. 1930. "Accounting for Investors." *The Journal of Accountancy,* 50(4), October.

King, Alfred M. 1976a. "Developing the Information for Replacement Cost Accounting." *Financial Executive,* August.

——. 1976b. "Solution or Problem?" *Management Accounting,* November.

Kohler, Eric L. 1933. Editorial. *The Accounting Review.* December.

Lemon, W. Morley, and Russell J. Peterson. 1976. "The S.E.C. and Replacement Cost Accounting: Implications for Financial Reporting." *Faculty Working Paper No. 324,* College of Commerce and Business Administration, University of Illinois at Urbana–Champaign.

McCormick, Edward T. 1948. *Understanding the Securities Act and the S.E.C.* New York: American Book Company.

Paton, William A. 1938. *The Journal of Accountancy.* March.

Peterson, Russell J., and W. Morley Lemon, 1976. "Financial Reporting Standard Setting—Public or Private Sector?" *Illinois Business Review,* 33(7), July.

Rappaport, Louis H. 1956. *SEC Accounting Practice and Procedure.* New York: The Ronald Press Company (pp. 27–28 of the 3rd ed., 1972).

Ripley, William Z. 1927, 1929. *Main Street and Wall Street.* Boston: Little, Brown and Company.

Sanders, Thomas H., Henry R. Hatfield, and Underhill Moore. 1938. *A Statement of Accounting Principles.* New York: American Institute of Accountants.

Securities and Exchange Commission. 1935. *First Annual Report, Fiscal Year Ended June 30, 1935.* Washington, D.C.: Government Printing Office.

——. 1936. *Second Annual Report, Fiscal Year Ended June 30, 1936.* Washington, D.C.: Government Printing Office.

——. 1939. *Fifth Annual Report, Fiscal Year Ended June 30, 1939.* Washington, D.C.: Government Printing Office.

——. 1940a. *Sixth Annual Report, Fiscal Year Ended June 30, 1940.* Washington, D.C.: Government Printing Office.

——. 1940b. In the Matter of McKesson & Robbins, Inc. Washington, D.C.: Government Printing Office.

——. 1941. *Seventh Annual Report, Fiscal Year Ended June 30, 1941.* Washington, D.C.: Government Printing Office.

——. 1945. *Eleventh Annual Report, Fiscal Year Ended June 30, 1945.* Washington, D.C.: Government Printing Office.

——. 1946. *Twelfth Annual Report, Fiscal Year Ended June 30, 1946.* Washington, D.C.: Government Printing Office.

——. 1948. *Fourteenth Annual Report, Fiscal Year Ended June 30, 1948.* Washington, Washington, D.C.: General Accounting Office.

——. 1950. *Accounting Series Release No. 70.* Washington, D.C.: Securities and Exchange Commission.

——. 1951. *Seventeenth Annual Report, Fiscal Year Ended June 30, 1951.* Washington, D.C.: Government Printing Office.

——. 1952. *Eighteenth Annual Report, Fiscal Year Ended June 30, 1952.* Washington, D.C.: Government Printing Office.

——. 1958. *Twenty-fourth Annual Report, Fiscal Year Ended June 30, 1958.* Washington, D.C.: Government Printing Office.

——. 1959. *Twenty-fifth Annual Report, Fiscal Year Ended June 30, 1959.* Washington, D.C.: Government Printing Office.

——. 1960. *Twenty-sixth Annual Report, Fiscal Year Ended June 30, 1960.* Washington, D.C.: Government Printing Office.

——. 1963a. *Twenty-ninth Annual Report, Fiscal Year Ended June 30, 1963.* Washington, D.C.: Government Printing Office.

——. 1963b. *Accounting Series Release No. 96.* Washington, D.C.: Securities and Exing Office.

——. 1964. *Thirtieth Annual Report, Fiscal Year Ended June 30, 1964.* Washington, D.C.: Government Printing Office.

——. 1965. *Thirty-first Annual Report, Fiscal Year Ended June 30, 1965.* Washington, D.C.: Government Printing Office.

——. 1967. *Thirty-third Annual Report, Fiscal Year Ended June 30, 1967.* Washington D.C.: Government Printing Offfice.

——. 1971. *Thirty-seventh Annual Report, Fiscal Year Ended June 30, 1971.* Washington, D.C.: Government Printing Office.

——. 1972a. *Accounting Series Release No. 124.* Washington, D.C.: Securities and Exchange Commission.

——. 1972b. *Accounting Series Release No. 125.* Washington, D.C.: Securities and Exchange Commission.

——. 1972c. *Thirty-eighth Annual Report, Fiscal Year Ended June 30, 1972.* Washington, D.C.: Government Printing Office.

——. 1974. *Fortieth Annual Report, Fiscal Year Ended June 30, 1974*. Washington, D.C.: Government Printing Office.

Storey, Reed K. 1964. *The Search for Accounting Principles*. New York: The American Institute of Certified Public Accountants, Inc.

Zeff, Stephen A. 1966. *The American Accounting Association—Its First 50 years*. New York: The American Accounting Association.

——. 1972. *Forging Accounting Principles in Five Countries, A History and Analysis of Trends*. Champaign, Ill.: Stipes Publishing Company.

Chapter 5

The Role of Costs in Public Regulation of Business

Herbert F. Taggart

Legislation and Legislative Propensities

Whenever a legislative body feels impelled to pass a law intended to govern the conduct of business enterprises in setting prices for their products or services, it is a practical certainty that an important criterion of acceptable pricing will be the cost of whatever is being sold. This makes sense if the cost calculations required need not be carried to too great a degree of particularity. For example, it is hard to see how public utility rates could be intelligently regulated without reliable knowledge of the overall costs of doing business.

The trouble arises when a law or regulation requires the calculation of costs in too great detail. And legislative bodies have seldom or never hesitated to do just that. There seems to be a widespread

conviction on the part of legislators that prices of goods and services are or ought to be based on cost. To the average legislator, cost is an exactly definable quantum, in spite of advice to the contrary by accountants, economists, businessmen, and others who ought to know.

An excellent example of this frame of mind occurred in connection with the consideration in 1951 of several bills that would have directed the Civil Aeronautics Board of the U.S. government to set rates for carrying airmail in terms of the cost of this service to the airlines. One such bill would have required that "[t]he rates . . . shall be based upon the necessary cost to the air carrier, under honest, economical, and efficient management, of the mail transportation services actually rendered." To ascertain such costs the airlines would have to install cost accounting systems that would determine separately the costs of transporting passengers, freight, express, and mail, all of which may be carried on the same planes.

This legislation was proposed in complete disregard of the experience of the railroads in attempts to do the same kind of thing. The conclusion of the Interstate Commerce Commission in a railway mail pay case was that "[t]he cost computed in the manner described is a hypothetical cost and not an actual cost."[1] In a 1949 decision the Supreme Court agreed: "Railroad accounting does not, and concededly cannot, accurately reflect actual operating costs of each type of service rendered."[2] One eminent commentator is reputed to have consulted the ultimate authority with this result: "God Almighty does not know the cost of carrying a hundred pounds of freight from Boston to New York."[3]

Despite opinions of this sort, the Senate Committee on Interstate and Foreign Commerce held hearings on the airmail rate bills at which a number of well-qualified witnesses testified. One of them pointed out that only 1 or 2 percent of the costs of operating an air line could be specifically identified with airmail. The other 98 or 99 percent of any cost figure arrived at would be the result of some more-or-less arbitrary system of prorations and allocations. The best result that could be hoped for would be an average cost per ton mile for all classes of cargo, a cost figure about as valid for pricing purposes as the meat packer's average cost per pound for hamburger and T-bone steaks.

The chairman of the committee was totally unimpressed:

I still come back to that original observation that if the over-all costs of air line operation may be determined, and you even say that it is possible to determine the costs of transporting a ton one mile, then it would seem to me that you could reduce it to the unit of pounds and go from there to whatever you were transporting, whether it were freight, express, mail, or passengers, and get a reasonable figure.[4]

None of these bills got through Congress in 1951 and no similar legislation has been passed since, although a message from the President once suggested that "compensatory rates for mail transportation should be based upon the cost of rendering mail service, plus a fair return."[5]

NRA: Cost Accounting with the Force of Law

There have been a number of more notable examples of a requirement for the use of the results of cost accounting with the force of law. One agency that was so involved was the NRA (National Recovery Administration), a federal agency, which existed only from 1933 to 1935, but which was very much in the public eye while it lasted.

[1] 214 ICC 66, Railway Mail Pay, Georgia and Florida Railroad Company.

[2] U.S.V. Jones, 336 U.S. 641, p. 654.

[3] A. T. Hadley, exact source unknown.

[4] Comment of Chairman of Senate Interstate and Foreign Commerce Committee during hearings on S. 1137 and related bills, 82nd Congress, 1st Session.

[5] H. Doc. No. 160, 83rd Congress, 1st Session.

The cost accounting generated by the NRA was not prescribed by the law but by the codes of fair competition adopted by many trades and industries. The Depression had brought about ruinously low prices for many products and services, and many code authorities felt that there must be some method of establishing price floors in order to keep desperate businessmen from committing commercial suicide. A number of different approaches toward achievement of this end were adopted. The most popular was some form of prohibition of selling below cost. For this purpose, cost had to be defined. Some industries were content to include a relatively simple definition of cost in the basic "code of fair competition." A few industries, such as gear manufacturing and photoengraving, had developed cost accounting manuals for their members. These were specified by the codes as the methods of ascertaining cost. Most industries, however, had no such manuals. Their codes called for the development of cost formulas or cost systems which their members would be required to use. No less than 357 industry codes contained some such provision.

These cost formulas or systems were all subject to the approval of the administrator of NRA, General Hugh Johnson. The General obviously needed help in deciding whether or not to approve such compilations, and for this he turned to his Research and Planning Division, which at first was headed by Robert H. Montgomery, a most respected leader in the accounting profession. That the job of reviewing these documents had not been placed in the most sympathetic hands is suggested by the following excerpts from a 1934 Montgomery speech:

If the world owes every man a living, if we can lift ourselves by our own bootstraps, if we can make silk purses out of sows' ears, then the adoption of a standard cost formula as a useful element in the fixing of prices will help us on the road to recovery.

In my opinion a uniform cost formula is impracticable because there are too many unknown and unknowable factors to produce an accurate result. In school we were told that in an equation we could have no more than one unknown factor or an accurate result would be impossible. The proponents of a uniform cost formula hand us from three to thirty unknown factors and ask us to produce a figure which we will use not only as a basis for fixing sales figures but the figures may be used as a limit below which you must not sell or you will go to jail.

Nevertheless, Montgomery realized that a job had to be done, and he therefore added to his staff an accountant who was designated as chief of the Cost Accounting Unit. For some time the unit consisted solely of the chief: there were no Indians. Later, two more accountants were employed, and all the work related to the cost formulas and systems was performed by these three. Montgomery soon resigned and was succeeded by Leon Henderson, an economist who described himself as a production-minded Democrat. He had little faith in plowing under piglets as a cure for the depression.

The systems and formulas presented for the administrator's approval varied widely, as might be expected. Some were little more than expressions of pious hope—so filled with obscurity and loopholes that their efficacy was no greater than that of a moral precept. These stood a good chance of approval, since they obviously placed no limitations on price flexibility. Others attempted to put rather specific props under minimum prices.

The funeral supply industry, for example, had been plagued by the backyard operator, usually a carpenter, who could nail a few boards together and produce a coffin whose cheapness had a great appeal to bereaved families during the Depression. Such operators, while they might be able to compute manufacturing costs after a fashion, had no recognizable selling and administrative costs. This lack was to be supplied, according to the proposed cost-finding method, by the adoption, by a 60 percent vote of members of the appropriate industry group, of flat, minimum percentages of sales "which shall be included in the costs of all members. . . ." This proposal never received the administrator's approval.

In all, approval of cost formulas was achieved by forty industries, ranging from boiler manufacturing, through imported date packaging, to smoking pipes. Even these approvals were for limited periods of time, to see how they worked out. Not more than half of them were still in effect when the Supreme Court wiped out the NRA in 1935.

The problems encountered in making the NRA no-sales-below-cost provisions work were multitudinous. One of them was reported by Baldwin Locomotive Works, whose foundry operations were subject to twenty-eight different codes. In a hearing on a proposed cost accounting system for the gray iron foundry industry, representatives of Baldwin expressed concern over how they were to remain in compliance with all these codes. Must they compute their costs by 28 different methods? If so, the problem of unemployment among cost clerks would soon be solved.

In spite of these and many other practical problems in the implementation of the policy of basing minimum prices on costs, the administration was assured by some volunteer advisers that this was really a simple matter. "There is no excuse for controversy as to what constitutes cost," wrote one. "It is a question of fact, not one of opinion. The fact is that all expenditures in the *proper* [his emphasis] conduct of a business are a part of the cost, including interest and depreciation." Another volunteer, who described himself as a "cost engineer" with long experience, defined the cost of a product as "the sum of the expenses involved in its production, nothing omitted, nothing added."

In view of such advice as this it is not surprising that legislators without experience in the intricacies of cost accounting or appreciation of the many points at which judgment or managerial policy, rather than objective criteria, determines cost allocations, are unable to see anything wrong with the apparently simple requirement that prices or price differences be based on costs.

Although NRA is gone, selling below cost is still taboo under certain circumstances. It may be a violation of Section 5 of the Federal Trade Commission Act, or it may violate one of the many state unfair practices laws. It is condemned in the trade practice conference rules adopted by many industries under the guidance of the Federal Trade Commission. Because the Federal Trade Commission Act is an antitrust statute, below-cost selling may even be a criminal offense under Section 3 of the Robinson-Patman Act. The definition and ascertainment of cost under such provisions have not proved to be simple, but the problems are too numerous and the history too complex to be dealt with here, especially since both laws and rules have had somewhat limited practical application.

Accounting in the Price Control Program of World War II

Five years after the Supreme Court swept the NRA *minimum*-price fixers out of Washington, many of the same cast of characters, including Leon Henderson, converged on the city again to establish an organization to control *maximum* prices. The Office of Price Administration made extensive use of cost data in its attempt to dampen the effects of wartime inflation. While the cost accounting staff of NRA never exceeded a half-dozen people, the accounting division of OPA reached a high of about 1400, with accountants scattered from Key West to Nome and from Honolulu to Portland, Maine. In addition to its own accountants, the OPA made extensive use of the accounting staffs of the Federal Trade Commission and the Tariff Commission.

By and large the role of costs during the OPA period was not to establish prices but to measure the legitimacy of increases in prices. The initial price-control device was the freeze. If, after prices were frozen, a seller or an industry desired an increase, studies by the accountants were aimed at measuring the extent of alleged cost increases. Price increases,

in general, were not permitted if cost increases did not justify them.

The status of accountants in the OPA was a considerable cut above that in NRA. The director of accounting bore the impressive title of Assistant Administrator. However, the OPA accountants were never in policy-making roles, although they may well have been consulted on occasion in the making of certain decisions. Instead, their function was to ascertain and report financial facts on which intelligent action might be taken. Accountants with some expertise in specific industries were attached to each industry group or division within the Washington offices of the agency, and other accountants were assigned to field offices throughout the country.

One problem that this arrangement gave rise to was that of divided jurisdiction. Those in charge of accounting operations in the top echelon felt that professional standards should be established and controlled at that level. Administratively, however, the accountants who were assigned to serve individual organizational units were necessarily responsible to the heads of those units. Where to draw the line between the two kinds of responsibility was not always clear. In a few case, where the findings of the accountants assigned to specific units did not please the heads of those units, other accountants, with philosophies more in line with those of the unit heads, were "bootlegged" into the units, disguised as economists or statisticians, for the purpose of providing data more to the liking of those in charge. The complications resulting from this practice may readily be imagined.

The principal work of the OPA accountants consisted of two kinds of studies. One was a study of the cost and profit picture of an entire industry or of some segment thereof. The other consisted of reviewing the records of individual companies to see whether their claims of increased costs or declining profits were valid support for requests to increase prices.

Another function performed for a time by the OPA accounting staff was to review all questionnaires before they went out. Mr. Henderson had begun to get complaints from industry that the demands for information by various segments of the agency had gotten out of hand. Business enterprises were being asked for complex data that either did not exist in any form or could be retrieved only by the expenditure of inordinate amounts of time and money. The appetite of OPA lawyers, economists, and statisticians for information was insatiable. The result was that the administrator turned over to the accounting division the task of screening all questionnaires for feasibility and probable impact on the recipients. The accounting division promptly became the least popular segment of the organization. It was a great relief when that job was taken over for the whole federal government by the U.S. Bureau of the Budget in the Executive Office of the President under the 1941 Federal Reports Act.

Still another duty of the OPA accountants was the collection of industry financial data. Such data were collected directly from some 20,000 companies by the use of forms devised for this purpose by the accounting division. In December 1942, some 18,000 annual reports had been received, plus about 30,000 interim reports. From these reports were compiled data concerning sales, profits, investment, and so on, by particular trades and industries for the use of OPA personnel in preparing price regulations and making rulings on requests for approval of price changes. The Financial Reporting Branch also was provided by the Treasury Department with cards which showed condensed financial data from about 75,000 companies over the five-year period 1936–1940. These data were useful in establishing profit comparisons and standards.

Cost studies made by the OPA accountants covered substantially all aspects of American trade and industry. This work was not done without encountering many problems and difficulties. The nature of some of these obstacles is suggested by one significant statistic which was derived from a review of the OPA accountants' activities made near the close of the agency's life. This review was inspired by proposed legislation which would have required that all prices established by OPA must provide for recovery of total costs plus a reasonable margin of profit, computed on an individual product basis. Such legislation would obviously have thrown an enormous burden on the OPA accounting division, and Paul M. Green, who was then Deputy Administrator for Accounting, asked two of his lieutenants to estimate what such legislation might mean, in accounting terms. Based on their findings, Green told the Banking and Currency Committee of the House of Representatives that "85 percent of all industrial companies do not allocate cost information on a product basis."[6] In only 15 percent of all industrial enter-

---

[6] Statement transmitted to Committee, April 4, 1946, but not published in the proceedings.

prises would OPA be able to find cost information that would make possible the implementation of the proposed legislation. The task would not have been made any easier by the fact that the proposal would have required not only the determination of current product costs and profits but the relating of these figures to product costs and profits of some earlier base period, such as 1936–1939.

The Clayton and Robinson–Patman Acts

OPA and its Korean successor, OPS (Office of Price Stabilization), are now only memories. Since the passage of the Clayton Act in 1914, however, there has been on the statute books a law that bases price differences, rather than prices themselves, on costs. This is Section 2 of the Clayton Act, which first made this principle a part of American antitrust policy. The Robinson–Patman Act, which amended Section 2 in 1936, forbids discrimination in prices charged to different customers, with certain exceptions. One of the exceptions is where the price differences are justified by "differences in the costs of manufacture, sale, or delivery resulting from the differing methods or quantities in which such commodities are to such purchasers sold or delivered. . . ."

The law makes no attempt to define what is meant by the term "costs." This is probably fortunate, since any congressional definition would raise more questions than it answered. Neither has the Federal Trade Commission, which administers the Robinson–Patman Act, laid down any definitions or rules that can be relied upon by respondents to complaints of price discrimination. (This is a slight exaggeration, since there exist a few negative rules—things that are not acceptable.) The commission appointed an advisory committee in 1953 with the hope that such a committee might be able to illuminate the murky area of cost justification, but when the committee's report was issued in 1956, the commission chose not to endorse it. As a result, each litigated case has been dealt with on an *ad hoc* basis, and what has been found acceptable in some instances has been rejected in others.

As a result, the cost defense has been found in practice to be "largely illusory."[7] The Supreme Court has agreed with this verdict. In its *Automatic Canteen* decision,[8] the court commented on "the intricacies inherent in the attempt to show costs in a Robinson–Patman Act proceeding" and observed the "elusiveness of cost data" which that effort entails. In fact, the court concluded, "proof of a cost justification being what it is, too often no one can ascertain whether a price is cost-justified."

One overriding difficulty with the Robinson–Patman cost defense is the fact that proof must almost invariably be in terms of distribution and administrative costs, a field that is still largely neglected in practice, in contrast to the manufacturing cost area, which has been explored at great depth, and in which,

---

[7] Former FTC Chairman Edward F. Howrey in a speech on October 18, 1954, and the report of the Attorney General's National Committee to study the Antitrust Laws, March 31, 1955.

[8] Automatic Canteen Company of America v. Federal Trade Commission, 346 U. S. 61.

comparatively speaking, there is far less room for disagreement. The vast majority of sellers make no real analysis of their selling costs, and most marketing managers resist attempts to control the costs of their operations by measures similar to those used in the factory. Selling—the creation and stimulation of customer demand—is a creative process, requiring imagination and inspiration. It would be unthinkable to hamper practitioners of this art by imposing the restrictions engendered by budgets, standards, and similar limitations on freedom of action.

What is involved in a Robinson-Patman cost study could be illustrated by a résumé of almost any actual case. This would make clear the technical accounting problems which have confronted those who have tried to isolate and measure cost differences under this legislation. Any such effort would unduly lengthen and complicate this essay, however, and perhaps bore those readers whose taste does not run to such esoteric matters.

Three Classes of Cases

Grouping of Customers, Orders, and Commodities

However, three examples of the kinds of problems confronting the preparers of cost defenses may make clear why this job is so frustrating. The first example deals with a very basic problem, the classification or grouping of customers, orders, and commodities. It requires little thought to perceive that if customers, for example, have to be dealt

with one by one, the problems of cost determination become unanswerable. This fact was recognized by the Supreme Court in the Chicago fluid milk case[9]:

Although the language of the proviso, with some support in legislative history,* is literally susceptible of a construction which would require any discrepancy in price between any two purchasers to be individually justified, the proviso has not been so construed by those charged with its enforcement. The Government candidly recognizes in its briefs filed in the instant case that "(a)s a matter of practical necessity . . . when a seller deals with a very large number of customers, he cannot be required to establish different cost-reflecting prices for each customer." In this same vein, the practice of grouping customers for pricing purposes has long had the approval of the Federal Trade Commission. We ourselves have noted the "elusiveness of cost data" in a Robinson-Patman Act proceeding. *Automatic Canteen Co.* v. *Federal Trade Comm'n,* 346 U.S. 81 (1958). In short, to completely renounce class pricing as justified by class accounting would be to eliminate in practical effect the cost justification proviso as to sellers having a large number of purchasers, thereby preventing such sellers from passing on economies to their customers. It seems hardly necessary to say that such a result is at war with Congress' language and purpose.

*For instance, the Chairman of the Conference on the Bill reported to the House: "The differential granted a particular customer must be traceable to some difference between him and other particular customers, either in the quantities purchased by them or in the methods by which they are purchased or their delivery taken." 80 Cong. Rec. 9417 (1936).

This strong language in favor of customer groupings was not, however, an invitation to group customers in any way favored by the seller. According to the court:

[9] U.S. v. Borden Co. et al., 370 U.S. 460 (1962).

But this is not to say that price differentials can be justified on the basis of arbitrary classifications or even classifications which are representative of a numerical majority of the individual members. At some point practical considerations shade into a circumvention of the proviso. A balance is struck by the use of classes for cost justification which are composed of members of such selfsameness as to make the averaging of the cost of dealing with the group a valid and reasonable indicium of the cost of dealing with any specific group member. High on the list of "musts" in the use of the average cost of customer groupings under the proviso of 2(a) is a close resemblance of the individual members of each group on the essential point or points which determine the costs considered.

In this regard we do not find the classifications submitted by the appellees to have been shown to be of sufficient homogeneity.

Borden's customer classification had put chain stores in one group and all independent stores in another. The court was convinced that many independent stores compared favorably in size (as measured by their intake of dairy products) with chain store units. To average these large independents with the "mom and pop" corner grocers was, in the opinion of the court, "like averaging one horse and one rabbit."

Since this decision, the FTC staff have been on the alert for other "horse and rabbit"situations. They were sure they had found one when American Motors (AM), accused of illegal price discrimination in the sale of Kelvinator electric appliances, compared the costs of doing business with four "favored" merchandise distributors with the average cost of serving some 6000 "disfavored" retail customers.[10] This must surely be an example of the FTC's favorite sin: too broad averaging. The trial examiner nevertheless accepted AM's cost defense. He was overruled by the Commission, but the latter was in turn overruled by the U.S. Circuit Court of Appeals.[11]

Very early in the game the attention of the commission was called to the sad plight of the marginal buyer, the one who was on the upper fringe of one volume group, but did not quite qualify for the next higher volume group. He would be subject to the unfair competitive advantage enjoyed by his competitor, who received a higher discount because he had barely achieved membership in the next-volume group. The Commission sensibly refused to be moved by this piteous tale, influenced, very probably, by the unlikelihood of any actual competitive situation answering to this description, and further by the obvious fact that a customer who is potentially the victim in such a case can forestall his handicap by ordering a few more product units. As a matter of maintaining good customer relations, in fact, salesmen who are on their toes will remind the customer what he needs to do to attain the higher discount.

In two treble-damage suits that were litigated before the Borden case, federal district courts had held that cost justification must be customer by customer. Both of these cases arose out of suits by customers of American Can Co. The first suit, brought under Section 4 of the Robinson–Patman Act, was by a customer known as Bruce's Juices, which

---

[10] American Motors. Docket No. 7357, 68 FTC 87.

[11] American Motors Corp. v. FTC 384 F. 2nd 247. Certiorari denied, 390 U.S. 1012.

claimed damages in the amount of $657,000. If these were tripled, American Can would be obligated to pay something over $2,000,000, after the addition of the complainant's legal expenses. Bruce's Juices prevailed in the district court.[12] The court remarked that American Can's customer classification system "completely disregarded the actual expenses incident to selling its individual customers." On appeal of this decision to the Fifth Circuit Court of Appeals, Bruce's Juices won again.[13] The court characterized the American Can discount plan as involving "too broad averaging," although the decision did not specifically favor individual customer accounting.

The second American Can case resulted from a suit brought in Arkansas by Russellville Canning Company. Plaintiff's counsel laid heavy emphasis on the failure of American Can's cost computations to disclose the costs of dealing with individual customers. The district court held for the plaintiff.[14] A quotation from the decision is indicative of the court's reasoning:

A literal interpretation of Section 2(a) would appear to call for consideration of the sales costs to individual customers and to individual plants of customers who operate more than one. It is difficult to see in what other manner price differentials can be limited to the sphere of actual costs. Certainly, if the chief purpose of the Act, the protection of small businesses, is to be achieved in any degree, some semblance of individual cost justification should be required.

In this case, however, an appeal to the Eighth Circuit Court resulted in a reversal and remand to the district court for a retrial. The appeals court's reasoning sounds much like that of the Supreme Court in the Borden case:

It seems to us that the applicable statute discloses no Congressional intent to authorize a District Court, in an action such as this, to reject a seller's attempted justification of its quantity discount system unless the justification meets all of the requirements which the District Court in this case evidently considered essential. If a manufacturer granting quantity discounts is required to establish and to continuously maintain a cost accounting system which will record the expenses incurred in selling every individual customer and all of the data which the plaintiff deems essential, the burden, expense and assumption of risk involved would seem to preclude the granting of quantity discounts, at least until the approval of the plan by the Federal Trade Commission had been secured. . . .

We think the District Court in the instant case, in determining the sufficiency of the defendant's attempted justification, applied too rigid a standard.[15]

No retrial ever occurred. It is to be presumed that both this and the Bruce's Juices case were settled out of court. Although these two cases were not tried before the Federal Trade Commission, there is little likelihood that the Commission would have accepted American Can's customer groupings. Canco classified its customers in three groups for pricing purposes. Group A, which received the highest discount, included only two customers; group B numbered

[12] Bruce's Juices v. American Can Co., 87 F. Supp. 985.

[13] American Can Co. v. Bruce's Juices, 187 F. 2nd 919 (1951). Certiorari denied 342 U.S. 875.

[14] Russellville Canning Co. v. American Can Co., 87 F. Supp. 484 (1949)

[15] American Can Co. v. Russellville Canning Co., 191 F. 2nd 38 (1951).

from 19 to 34 in various years, and group C, which received no discount, included approximately 2700 customers.

These examples are perhaps enough to illustrate sellers' problems in classifying customers for pricing purposes. They also indicate the desirability of carrying on cost studies in advance of complaints by the FTC or unhappy customers. If a differential price schedule is adopted without reference to costs and a complaint ensues, the cost analyst is faced with the problem of trying to justify that particular schedule. He may find this to be a formidable task. A study of differential costs made prior to the adoption of a price schedule, on the other hand, can very readily be so constructed as to throw light on the relation of costs to a wide selection of possible price brackets, and make it possible to adopt a pricing system that will be defensible in the event of a complaint.

Cash Discounts

The second item illustrating the kind of problem that may be faced by a respondent to a price-discrimination complaint relates to a matter about which it would seem that there could be no controversy: the treatment of cash discounts. Cash discounts became an issue in the complaint against Sylvania Electric Products (Docket No. 5728). Sylvania offered all customers a 2 percent discount for prompt payment. To Sylvania's accountants this meant that if the base price of a radio tube was, for example, $1.00, the net price to customer A in the no-discount bracket was 98 cents, no matter whether he took the discount or not. If, because of bad management or a lack of ready funds, he actually paid $1.00, the extra 2 cents

was the price of the credit extension, not of the tube. If customer B was in a volume discount bracket that entitled him to a 10 percent discount, his net price was 88.2 cents because his cash discount was 1.8 cents. The effective price difference between A and B was therefore 98 cents minus 88.2 cents, or 9.8 cents, and not 10 cents.

The transcript of the Sylvania hearings includes some 300 pages devoted to the Commission accountant's insistence that the price difference was really 10 cents. He was positive that cash discounts should be ignored. The result, of course, was to make Sylvania's price differences greater than they would have been if the cash discount item had been handled properly. Therefore, the cost difference had to be correspondingly greater.

Sylvania counsel were never able to shake the Commission accountant from his position, even with evidence that he had not always been consistent in it. When it came time for briefs, the Commission counsel cited legislative history. The House Conferees' report on the Robinson–Patman amendment had read in part as follows:

The Senate amendment made it unlawful to discriminate between purchasers 'in price or terms of sale.' The House bill did not contain the words 'or terms of sale.' The Senate receded, and the words 'or terms of sale' were stricken. *The managers were of the opinion that the bill should be inapplicable to terms of sale except as they amount in effect to indirect discriminations in price within the meaning of the remainder of subsection (a).* [Emphasis supplied by counsel.]

He also cited the Commission's definition of "net realized price" in U S. Rubber et al., FTC 1489 (1939). This definition read as follows: "the net amount of money paid by a purchaser

. . . after taking into account all discounts (excepting uniform cash discounts available to all purchasers), commissions, rebates, refunds, and other price adjustments."

It was counsel's contention (and that of his accounting colleague) that cash discounts available to all customers at a uniform rate result in no price discrimination. As a matter of fact, they do, but the discrimination is in favor of the customer who pays the higher base price. His discount will be higher than that of a customer in a higher volume bracket since his base price is higher. The example used above demonstrates this. Customer A gets a 2-cent cash discount, while customer B gets a cash discount of only 1.8 cents.

In the Sylvania case the amount that was being argued about was 0.22 cent. This seems like a rather small item to justify devoting to it 300 pages of record, but it was almost exactly one-fourth of what the Commission accountant claimed was Sylvania's failure to justify. The Commission accountant's cost difference was 13.91 cents per radio tube and the price difference was 14.78 cents. The alleged failure therefore amounted to 0.87 cent.

The Sylvania case was not the only one in which Commission staff firmly stuck to the position that cash discounts had nothing to do with price, but it is by all odds the best and most remarkable example. It had been concluded in 1954, while the Advisory Committee on Cost Justification was in existence and was therefore fresh in the committee's mind. As a result, the committee report included the following language:

Whether or not the buyer pays his bills in time to receive a cash discount does not in any way affect the price. Where a careless or ill-financed buyer fails to take a cash discount, the excess is a payment for credit accommodation, and not a payment for goods. Thus, if the invoice price to buyer A is $10, and buyer B is $9, and each is entitled to a two per cent discount for cash payment within a specified period, the effective price to A is $9.80 and to B is $8.82. The price differential to be justified is 98 cents, no matter whether either A or B takes advantage of the discount. Similarly, if the invoice price to both A and B is $10, A's invoice being subject to a two per cent cash discount and B's price being net, the price differential in favor of A is 20 cents, whether or not A takes the discount.

Although the Commission exonerated Sylvania, it did not decide the cash-discount question. Interestingly enough, however, it has subsequently changed its definition of net price. For example, in the Philadelphia Carpet Company decision (Docket No. 7635), handed down in 1964, the determination of net price requires the following: "there shall be taken into account discounts, rebates, allowances, deductions or other terms and conditions of sale by which net prices are effected." Significantly absent is any language that would exclude cash discounts from this treatment.

Cost of Capital

A third area in which respondents and the FTC have run a collision course is cost of money, or cost of capital. As the situation presently stands, the Commission denies that there is any such cost, or at least that it can be taken into account in a Robinson–Patman proceeding. Every accountant, economist, or business manager would agree that capital has a cost. It is not a free good. That this cost should be taken into account in cost-justification calculations has been proposed, to date, by four respondents: Thompson Products Company, The

Borden Company, Sperry Rand Corporation, and Forster Manufacturing Company. The Commission rejected the claims of the first two, but the complaints in the other two cases were dismissed for reasons not related to the cost defense. The Commission therefore did not rule on the cost-of-money question.

In all cases, the respondent based the cost-of-money claim on a showing that investments in certain assets needed for serving the "disadvantaged" customers were not needed, or needed in smaller amount, to serve the class of customers who were charged the lower prices.

Thompson Products sold automotive parts both to original-equipment manufacturers (OEMs, mainly automobile companies) and to a large group of auto-parts distributors. The OEMs were charged prices that averaged more than 39 percent lower than those charged to distributors for the same assortment of items. Thompson's accountants found distribution costs to the distributors (exclusive of the cost of money) to be 38.31 percent of sales. The corresponding expenses of dealing with OEMs were a mere 0.16 percent. The operating-cost differential was therefore 38.31 percent—not quite enough to justify a price difference of 39.28 per cent. In addition to this relatively small failure of cost justification on the whole line of OEM business, Thompson was faced with the fact that the prices charged to individual OEM customers varied from two cases in which the distributors received lower prices than certain OEMs to one instance in which the OEM's price advantage was 60.94 percent. Out of a total of 22 OEM customers, 14 had a price advantage in excess of 38.15 percent. The average

advantage of these customers was 43.10 percent. It was clear, therefore, that if the OEM customers must be looked at individually, and not as a group, Thompson was in trouble. And most of Thompson's really big OEM customers—Ford, Chrysler, General Motors—fell in this high-advantage group. Furthermore, the FTC staff were insisting that these customers must be justified individually—they could not be treated as a group.

To take care of all these problems, Thompson proposed the recognition of an item sometimes called "cost of money" and sometimes "return on investment." In order to serve its distributor customers, Thompson had in 1955 an investment of something like $8.8 million, consisting of inventories, accounts receivable, working funds, and warehouse plant and equipment. No such investment was required to service the OEMs. The rate proposed to be applied to this investment was equal to the company's rate of earnings before interest and taxes on total assets, less non-interest-bearing liabilities. This rate was 20.8 percent. Applying this to the $8.8 million produced a dollar amount of some $1.8 million, which was 10.64 percent of the sales to which it was to be related. This, added to the 38.15 of cost difference otherwise computed, would take care of every individual OEM except one, sales to which were negligible, and two others, where the failure would be less than 1 percent.

As can easily be imagined, this proposal was greeted by the Commission counsel with little short of horror. The hearing examiner, though he admitted testimony on the subject, pointed out what he thought was the basic weakness in the argument. If return on investment was profit, as he seemed to think, and if a profit was needed to justify price differences, then the company that made no profit would not be able to show justification.

Commission counsel quoted from Senate Report 1502, 74th Congress, in part as follows: The language of the bill was designed "to preclude . . . differentials based on allocated or imputed, as distinguished from actual, differences in cost." This, he thought, effectively barred cost of money from consideration. Taken literally, it would preclude much more. The Commission has never been hesitant to accept allocated costs. All indirect costs must be allocated and, according to Kohler, in *A Dictionary for Accountants,* even the process of charging direct costs to the object for which they are expended constitutes allocation. His definition of "allocate" reads in part as follows: "To charge an item or group of items of revenue or costs to one or more objects, activities, processes, operations, or products, in accordance with cost responsibilities, benefits received, or other readily identifiable measure of application or consumption" (Kohler, 1970, p. 25). It is worthy of note that there is no suggestion in this definition that allocated costs are unreal, or the opposite of actual. The Commission, of course, has never considered them as such. There may have been arguments about the methods of allocation, but never about the process itself.

Since the objection to Thompson's cost-of-money item was surely not that it was allocated, one must assume that the objection arose out of the fact that it was imputed. Here can be found some support for counsel's position in Kohler's dictionary. His definition of "imputed interest" is as follows (Kohler, 1970):

> The return on capital assumed to be a part of the net income of an enterprise; normally not separated and usually regarded as inseparable from the balance of net income as pure profit because of (a) the absence of any contractual obligation therefor, and (b) the impossibility of selecting any realistic amount that represents such return (pp. 224, 225).

Although this definition does not specifically characterize imputed interest as unreal, the implication is conveyed by the absence of contractual obligation and the impossibility of measurement. Unfortunately, the Kohler dictionary does not define cost of money or cost of capital.

When the Commission came to passing judgment on Thompson's cost defense, it was rejected. An important reason was agreement with Commission counsel that each OEM customer should be considered separately. Another was total rejection of Thompson's cost-of-money theory. "This amount," said the Commission, "is essentially an allocated portion of the total profits of the company from all sources, including export sales, defense contract sales, and sales of automotive parts. . . . The return rate factor or element here claimed is thus entirely outside the sphere of actual cost differences."

Borden took a different and more modest approach. It claimed as cost of money 8 percent of the capital employed in the sale of its branded evaporated milk, which was required in lesser amounts in the sale of milk bearing customer brands. The 8 percent rate was described as "the one which the company used in connection with its incentive compensation plans." This rate was applied to two asset items: inventories and accounts receivable. Inventories of Borden brand milk far exceeded those of private label. Accounts receivable from Borden brand customers, on the other hand, were decidedly lower (per unit of product sold) than were accounts receivable from private-label customers. Thus, the two elements of investment offset each other to some extent. The net result was an investment cost of the Borden brand business (the higher-priced line) about 0.4 cent greater than that attributable to the private-label (lower-priced) business.

As might be expected, the Commission rejected this portion of Borden's cost study. It cited the Thompson Products decision as precedent and remarked: "The fallacy in this position is that the so-called investment cost is not an actual, incurred cost at all; it amounts to a return on capital investment. Accordingly, this item is rejected for cost justification purposes."[16]

The corresponding claims of Sperry Rand and Forster were merely for bank interest which they would have had to incur if the "favored" customer had not made its purchases and paid its bills in such a way as to relieve the respondent of the necessity of carrying inventory and, in the Sperry Rand case, of waiting for its money. Both companies financed themselves in part by bank loans, and their claims were based on the rates which they would have had to pay if their "favored" customers had not relieved them of the necessity of borrowing.

Without going further into details,

here, at last, were cost-of-money claims that bore no stigma of imputation. Assuming that the assumptions on which they were based could be adequately substantiated, they were claims for out-of-pocket money which the respective respondents did not have to spend. They were on all fours with the types of cost items claimed by other respondents and accepted by the Commission.

Commission counsel nevertheless attacked these claims, basing criticism partly on the Thompson Products and Borden decisions. As a matter of logic, this criticism had little merit. A claim for unspent bank interest was not even a distant relative of the Thompson calculation and bore little resemblance to the Borden 8 percent.

If it was return on investment, it was return on the bank's potential investment in Forster's or Sperry Rand's business. As such, it far more resembled wages that did not need to be paid or other expenditures that became unnecessary, which are the savings generally claimed by respondents who submit cost defenses.

The hearing examiner in the Sperry Rand case nevertheless agreed with Commission counsel. His reasoning is of interest:

The hearing examiner has concluded that the intent and purpose of the Commission in its two said decisions was to exclude interest calculations of any sort for any purpose in cost justification defenses as "entirely outside the sphere of actual cost differences." The Commission construes the Act's pertinent proviso as "limited to permitting cost differentials making only due allowance for differences in cost of manufacture, sale and delivery *resulting from the different methods or quantities*

---

[16] The Borden Co., Docket No. 7129, 62 FTC 130.

in which the commodities are sold or delivered to purchasers." (Italics supplied; *Thompson Products, supra,* P. 1276.) While borrowing money and paying interest thereon may well increase the cost of sale or delivery of commodities in a general business sense, such interest does not result from "different methods or quantities" in the sale or delivery of such commodities to purchasers as the Act prescribes. In view of the legislative history of the Act and its express and limited language, the Commission has clearly indicated it does not intend to expand any allowance of cost justification claims to include interest under whatever momenclature it may be presented.

Unfortunately, the Commission was not required to consider this item in either case. The Sperry Rand complaint was dismissed because the Commission was convinced that the transactions involved were of so unique a character that they stood little chance of being repeated.[17] The portion of the complaint against Forster that involved the cost defense was dismissed because of an inadequate showing of injury to competition.[18]

Robinson–Patman:
Some General Considerations

In spite of what many people seem to think, cost is not an objectively determinable quantum, but instead is what someone says it is. In all Robinson–Patman cases, two sets of people have a say as to cost. One set is the accountants for the respondent and the Commission accountants constitute the other set.

Where these two groups agree, as they have on several occasions, the decision is relatively easy. Where they fail to agree, as has also happened, the administrative law judge, who first hears the evidence and prepares an initial decision, must choose between them. It is a significant fact that almost never has the judge failed to agree with the Commission accountants. He disagreed in the Goodyear–Sears Roebuck case[19] under old Section 2, in which the judge (then called trial examiner) refused to accept a few of the more outrageous accounting propositions laid down by the Commission accountant. In only one recorded instance under the Robinson–Patman Act has the judge failed to go along with the Commission accounting staff's analysis. This was in American Motors (Docket No. 7357). The Commission in that instance overruled the judge. In no other instance has respondent, no matter how much money was spent or how much accounting talent was brought to bear, been able to prevail with the judge against the accountants employed by the Commission.

The Commission itself must accept or reject the findings of the judge and the opinions of the accounting experts. In the Goodyear case, the Commission went somewhat further than the judge in rejecting certain of the opinions of the Commission accountant. In the Sylvania case,[20] decided in 1954, the Commission disagreed with both the judge and the Commission accountants on one vital

---

[17] Sperry Rand Corp., Docket No. 7559, 64 FTC 842 (1964).

[18] Forster Manufacturing Co., Docket No. 7207; 62 FTC 852.

[19] 22 F.T.C. 232.

[20] Docket No. 5728, 51 F.T.C. 282.

point. These represent the only two cases in which the Commission has disagreed with its own accounting staff.

In the Niehoff case,[21] decided in 1955, the judge ruled for the respondent on one cost item and was overruled by the Commission. This probably is another case in which the judge disagreed with the Commission accounting staff, but the public record is silent with respect to the accounting staff opinion, since no Commission accountant testified on this point. It is not difficult, however, for one familiar with the accounting staff's general point of view to surmise what its opinion was on the point in question.

There is intended in this description of the remarkable success of the Commission accounting staff no suggestion that the result has necessarily been wrong or bad. Such an extraordinarily high batting average should suggest to any respondent, however, that the success or failure of any cost study depends almost exclusively on its ability to make a favorable impression on the Commission accountants.

It is often assumed that it is practically impossible to secure dismissal of a complaint through presentation of cost evidence. The facts do not bear this out. In the first 20 attempts at cost justification under price-discrimination complaints, 9 respondents were successful, 10 failed, and in one case the respondent was successful in one cost issue and failed in another.[22] Thus, the balance between success and failure was remarkably even. In addition to cases on the

record, informal, off-the-record cost presentations have been made by many sellers, but such proceedings are confidential and no measure of the degree of success exists.

It is significant, however, that the cost defense has been resorted to in extremely few recent cases. (Of course, the number of price discrimination cases has shrunken to almost zero in the immediate past.) Of 18 respondents in 1957 only one offered the cost defense. This one happened to be successful. None of the 20 respondents to complaints in 1958 attempted to defend on the cost basis. The reasons are easy to understand: the outrageous cost of such defenses, coupled with the unlikelihood of their success.

Summary and Conclusions

This review of some of the applications of cost accounting to the mutual problems of business and public authority has necessarily been very sketchy. It has demonstrated, however, a few matters that appear to be both clear and significant. One is that basing price decisions on costs has a great appeal to legislators. Cost as a criterion for price appears to the average legislator to be both fair and simple. Mr. Patman, for example, writing about the law of which he was coauthor, admitted that sellers might have to do a little speculating about costs when considering future transactions. "In event of litigation, however," he said, "purchases will not

---

[21] Docket No. 5768, 51 F.T.C. 1114.

[22] Thompson Products, Inc., Docket No. 5872.

be *prospective* ones. The transactions will be past history. Costs will not be theoretical or estimated. They will have been incurred and recorded" (Patman, 1938, p. 18). The implication seems to be that actual costs are objectively and exactly determinable and that there is or should be no room for argument. Mr. Patman makes it clear, however, that he realizes that there will be arguments just the same. "The definition of costs," he says, "sometimes takes on strange constructions when the phrase-twisting experts play with it" (p. 19).

In point of fact, the determination of costs of individual products or services, especially when related to particular transactions, has always proved to be extraordinarily difficult. Respondents in Robinson–Patman cases have been known to spend hundreds of thousands of dollars on cost studies that might just as well never have been made. And this money was spent not because the respondents merely wanted to throw up an elaborate smoke screen but because the subject of the study is extremely difficult and elusive. It is one thing to agree on costs among businesspersons where litigation is not involved and quite another to make the kind of showing of costs which will stand up under the kind of testing that it receives in a courtroom.

Another fact which needs to be kept in mind is that costs, far from being precisely measurable by objective criteria, are actually the product of the judgment and *bona fides* of the people who prepare them. They are therefore only as good and as reliable as the accountants to whom this task is assigned. Really capable accountants are scarce, both in and out of government, especially in view of the fact that their time is already well occupied with the preparation of figures and reports for the assistance of management and for taxation and other financial purposes. Added burdens should not be lightly regarded.

Although it is too much to suppose that implementation of public policy through costs will assume appreciably less importance than it now has, it is to be hoped that we shall not see too much in the way of increased dependence on costs for this purpose in the future.

References

Kohler, E. L. 1970. *A Dictionary for Accountants*, 4th ed. Englewood Cliffs, N. J.: Prentice-Hall, Inc.

Patman, Wright. 1938. *The Robinson-Patman Act.* New York: The Ronald Press Company.

Part III

Some Fruits of Practice

Chapter 6

Eric L. Kohler, Comptroller of the Tennessee Valley Authority (1938-1941)*

Jerry F. Stone

The "Bookkeeper"

Chartered by Congress in 1933 as a fully owned government corporation, the Tennessee Valley Authority was assigned responsibility for a massive program of developing the Tennessee River and its tributaries. More specifically, it was required to undertake construction and operation of a chain of multipurpose dams for improving navigation, creating flood controls, and providing facilities for the production and distribution of hydroelectric power—and later, the construction and operation of steam power plants. Also authorized were the improvement and operation of an already existing government-owned chemical plant at Muscle Shoals for the production of fertilizers and, subsequently in the war years, explosives. Still other programs were authorized for the preservation and improvement of the valley's ecology and for raising the economic level of the valley's inhabitants.

The TVA area is large. The Tennessee River rises in tributaries from the mountain streams of southwestern Virginia and western North Carolina and flows south from Knoxville across Tennessee to Chattanooga, west through northern Alabama and Mississippi, then north, recrossing Tennessee and joining the Ohio River at Paducah, Kentucky. Depression-born, the TVA objective was hailed politically as the construction of an "American Ruhr."

An important provision of the act was

*The author is indebted to W. W. Cooper and Y. Ijiri for their extensive help in writing this chapter.

the prohibition, strictly adhered to, of political consideration as a basis for employment. This stipulation was to raise the ire of local politicians, notably U.S. Senator Kenneth McKellar, who, by virtue of seniority, was a powerful figure of the time. This and the character and magnitude of TVA's prospective operations stimulated the imagination and made available people who otherwise might not have sought or accepted government employment. The result was a highly competent staff. Notable examples were Theodore Parker, who later became Dean of Civil Engineering, Massachusetts Institute of Technology; attorney Henry Fowler, destined to become Secretary of the Treasury and now a prominent investment banker and a Goldman Sachs partner; and David Lilienthal, who, during the first 13 years, was probably the most important contributor to the development of TVA's early policies.

Strangely, this attraction of personnel either had not extended to key accounting people, or management was unfortunate in its selections. This may have been because the creative mind, engrossed in plans for changing the geography and economy of a vast area, does not long dwell on such matters, which it may think of as simple "bookkeeping."

As a result, those who directed TVA's accounting had developed some strange notions: among them, that commercial concepts of a balance sheet, an income statement for power operations, and interim reports necessary for the authority's administration were impossible. However, records of money transactions and basic documentation had been carefully maintained, the fault being that the results had not been consistently or meaningfully reported.

There were, of course, exceptions. In this connection, it must be said that TVA's Construction Accountant was one of those highly competent, plain-spoken people frequently found in the construction industry. He organized field construction accounting offices at major construction sites, staffed them with his own brand of "hard hats," and installed adequate time-keeping and payroll methods which, with good inventory controls, produced good construction cost accounts at the field level. It could be that his success was due to the fact that his activities were removed from the central office and he received little or no supervision. He knew what the construction people required for cost control, and he supplied it.

Running Battle with the GAO

In 1938, a congressional investigation was triggered by FDR's dismissal for "contumacy" of Arthur Morgan, the Authority's first chairman. Morgan and David Lilienthal had disagreed on basic policy and Lilienthal won. This investigation was fanned into a full-blown inquiry, some might call it an inquisiton, by both the opponents of public power and by wrathful politicians unable to secure jobs for their constituents. These powerful forces quickly recognized that the inadequacy of financial records and reporting was the "monster's" Achilles' heel.

That this was a vulnerable focal point was made more apparent by an audit report issued by the General Accounting Office. From the outset the Comptroller General and TVA management had engaged in a five-year running battle. The GAO insisted that all government agencies, including TVA, transmit their vouchers to Washington for pre- or post-audit. Such audits might result in "exceptions." An exception meant that, until explained or cleared, the amount became the personal debt of the disbursing officer signing the check. Such exceptions were taken for various reasons, a common one being that something was lacking in the record, such as a signature or certification, or perhaps an emergency purchase had been effected without submission of bids.

TVA's management stoutly maintained that its corporate powers exempted it from the accountability procedures of the GAO. However, without admitting jurisdiction, it did permit an office examination of the vouchers and visits from a so-called field audit force.

The exceptions piled up—thousands of them—some on the most ridiculous bases. For example, the writer once encountered a GAO audit clerk who said, waving a voucher, "Look here, this invoice has an item on it for P-PINS, the purchase order doesn't order any P-PINS, and the receiving report does not show the receipt of any such pins." The fellow was told that P-PINS is an abbreviation for parcel post and insurance. Here at least an encounter in the field forestalled one such "exception."

The Comptroller General issued a voluminous report listing his thousands of exceptions together with the report of his field auditors. More investigators than auditors, the work of even this field staff did not culminate in audited balance sheets and income statements, but in a disconnected narrative full of charges of grave misdoings, such as: "In countless instances moneys were received which were not deposited in the Special Deposits Account of the Treasury, as required by law." The law referred to is a requirement that all returnable moneys received, such as bid bond deposits and other items of this nature, shall be identified and deposited in the U.S. Treasury, reimbursements to be made by Treasury check.

The "countless instances" were truly countless. They included nickel bottle deposits left by workmen at dam-site commissaries. If a workman wanted to buy a bottled soft drink and take it off the premises, he would leave a nickel bottle deposit, which nickel was tossed into a cigar box, from which it was returned when the bottle came back.

The writer knows that this kind of thing was the basis for a good many such "audit remarks" because he was in a dam-site canteen with the chief of the field audit party when this outrageous impropriety was discovered. Vividly recalled is the conversation concerning the absurdity of identifying each nickel depositor, sending the money to the Treasury and later, much later, drawing and delivering 5-cent checks. The writer also remembers the looks of disbelief on the faces of the TVA board of directors when he explained this part of the audit report.

The Watchdog's Bark

Of course, the GAO report was seized upon by hostile members of the Congressional Investigating Committee, and it was given wide circulation by the private power people, notably the Edison Electric Institute. It was said to be evidence of a truly scandalous situation involving the criminal mishandling of funds and flagrant violations of the law.

These exceptions were fascinating because they were *all* unimportant and involved different kinds of paperwork from which the GAO's audit clerks had drawn conclusions that were both fantastic and irresponsible. They constituted an indictment of such a volume of trivialities that, if answered in detail, no one would read it or comprehend it. At the same time, they could not be ignored. Something had to be done.

To understand how such audit reports could come to be produced, we have to look at the background of the GAO. Established under the Budget and Accounting Act of 1921, its director was designated Comptroller General. He was intended to be, and was labeled, "the watchdog of Congress." It is doubtful if those who framed the act had any concrete ideas as to how the office would function. Certainly, the first Comptroller General did not. He was not an accountant, nor had he any business experience that would assist him in dealing with financial matters. His appointment by Warren Harding for a 15-year term stemmed from political considerations. He once summed up his conception of his responsibilities as follows: "If Congress should direct that 1 million dollars be thrown into the Potomac River from the right bank, my concern would be that the money be thrown from the right bank and not the left bank.[1]

The man was lost and did not know enough to realize the need for professional guidance. His total effort seemed to be directed toward making Congress believe that he was on the job. To do this, he had to produce something, and all that he and his clerks could produce were trivia to balloon out of all proportion and to surround with innuendos of gross misdeeds; thus was the "watchdog's" bark heard. Overlooked entirely was the wonderful opportunity to overhaul the archaic budget and accounting practices of government.

The Problem of Joint and Common Costs

If this were not enough, there were other vexing problems affecting financial reporting, some of which involved complexities that could only be addressed, if at all, by the most sophisticated accounting tools available. Others required invention in order to extend the state of the art of accounting. And so on.

The water control program for the Tennessee Valley was conceived as a series of high reservoir dams on tributaries of the Tennessee River to regulate a constant flow through a series of lower, main-river dams. The whole was to form an interconnected system and was to be designed and operated accordingly. Before the spring flood season, the reservoir dams were to be drawn down to provide capacity for withholding the flood waters that had long devastated the basin. When safe to do so, the reservoirs were to be filled and a constant stream maintained for the generation of power and the provision of a navigable depth of 9 feet in the main stream.

Thus, to the system of interconnected

[1] From two articles entitled "Government-Run Everything." *Saturday Evening Post*, October 3 and October 17, 1936.

water operations, with attendant costs and benefits, was added the multiple-purpose character of objectives involving flood control, navigation, power, and other activities, such as recreation and regional development. The drawing down of reservoirs for flood control was, and is, the first priority—performed rigidly under a "rule curve" developed from a many-year record of rainfall in the valley. Such an operation is not consistent with the maximum production of electricity. Reservoir capacities have to be reserved for flood control and also to maintain the requisite navigation depths. This means that there is always a risk that the rain pattern will change and therefore that drawn-down reservoirs will not refill. This has happened. Thus, to any except the most jaundiced eye, the water control program is not directed only to power production. It is multipurpose, as designed and operated, with the already indicated priorities.

With this view of the system to be developed, the TVA act *required* that the Board allocate its investment in multipurpose projects as between navigation, flood control, power, and national defense. At the time of the crisis associated with the joint House–Senate investigation of the TVA, the legally required allocation had not been made, and failure to comply with this requirement was a point of criticism.

A whole corps of people had been working on the problem, including a host of eminent outside consultants, such as James C. Bonbright and Martin Glazer. It was not difficult to resolve that:

1. The cost of intakes, power houses, and

appurtenances should be allocated to the power program.
2. The cost of locks and channels belong in the navigation program.
3. The excess reservoir capacity is patently for flood control.

But then the real issue emerges. How should the great mass of the system costs common to all purposes be allocated? This was the question facing the experts. Upon its solution depended the distribution of depreciation expense and other costs as directed by the act but, of course, there was no "accounting" solution to this problem—or any other solution—that would meet with everyone's approval.

Taking the Wind Out of the Sails

To recount, in the spring of 1938, after five years of existence and the expenditure of millions of dollars, TVA could produce no worthwhile financial statements. It was under attack by members of Congress, the Edison Electric Institute, the U.S. Chamber of Commerce, and the U.S. General Accounting Office. In this situation, the board of directors in May 1938 brought in Eric L. Kohler as Comptroller to effect a complete reorganization of the accounting processes. Kohler was a widely recognized authority, the author of accounting texts, a former president of the American Accounting Association, and a former manager in the nationally known public accounting firm of Arthur Andersen & Co. His reputation was that of one of the country's outstanding accountants.

Kohler's first task was to recast the millions of dollars of transactions for the first five years of TVA's existence, and to produce financial statements that would meet professional standards. He insisted upon the employment of an independent public accounting firm to audit these statements once they had been produced. This resulted in a report containing an *unqualified*[2] auditors' report confirming the propriety of the first five years of TVA's transactions. This, I might say, constituted a "first," not only in the form of the accounting report prepared but also in the type of audit utilized. No Federal agency or corporation had ever before submitted its accounts for audit by a firm of independent public accountants. To this day, Coopers & Lybrand continue to audit TVA's operations and to this day the TVA continues to utilize the types of statements which were prepared for this first release.

This audited report was presented to the Joint Congressional Committee by Mr. Kohler along with a great deal of other material in the course of week-long testimony. In this testimony, Mr. Kohler's remarks concerning the General Accounting Office's auditing methods as applied to the TVA were devastating. The GAO's reports could only be answered by a broad response exposing its methods; a detailed response would have been futile. This solved the GAO annoyance at the time, and the financial statements and audit report took some of the wind out of the sails of TVA's critics. It was, in a measure, instrumental in the survival of TVA in the face of a massive attack and, in a measure, it was also to have other consequences contributing, subsequently, to a recognized need for overhauling all of the GAO's accounting and auditing practices (see the chapter by Cooper and Frese).

The financial statements did bring new controversy in the form of the allocations utilized. Kohler, as chairman of the TVA's allocation committee, had an important part in the solution which resulted in a judgmental allocation based on numbers and other considerations but not strictly the result of a mathematical computation. The result was not stated to be "*the* way" but "*a* way" of accomplishing the purpose, since, as the report itself recognized, there was not—and, indeed, could not be—any objectively determined way of allocating such common costs, which ranged from the fixed costs of dam construction to the joint costs of systems operations. The allocation was completely explained and justified along these lines. The method of application in the schedule of fixed assets and in the income statement, however, was effected in such a manner that the reader could form his own opinion

---

[2]*Editor's Note:* There was, however, an exception, in that their annual report, explicitly noted in Vol. II, Financial Statements, p. 24, of the *Annual Report of the Tennessee Valley Authority for the Fiscal Year Ended June 30, 1938:*

The allowances for depreciation, and the amounts expended for maintenance, of completed dams and other property common to the navigation, flood control and electric power programs have been charged against the operations of such programs on the basis of the allocation of the investment in such property stated in the Authority's report of June 9, 1938, to the President of the United States. Other common expenses have been allocated to the respective programs in the manner indicated in Schedules C and D. We express no opinion respecting such allocation of property investment and of common expenses, nor upon the legality of expenditures by the Authority, inasmuch as these matters involve interpretation of the Tennessee Valley Authority Act and questions of public policy.

and reallocate these costs to the various programs accordingly. This could be done in a fairly easy manner.

The result was a thoroughly informative statement which effected the allocations required by law while making it possible for a user of these statements to effect other allocations, if desired. This was an ingenious solution to a legal requirement that really admitted of no objective determination, with the result that the "bottom line"—across all programs—would be the same whatever allocation routes might be followed. See Appendixes A and B.

Attempts at Product Costing

With the problem of external financial reporting thus resolved, the next task of the new accounting management involved the installation of a system of internal accounting and reporting for management control and budget administration. Kohler's predecessors had become engrossed with punched cards and other such mechanisms in their attempts to produce the analogue of a "product costing" system. This involved a series of allocations and imputations across a variety of administrative services and "product units" even where the latter could not be readily identified. For example, the operations of TVA were administered by departments pursuing each major endeavor—such as the Office of the Manager of Power, subdivided into divisions for: General Administration, Systems Operation, Power Production, Power Resources Planning, Transmission Planning and Engineering, and Power Construction. Each of these divisions was, in turn, further subdivided into sections and then into

units, the latter representing the lowest echelons in the division of work. A section of the Power Production Division existed at every generating station, where the work was subdivided and assigned to units.

The Accounting Division, in trying to arrive at its concept of "cost," added to the payroll cost of the departments a percentage arbitrarily selected to cover the cost of general administration for the entire TVA. To division payrolls, it added a percentage for department overhead and so on to sections and units. This attempt at "costing" resulted in a melange from which it was impossible to find the direct cost or expense of anything or to pinpoint the person responsible for its incurrence. It was inextricably bound up in allocations and reallocations that could not be unraveled. Comparisons with budgets were impossible because people can plan only for their own direct expenditures.

This situation, as described only for the power operations, became even more vague and confused with attempts to extend it to other areas, such as engineering and construction. It was clear that a complete revision of the accounting system was called for. A large roomful of tabulating equipment, alphabetical printers, keypunch machines, and sorters was wholly replaced with NCR bookkeeping machines, upon which direct transactions were posted without being subjected to allocations in a muddy concept of cost distribution. This could have been accomplished with the use of the tabulating equipment, of course, but two considerations militated against doing this: (1) there was not enough secondary use of the cards to make it economical, and (2), and more important, the keypunch equipment had become so identified with the costing procedures that changing it helped to reorient the people involved so that they could be brought back to more basic concepts of record keeping and accounting.

Activity Accounting and Responsibility Costing

In such an environment, about 1938, "activity accounting" was born.[3] It is basically "responsibility accounting," with some significant differences. The concept embraces the idea that every transaction, no matter what its importance, is controllable and that some one person is responsible for it; that it originates within recognized departmental organizations or suborganizations; and that it contributes to the performance of such "functions" as capital additions, revenue production, and operating expenses, including the various types of overhead. It involves the recognition and organization of the accounts by reference to the organization units conducting the activities, in such a way that they can be summarized upward by superior organization units, rather than allocated and prorated downward to "products," and also so they could be cross-classified into the functions that these organizational units participated in. Such a compilation makes possible budget comparisons for persons responsible for cost incurrence at every level and reports them in functions.

Thus, from the standpoint of internal accounting and management control, activity accounting represents an approach that might be called "organization costing" and control, to contrast it with the "product costing" and control that Kohler's predecessors had tried to develop. As such, it also facilitated the process of budgetary preparation and control at any level of organization activity or function by (1) tying the accounts directly into the wanted budgeted comparisons, and (2) arranging the compilations indicated in the preceding paragraph.

Note that such compilations could be synthesized from the lowest organization unit up through divisions and departments to the entire organization. Similar compilations could be arranged by functions with intersections between organization units and functions used to precipitate other details of interest for comparative analyses either across functions or across organization units. Finally, the arrangement of the financial results of functions was designed to produce balance sheets, income statements, and funds flow statements all from the same basic data matrix.

Controllability of all costs was at the core of activity accounting. This was to be achieved by an explicit organization design with all job-related functions explicitly specified. Budgets were also related to these assignments by individuals, and the accounting system was used to collate both. In particular, the

---

[3] The basic concepts of activity accounting, as outlined in Kohler's testimony before the joint House Senate investigating committee, were subsequently reproduced in the description of "activity accounting" that appears in Kohler (1975, pp. 19-22). As is well known, Arthur Andersen & Co. subsequently became a leading proponent of Responsibility Accounting and, indeed, Leonard Spacek was retained as a consultant by Kohler to help in the development and installation. It seems to be unknown, however, whether Kohler was associated with the development of the concepts and methods of responsibility accounting at Arthur Andersen & Co. either before or after his tenure with that firm.

principle of account design, in addition to the ones already indicated, was to assign accounts to the lowest possible level of organization and budgetary responsibility so that the accounting system conformed to the requirements of both budgetary administration and organization design at all levels. The costs incurred by responsible units of organization were reported to this lowest level for budget administration as well. Reports to higher echelons were then synthesized from the lower-level units after adding costs or charges for which the higher, but not the lower, levels were responsible. Kohler's theory was that a person should *not* be held responsible for something not under his or her control. That is, the higher echelons were viewed as responsible for lower-level expenditures and expenses—but not vice versa.

To quote from the latest edition of Kohler's *A Dictionary for Accountants* (Kohler, 1975):

Activity account: An income or expense account containing transactions over which an activity supervisor assumes responsibility and maintains control. The transactions may include materials and services, but not overhead or other items that are the responsibilities of other persons. To insure the following of a performance design predetermined [with] higher authority, limitations in the form of permissible objects and ranges of expenditure, the number and qualifications of employees and adherence to standards of operation and output are commonly imposed on the activity [as part of the system of organization and operating controls] (pp. 19–20).

This statement emphasizes the organiza-tion aspect of activity accounting and the way it relates to the organization's budgeting and performance controls. This could be accomplished to obtain any wanted syntheses and comparison, from the lowest organization units up to the top, in a straightforward manner. Alternatively, a synthesis across orga-nization units could be used to obtain expenditures and costs by function for both budgetary and accounting pur-poses.[4] In fact, continuing this synthesis by function produces the income and ex-pense summaries for the major pro-grams—power, flood control, naviga-tion, recreation—from which the TVA income and expense statements are formed.

Fundamentally, Kohler's idea was to avoid cost allocations and reallocations as much as possible. This could be sub-stantially achieved within the program accounts, where the expenditures were confined to operating costs, by and large. The closer one came to con-struction activities, however, the more difficult it became to avoid allocations. Indeed, it became desirable to give accounting recognition to such alloca-tions and reallocations because the construction engineers formed their estimates in this manner and hence comparability was needed from the accounts as well. However, overall project control was entirely susceptible to the plan, because such accounting allocations were entirely within the total project.

To deal with this problem, a distinc-tion was made between "programs" and "projects," where the former re-

---

[4]The synthesis is analogous to the ones obtained from the "crosswalk tables" in modern PPBS, "program planning budgeting systems." See, for example, Alioto and Jungherr (1971).

ferred to operations and the latter to capital-asset acquisitions (Kohler, 1975):

A *project* is a major property acquisition. Expenditures under a project are asset additions. An expenditure may involve the purchase of different kinds of assets . . . or it may relate to "own" construction.

A project budget, the result of planning and programming [sic], bears the approval of top management in advance of commitment; prospective unit costs are a feature. Examples of such units are material weights, labor hours, types of operation and completed parts of structures.

As the project is being acquired or is building, quantity and cost records are maintained [and reported, with relevant comparisons, up to and including] the completed-project cost report. Total reported cost is identical with the project cost reflected in financial statements (pp. 20–21).

Thus, for both projects and programs, the activity accounting system provided the requisite information for internal organizational and budget controls as well as the external financial reports (Kohler, 1975):

One synthesis of activity accounts yields *financial* (functional) *statements* of projects and programs; another, capital outlay, income and expense by organizational divisions, ordinarily required for budget comparisons (pp. 20–21).

Evidently various subtotals and additional comparisons could also be obtained for a variety of special reports as well. For instance, even such detail as across-organization or across-function costs of clerical operations could be obtained as well as special-purpose reports on such major items as power production and transmission or dam construction by subproject detail. Thus, regularly recurring as well as special-purpose reports were also supplied with a wealth

of buttressing detail conveniently available, when wanted, in this (then) new and original system of account design.

The Early Accomplishment

Kohler was a purist in many respects, and this was particularly true in implementing the idea of activity accounting. Nevertheless, he was forced to compromise in many areas in its implementation, as when, for example, it was not practically possible to distinguish various expenditures resulting from activities undertaken jointly by several organization units. Yet Kohler believed that imperfect though it might be, the implementation of the concepts of activity accounting was essential for securing economical performance and proper accountability in an organization like the TVA. Failing this, the requisite management controls were not likely to be forthcoming and, indeed, there would even be an attenuation in the accountability needed for the organization to survive in the tough, adversary political climate that TVA was compelled to live in.

Although the related concepts of responsibility accounting have now been developed and implemented in many types of organization, Eric Kohler had to make a pioneering effort to develop a similar system for accounting in the late 1930s and early 1940s. His experience in this area was considered to be so valuable that Leonard Spacek of Arthur Andersen strongly urged Kohler to write a monograph on responsibility accounting. In fact, Mr. Kohler was commissioned by Arthur Andersen to write such a monograph, but, for a variety of reasons, it never materialized. Had he written the monograph, there is no doubt that it would have been regarded as a milestone not only in the area of Responsibility Accounting but also in the whole field of managerial control.

The Controller

Kohler was a man of discipline. From the day he took over as Comptroller, he was determined to provide an adequate basis for control over the operations of the TVA, and Activity Accounting was the main tool he forged to achieve this much-needed control over the huge and complex operation of the TVA. Almost from scratch, he developed a system of accountability for both internal and external control and reporting which could withstand the strong pressure for laxity of management or diversion of resources from both inside and outside the TVA—a system that continues to function in a model way even to this day, two generations later.

Kohler's technical accomplishments, which were impressive by any standard, achieve even greater stature when it is realized that they were all undertaken at an early date and achieved in a very short time under severe pressure. Kohler's character and work habits were equally impressive. I, like others, stand in awe of them even to this day. I remember Kohler with affection as well as respect and here I have gone back to these very vivid experiences, in order to provide others with some of the flavor of what it was like to work with him and to experience the satisfactions and rewards of the resulting accomplishments.

Appendix A

Tennessee Valley Authority
Fixed Assets*
June 30, 1938

		Cost				Depreciation		
							Depreciation expense	
Completed dams	Wilson	Norris	Wheeler	Total	Accrued at acquisition	Year ended June 30, 1938	Entire period	Balance in reserve at June 30, 1938
Multiple-use facilities								
Reservoir land and land rights	$ 564,125.00	$ 9,033,679.80	$ 5,329,638.49	$14,927,443.29				
Relocation, removals, and backwater protection	—	4,218,403.42	2,059,635.90	6,278,039.32				
Total land cost	$ 564,125.00	$13,252,083.22	$ 7,389,274.39	$21,205,482.61				
Reservoir clearing	890,243.00	1,846,305.63	3,625,010.47	6,361,559.10				
Dam structure, excluding intake section	11,757,794.00	10,439,132.20	8,489,742.08	30,686,668.28	$1,684,253.00	$ 425,917.00	$1,294,664.00	$2,978,917.00
Roadways	1,899,384.00	276,627.88	764,220.84	2,940,232.72	260,782.00	51,755.00	190,883.00	451,665.00
Other structures and improvements	—	206,209.40	134,915.46	341,124.86	—	19,468.00	36,309.00	36,309.00
Total	$15,111,546.00	$26,020,358.33	$20,403,163.24	$61,535,067.57	$1,945,035.00	$ 497,140.00	$1,521,856.00	$3,466,891.00
Deduct direct flood-control investment, contra below		2,600,000.00†		2,600,000.00†		25,284.00†	48,697.00†	48,697.00†
Add nonoverflow sections to replace other sections, contra below								
Intake section	3,902,000.00	—	774,000.00	4,676,000.00	392,325.00	53,783.00	242,916.00	635,241.00
Lock section	125,000.00	—	202,000.00	327,000.00	12,568.00	3,495.00	10,690.00	23,258.00
Total multiple-use facilities, allocated below	$19,138,546.00	$23,420,358.33	$21,379,163.24	$63,938,067.57	$2,349,928.00	$ 529,134.00	$1,726,765.00	$4,076,693.00
Navigation facilities								
Lock	$ 2,684,276.00	—	$ 1,734,038.34	$ 4,418,314.34	$ 323,607.00	$ 63,700.00	$ 234,360.00	$ 557,967.00
Bridge across lock	94,921.00	—	178,907.69	273,828.69	21,780.00	5,368.00	17,929.00	39,709.00
Channel improvements			44,097.79	44,097.79	—	—	—	—
Total	$ 2,779,197.00	—	$ 1,957,043.82	$ 4,736,240.82	$ 345,387.00	$ 69,068.00	$ 252,289.00	$ 597,676.00
Deduct nonoverflow section to replace lock section, contra above	125,000.00†	—	202,000.00†	327,000.00†	12,568.00†	3,495.00†	10,690.00†	23,258.00†
Total before allocation of multiple-use facilities	$ 2,654,197.00	—	$ 1,755,043.82	$ 4,409,240.82	$ 332,819.00	$ 65,573.00	$ 241,599.00	$ 574,418.00
Add allocation of total multiple-use facilities, shown above (35%)				22,378,323.65	822,474.80	185,196.90	604,367.75	1,426,842.55
Total navigation facilities after allocation				$26,787,564.47	$1,155,293.80	$ 250,769.90	$ 845,966.75	$2,001,260.55
Flood-control facilities								
Direct flood-control investment, contra above		$ 2,600,000.00		$ 2,600,000.00	$ —	$ 25,284.00	$ 48,697.00	$ 48,697.00
Add allocation of total multiple-use facilities, shown above (25%)				15,984,516.89	587,482.00	132,283.50	431,691.25	1,019,173.25

Total flood-control facilities after allocation				$18,584,516.89	$ 587,482.00	$ 157,567.50	$ 480,388.25	$1,067,870.25
Power facilities								
Powerhouse, including intake section	$11,012,729.29	$ 1,422,972.71	$ 5,132,077.65	$17,567,779.65	$1,172,417.00	$ 223,701.00	$ 820,964.00	$1,993,381.00
Utility building	224,109.00	—	—	224,109.00	25,229.00	2,981.00	14,905.00	40,134.00
Intake gates	407,601.00	642,477.79	915,086.14	1,965,164.93	93,526.00	65,844.00	143,677.00	237,203.00
Turbines and generators	3,701,668.21	2,091,326.34	2,224,087.87	8,017,082.42	833,608.00	211,769.00	694,581.00	1,528,189.00
Accessory electrical equipment	1,369,582.02	328,105.58	568,061.83	2,265,749.43	275,388.00	77,955.19	240,380.53	515,768.55
Other power-plant equipment	237,863.31	244,535.59	387,043.90	869,442.80	50,931.00	28,172.00	65,798.00	122,341.80
Railroad to powerhouse	145,495.00	—	—	145,495.00	33,384.00	4,161.00	20,805.00	54,189.00
Total	$17,099,047.83	$ 4,729,418.01	$ 9,226,357.39	$31,054,823.23	$2,484,483.00	$ 614,583.19	$2,001,110.53	$4,491,206.39
Deduct nonoverflow section to replace intake section, contra above	3,902,000.00†	—	774,000.00†	4,676,000.00†	392,325.00†	53,783.00†	242,916.00†	635,241.00†
Total before allocation of multiple-use facilities	$13,197,047.83	$ 4,729,418.01	$ 8,452,357.39	$26,378,823.23	$2,092,158.00	$ 560,800.19	$1,758,194.53	$5,855,965.39
Add allocation of total multiple-use facilities, shown above (40%)				25,575,227.03	939,971.20	211,653.60	690,706.00	1,630,677.20
Total power facilities after allocation				$51,954,050.26	$3,032,129.20	$ 772,453.79	$2,448,900.53	$5,486,642.59
Total completed dams	$34,989,790.83	$30,749,776.34	$31,586,564.45	$97,326,131.62	$4,774,905.00	$1,180,791.19	$3,775,255.53	$8,555,773.39

*Footnote explanations have been omitted
†Red

95

Appendix B

Tennessee Valley Authority
Statement of Expense Common to Navigation, Flood Control, and Power Incurred in the Operation of Dams, Reservoirs, and Waterways
June 16, 1933, to June 30, 1938

Nature of expense	Year ended June 30, 1938				Entire period			
	Wilson	Norris	Wheeler	Total	Wilson	Norris	Wheeler	Total
Common operating expense of dams and reservoirs								
Malaria prevention	$ 18,503.60	$ 27,651.30	$174,043.47	$ 220,198.37	$ 159,393.64	$ 44,972.70	$ 260,160.85	$ 464,527.19
Policing and service to visitors	28,718.49	31,768.25	22,771.90	83,258.64	115,756.10	53,143.21	22,771.90	191,671.21
Operation of dams	8,583.21	1,033.83	8,276.46	17,893.50	68,296.14	2,294.94	13,788.02	84,379.10
Upkeep of roads and grounds	5,241.55	9,798.76	2.17	15,042.48	34,729.37	13,878.50	2.17	48,610.04
Operating studies and data	730.31	4,707.32	3,478.29	8,915.92	9,197.46	8,711.35	7,050.72	24,959.53
Totals	$ 61,777.16	$ 74,959.46	$208,572.29	$ 345,308.91	$ 387,372.71	$123,000.70	$ 303,773.66	$ 814,147.07
System expense, prorated (Schedule D)				147,311.65				338,280.91
Total common operating expense except for maintenance and depreciation				$ 492,620.56				$1,152,427.98
Maintenance of structures and equipment	$ 18,441.35	$ 3,283.06	$ 3,304.03	$ 25,028.44	$ 47,097.87	$ 3,370.54	$ 3,809.02	$ 54,277.43
Depreciation common plant	243,425.00	143,131.00	142,578.00	529,134.00	1,217,125.00	275,670.00	233,970.00	1,726,765.00
Total common operating expense				$1,046,783.00				$2,933,470.41

Allocation of common operating expense*

Nature of expense	Year ended June 30, 1938				Entire period			
	Navigation	Flood control	Power	Total	Navigation	Flood control	Power	Total
Common expense (½ or ⅓ to each purpose)	$164,206.85	$164,206.85	$164,206.86	$ 492,620.56	$ 441,465.09	$269,497.79	$ 441,465.10	$1,152,427.98
Maintenance 35%, 25%, and 40%	8,759.95	6,257.11	10,011.38	25,028.44	18,997.09	13,569.36	21,710.98	54,277.43
Depreciation	185,196.90	132,283.50	211,653.60	529,134.00	604,367.75	431,691.25	690,706.00	1,726,765.00
Totals	$358,163.70	$302,747.46	$385,871.84	$1,046,783.00	$1,064,829.93	$714,758.40	$1,153,882.08	$2,933,470.41

*Of the common operating expenses shown, the first five items can be directly ascribed to individual dams. Their total, plus system expenses, the details and distribution of which appear in Schedule D, have been allocated one-half to navigation and one-half to power during the years Wilson Dam was the only dam in service, since the operation of Wilson Dam alone made no material contribution to flood control; and one-third to each of the three purposes commencing in 1937. The percentages adopted for the allocation of investment in plant used in common for the three purposes are those appearing in the Authority's report of allocation to the President of the United States dated June 9, 1938, and are applied to the common investment in the system of dams and reservoirs in operation as an integrated unit without reference to the contributions of the individual dams to the several purposes. Accordingly, maintenance and depreciation on the common investment in plant have been allocated on these percentages: 35% to navigation, 25% to flood control, and 40% to power, irrespective of the number of dams in service.

References

Alioto, R. F., and J. A. Jungherr. 1971. *Operational PPBS for Education.* New York: Harper & Row, Publishers.

Kohler, Eric L. 1975. *A Dictionary for Accountants,* 5th ed. Englewood Cliffs, N.J.: Prentice-Hall, Inc.

Chapter 7

Eric Kohler in the Marshall Plan

Samuel Nakasian

Background

Eric L. Kohler had recently been appointed as Controller of the newly born ECA—Economic Cooperation Administration (Marshall Plan)—when I met with him for an interview in early 1948. As Controller, Kohler had a mandate to ensure the integrity and efficacy of the Agency's expenditures. Despite the tumult and pressures of organizing a new agency on a worldwide basis, the speedy delivery of goods and services took precedence, notwithstanding that such haste was likely to result in waste and abuses. This was the challenge facing Kohler when he was appointed by Paul G. Hoffman, the ECA administrator.[1]

Hoffman was a practical and experienced business executive who had moved from extraordinary success as a car salesman to President of the Studebaker Corporation, which he then restored to success from the brink of failure. An idealist, too, Hoffman was instrumental in developing the then-new Committee for Economic Development (CED) to enable the business community to organize its energies for attention to problems of public policy. Under his leadership, the CED became a formidable voice in molding progressive public policies. Innovative and perceptive, Paul Hoffman undertook to join the best of scholarly research with the best of business judgment and statesmanship

---

[1]Officially designated as Administrator of Economic Cooperation under Title I, Section 104(a), of the Economic Cooperation Act of 1948, also known as the Foreign Assistance Act of 1948, 62nd Statute, 80th Congress, 2nd Session, Ch. 169, April 13, 1948.

for this purpose and then forged them into an organized, going concern. The CED still functions and is remarkably effective, influencing policy with in-depth intelligence and wisdom in many important problem areas of our society.

These accomplishments naturally attracted attention to Paul G. Hoffman for appointment as administrator of the yet-to-be-formed Economic Cooperation Administration for the urgent rebuilding of devasted Europe. His qualities and talents were sorely needed to head the largest peacetime undertaking in America's history.

History will record the fact that his blend of pragmatism and idealism, as well as his choice and use of staff, produced a successful program that rebuilt Europe and secured its place in the free world for the next three decades and beyond.

Some idea of what Paul Hoffman was confronting in managing the Marshall Plan can be gained by considering the record of some of the preceding aid programs: One such program, UNRRA (United Nations Relief and Rehabilitation Administration), formed as a separate agency, mainly with U.S. funding, administered by Fiorello H. La Guardia;[2] and another, the Greek–Turkish aid programs,[3] administered by special U.S. missions. Neither offered very much in the way of attractive precedent. Waste, graft, and ill-designed efforts prolonged the suffering of the war's victims and undermined the confidence of Americans that their hard-earned taxes could be trusted to public agencies to meet urgent human needs. The fact that these programs had to be mounted with dispatch offered very little consolation, as subsequent audits by the General Accounting Office (and our findings as well) revealed a bleak pattern of management failures and abuses.

Hoffman was determined to avoid a similar result, if at all possible, and it was against this backdrop that he was led to the selection of Eric L. Kohler for Controller of the Marshall Plan.[4] This also explains the mandate with which Hoffman endowed the Controller's office, and it may also explain some of the steps that Kohler took at an early date in forming his own program. Two ideas that were prominent in Kohler's approach to the functioning of the Controller's office revolved around (1) an extensive and imaginative use of the audit function, including an "end-use audit" which extended to the ultimate disposition of the goods and services that were financed; and (2) a systematic vigilance over prices charged and quality delivered.

It was in connection with the latter function that I came into the picture, recommended by W. W. Cooper, who had been asked by Kohler to help ini-

---

[2] Its controller was Harry Howell.

[3] As far as I know, this program had no controller as such. See "An Act to Provide for Assistance to Greece and Turkey," 80th Congress, 1st Session, Ch. 81, May 22, 1947, Public Law 75.

[4] W. W. Cooper told me that Hoffman once related to him that he was seeking a person with practical experience who could be regarded as "the conscience of the American accounting profession." The fact that he was also securing the services of an accountant with a reputation as a scholar and with a wealth of government (as well as private sector) experience were added bonanzas.

tiate these activities. Cooper and I were colleagues during the war at the U.S. Bureau of the Budget,[5] where we supervised, among other things, price–cost accounting and the related information functions of civilian wartime agencies: Office of Price Administration, War Foods Administration, and the subsidy functions of the Reconstruction Finance Corporation. It was in this way that I came to stand before Eric Kohler in April 1948 as a consultant to the agency, later to be Chief of what was called the Price Branch, reporting to the Controller of the Marshall Plan.

I would like to record some of my experiences in a way that may help to cast light not only on the internal functionings of parts of this great program but also on ways in which the character and perceptions of two men (Hoffman and Kohler) influenced the outcome of what must be regarded as a remarkably successful program (see the Appendix). On the other hand, I shall only do this in a way "writ large," so to speak, and from the standpoint of a member of the Controller's office. Hopefully, this will add something in the way of insight, which can then be blended into the views that others can supply from "outside"—perhaps more objective—appraisals of what was involved in the Marshall Plan's record of accomplishment.

Before proceeding to my narrative, however, I would like to recount one incident from my initial interview with Kohler. The Economic Cooperation Act had just been funded, at a level of some $5 billion,[6] to start its task of helping to rebuild a war-devastated Europe. There was, however, almost overwhelming opposition in the U.S. Congress to this appropriation, which was highlighted by references to reports of graft and waste of public funds in UNRRA and the Greek–Turkish aid programs. Finally, the U.S. House of Representatives passed the appropriation bill by a margin of *one* vote, a fact that thereafter had always to be born in mind.

To facilitate passage, Section 202 was inserted in the appropriation bill:

> No funds made available under the authority of this Act shall be used for the purchase in bulk of any commodities . . . at prices higher than the market price prevailing in the United States at the time of purchase adjusted for differences in the cost of transportation to destination, quality and terms of payment.

In the course of the interview, Kohler reported to me that some of the members of the ECA staff held the view that Section 202 was impossible to administer and should be circumvented in the "greater interests" of the main purposes of the Marshall Plan. He asked me to express my opinions along the following lines: (1) was 202 a desirable limitation, and (2) could it be administered considering other sections of the act, which directed that the aid program of goods, services, and capital facilities be undertaken to the maximum extent possible through private channels?

After leaving this meeting, I realized

---

[5]Involving administration of the then-new Federal Reports Act, among other functions.

[6]See the Foreign Aid Appropriation Act, Public Laws Ch. 685, 62nd Stat., 80th Congress, 2nd Session, June 28, 1948. Interim financing had previously been provided by the Reconstruction Finance Corporation, and supplemental appropriations carried this initial amount to some $6.5 billion.

that Kohler was actually less concerned about the difficulties of administering 202 than in learning of my conception of public service—its duties and opportunities. This realization offered me insight into Kohler's own character and priorities. When Cooper once asked me how I was able to get Kohler's concurrence on so many complex and troublesome matters, often under conditions of turmoil and dispute with others, I recalled this interview and articulated my guiding principles as follows:

First, clearly identify the objectives of the recommended proposals with high moral principles. Second, demonstrate that the suggested methods of implementation would carry out the spirit of congressional mandate and especially that it would work with the least possible detrimental effects to the legitimate interests of private companies while protecting the government's integrity. Finally, if this did not produce concurrence, then try to demonstrate this position to be more virtuous than any other alternatives.

I would be remiss if I left the impression that this approach was a "gimmick." It was not intended to be cute or clever. It was intended rather as an application of Kohler's own principles, which were always oriented toward moral considerations with a heavy insistence on practicality in the implementing of his own conceptions of the public service.

"Macroeconomics" Versus "Individual Accountability"

The newly assembled staff for administering the Marshall Plan was soon tested by lively and often-heated debate. A group within ECA headed by Richard Bissell, Assistant Deputy Administrator for Programs and Operations[7] had come to hold a "macroeconomic" view of the aid program. Bissell, who had helped direct the background studies for the Marshall Plan, held to the position that the aid program should be viewed primarily as a financing mechanism to help cover Europe's balance-of-payment deficits. Apart from certain priorities for types of goods and services or industrial plants and other capital facilities, as established by the Office of Program Planning, the decisions of private enterprise should be relied upon under the play of markets to accomplish the act's objectives.

Kohler, on the other hand, believed that ECA should take a businesslike approach, with full accountability for all transactions, as if ECA were the fiduciary of the public. ECA should, of course, commit funds to approved requisitions, using private channels of trade, for goods, services, industrial plants, and so on, within the scope of already approved programs.[8] In addition, it should make sure that payment

[7]A listing of the original top-level staff and their titles may be found in "Opening Statement" by Paul G. Hoffman, Administrator for Economic Cooperation, to the Senate Appropriations Committee, May 13, 1948.

[8]We will not deal here with the European office under Averell Harriman, as the United States Special Representative in Europe, or the individual country offices which also entered into these program developments and policies. See "Opening Statement" by Paul G. Hoffman, Administrator for Economic Cooperation, to the Senate Appropriations Committee, May 13, 1948.

be made for prices, qualities, and other terms no less favorable than sales by the supplier to other "like" classes of *unsubsidized* purchasers.

With respect to Kohler's concepts of end-use (and other) audits and price justification, or even accountability, the ways in which these issues were resolved might well be decisive. Fortunately, Paul Hoffman and his deputy, Howard Bruce, personally heard and evaluated the "pros" and "cons" from the Bissell group and from Kohler and me. Hoffman's answer was short but clear: This was not to be a "give-away" program. It must be conducted in a businesslike way. No payment would be made unless the price was right for the quality and quantity delivered. How to accomplish this was up to the Controller's office, but it must be done expeditiously and in a manner that did not introduce delays in accomplishing program objectives.

The Bissell group was surprised. They had not understood the reasons underlying Hoffman's selection of Kohler and they had a great deal of trouble placing the functioning of his office in their concept of the program. In fact, throughout the program, as we shall see, they seemed constantly to regard our emphasis on lowest competitive cost as prejudicial to private industry.

Within the limits established by Hoffman's statement, Kohler exhibited his creativity as well as his zeal. He insisted that suppliers must be paid promptly, if lowest costs were to be obtained, but not at the sacrifice of accountability for compliance. "Make quick payment, but subject to ECA post-audit," became the *modus operandi.*

To help expedite these payments, Kohler met with the banking community and marshalled its members to handle the letters of credit, to ensure that the importer had deposited his payment in local currencies,[9] and to assemble the invoices and shipping and other documents needed to justify payment. Private banks made payment to suppliers *immediately* against these documents and were in turn reimbursed, also immediately, by a draft on ECA's account at the U.S. Treasury. Once under way, this was an almost flawless system.

It all looks simple, by hindsight, but it required the deft and sure knowledge of business practice, and how it might respond to new challenges, which Kohler (and Hoffman) both possessed to a remarkable degree. At the outset, in fact, this kind of prompt payment mechanism (including installation and implementation) appeared impossible to achieve for the thousands of ECA cargos that were involved.

Closely associated with this payment mechanism, however, were the audits that Kohler also instituted, which covered all phases of these transactions from inception and financing, down to end uses, which uses were visualized as occurring when these goods and services were either finally consumed or else entered into the normal flow of commerce and trade within each country. Correlatively, it was the function of the price analysis unit (which I directed) to maintain a continuing flow of studies

---

[9]These became the "counterpart funds" (in foreign currencies), which, among other things, have served to finance a generation of scholars under the Fulbright resolution as well as local public works. Each dollar of Marshall Plan created an equivalent amount of local currency, with the result of a $2 impact for each $1 spent.

and evaluations on all price-related aspects of these transactions. A system was designed to scrutinize transactions for possible reconsideration and re-capture, if necessary, and as a part of the expected full accountability which Kohler wanted in any case.

ECA Regulation I

Kohler decided, at a very early date, that considerations of Section 202 should be formalized and officially promulgated for the guidance of all concerned both outside and inside the ECA. ECA Regulation I, was the result.[10]

This regulation consumed more than three months in its preparation—with attendant burdens on our already over-occupied time and attention—largely because of the opposition of certain industry groups, especially oil, expressed as much by staff within ECA as by external industry spokesmen. Most troublesome were the proposed price and quality provisions, which made ultimate payment to the supplier contingent upon assurances that his performance was no less favorable as to price and quality than any other like class of sale to an unsubsidized buyer.[11] At times the discussions were heated and sometimes even acrimonious, as when, for instance, Kohler and I were openly accused of wanting to resurrect the recently disbanded Office of Price Administration and, by innuendo, of

concealing possibly even more obscure designs in the positions we were taking. Throughout this period, Kohler was quick in his grasp of all points, and imaginative as well as incisive in his response to the oncoming challenges.

When the final showdown on the approval of ECA Regulation I took place before Hoffman, the Bissell group made a last-ditch effort to water it down. As a result, Hoffman approved ECA Regulation I, but withheld approval of our proposed ECA Supplier's Certificate 100. He yielded to Bissell's plea that industry would never accept it and, at best, the program would be stalled and the agency embarrassed. To avoid engaging in a contest of guess and conjecture, Kohler and I responded by suggesting to Hoffman that we invite a cross section of industry representatives to meet in Washington to review the proposed Certificate, and he concurred.

The Certificate was designed to facilitate self-compliance with Regulation I and to be submitted as an essential document for payment by ECA. It was a 5- by 7-inch form requesting certification by a corporate officer or owner of the supplying company that the price and quality was in compliance with ECA Regulation I, and requesting the amount of commission paid, or payable, to supplier's agents who were also to be named. A false certification was denoted as a federal crime.

Kohler was not eager to put private management in this precarious position,

---

[10] See the *Federal Register*, 13(96), May 15, 1948, pp. 2653ff.

[11] See, for example, the memo of R. M. Bissell, Jr., "ECA Pricing Policy," dated October 18, 1948, and the memo of February 28, 1949, from the Controller to the Assistant Deputy Administrator and General Counsel of the ECA. See also the letter to the U.S. Comptroller General from Howard Bruce, Acting ECA Administrator, dated July 21, 1948, and the reply by Frank Yates, Acting Comptroller General, dated August 6, 1948. See also the letter from Howard Bruce to Lindsay Warren, dated August 6, 1948.

and so he, too, was understandably concerned about this form and its implications, yet finally concurred with me in its necessity to achieve compliance.

A meeting of some 30 industry representatives responded to our invitation. Among other items, we suggested to them that adoption of the Certificate would prevent suppliers from raising invoice prices for the purpose of paying higher commissions to foreign agents and/or clandestine payments to public officials. This was common practice under UNRRA and the Greek-Turkish aid programs, with the result that from 10 to 20 percent of their expenditure was estimated to have been spent on improper payments. In the postwar period, American aid was a convenient method for European importers to convert into dollars their local currencies, whose value was uncertain under prevailing economic and political conditions. Since importers could choose among a number of suppliers, they were in a position to dictate the terms to their advantage.

The meeting with these industry representatives was *not* conducted on a "take-it-or-leave-it" basis. The business committee could have turned down the proposed certificate or emasculated it with changes. To our gratification it was approved as submitted, however, and overwhelmingly so, with only one or two abstentions. Kohler expressed no surprise with this result, believing that in the end most businessmen would prefer competition within an honest game plan. As a final note, we might now also observe that Supplier's Certif-

icate 100, adopted in 1948, has been in continuous use for almost 30 years by the several foreign aid agencies succeeding ECA.[12]

Another practice, alas, was less steadfastly maintained by these successor agencies. This was the practice of maintaining fully "open books" as part of Kohler's policy of full and public accountability on all transactions. Since the public was paying the bills, the public—including competing companies, customers, stockholders, public officials, or whoever—was entitled to know what was being charged and received for supplies, equipment, and services. In fact, to facilitate public inquiry, the Controller's office published and made available for free distribution on a periodic (almost daily) basis the list of all ECA-financed transactions, together with pertinent prices and other relevant information.

The Issue of Financing Marine Insurance

In public office, Kohler performed as if he were the fiduciary of the public trust and expected no less from his staff and colleagues. In this role, he was always probing, searching for something undiscovered that might need doing to fulfill his sense of duty.

Early in the program, I recall W. W. Cooper proposing to Kohler that we consider the marine risks of transporting ECA supplies and equipment to Europe. Under the Marshall Plan, importers paid in local currency (counterpart funds) for

---

[12] The vigilance standards of some executive agencies have apparently greatly eroded, as witnessed by the exposé of "corporate bribes" by American arms and aircraft manufacturers, whose sales abroad in many aspects involve one or more U.S. federal agencies.

shipments received from suppliers, who were paid in dollars by the ECA. We undertook an in-depth analysis which revealed the following. If the importer purchased CIF (Cost, Insurance, and Freight), he incurred no risk of his counterpart funds because payment was conditioned on delivery of the cargo to him. If the importer bought FOB (Free on Board) or C and F (Cost and Freight), he did risk his payment (made in local currency, not dollars). However, he could insure this risk in his own currency without cost to ECA. In *any* supply contract, ECA guaranteed the supplier dollar payment when he delivered the cargo to the carrier. Therefore, only ECA bore the dollar risk of marine casualty to the cargo. That being the case, why should not ECA be the marine self-insurer on the thousands of cargos shipped to Europe? As self-insurer the savings should be equal to at least one-half the estimated $20 million payable in premiums. Kohler readily agreed and opted for the savings.[13]

This action prompted the President of the Marine Underwriters to make a personal appeal to Hoffman. Kohler and I were invited to attend this meeting. After the underwriters' case was made, Hoffman, in his low, casual voice, said "Mr. . . .: I would like to make myself very clear; I represent you as a taxpayer and not as an underwriter." Kohler beamed with pride at his kindred public servant.

Kohler succeeded at the agency level but lost partially in Congress the following year. In a rider to the next appropriation bill, Congress authorized payment of dollars for marine insurance when importers requested it. Kohler's faith in our government "of the people and for the people" was somewhat bruised by this experience—but he firmly believed in the process—if only officials would conscientiously perform their functions. Under the regulations we drafted to carry out this congressional authority, we provided that any dollar settlement of marine losses be reimbursed to ECA. As a result, importers chose to insure their cargoes in local currency at their own expense rather than in dollars.

Oil, Of Course

Kohler gained little solace from merely the appearance of good administration or a recital of its principles. He kept probing through the surface and always applauded the analytical mind that revealed something important that was not otherwise evident. We can illustrate this by means of the problem of oil pricing in the Middle East and at the same time help to illuminate how the price analysis unit functioned.

Thirty years ago, as now, the price of oil was a big item in Washington. Postwar Europe represented an enormous potential market for petroleum, but the war had consumed its reserves of dollars and gold and largely destroyed its productive plants capable of generating foreign exchange. Marshall Plan funds available for both petroleum

---

[13]Other complex issues included the possible "moral hazards" associated with premium payments in one currency and compensation in another. See Memo of August 24, 1948, to E. L. Kohler from ECA Advisory Committee on Insurance setting forth its "Recommendations for ECA Financing of Insurance."

and its transport created a bonanza for the largely shut-in production of the Middle East needed to fuel Europe's reconstruction.

In early 1948, the major oil companies faced the problem of how to price Middle East crude for Europe, which, prior to the war, had been largely supplied from the Caribbean and U.S. Gulf. The Middle East was needed to replace this source of supply, now substantially committed to the United States and other western markets.

The first shipment of crude from Ras Tanura, Saudi Arabia, was priced at $2.23 f.o.b. by Standard Oil (now Exxon) for shipment to its affiliate in France. The $2.23 price plus freight was rationalized as equating with the delivered price to Europe of shipments if they were made from U.S. Gulf–Caribbean sources. To embellish this idea, the concepts of "watersheds" and competing sources were introduced and argued to justify the posted Middle East price on essentially a basing-point system of pricing.

Major oil companies felt they were meeting the market-competition test by demonstrating that Europe would pay no less, and probably more, if supplied from the U.S. Gulf and Caribbean.

Despite this persuasive argument, Kohler and I, supported by Hoffman, did not believe that we could maintain the integrity of the Marshall Plan in Congress and before the public by ignoring the fact that just prior to the appropriation of funds by Congress, Middle East crude oil was being offered for less than half the $2.23 price.

Kohler was fascinated by this disclosure and the fact that Standard and four other companies were the sole crude-oil suppliers under the program.

They could, in fact, set their own price in the market created by the funds supplied by U.S. taxpayers, and the rationale of the basing-point system failed to win our agreement that the resulting price could be explained to the Congress.

The issue was brought to a crisis point by our instruction *not* to make payment to Standard Oil. The General Counsel of Standard Oil failed to convince us that $2.23 was the "market price," and the several officials in the agency—"expert" in the "economics of Middle East Oil"— also failed in their attempts to support Standard's position.

Within 48 hours, Eugene Holman, President of Standard Oil, was in Hoffman's office explaining to Hoffman, Kohler, and me how pricing and competition works in the oil business. Hoffman replied to his friend (and CED colleague): "Gene, let me be crystal clear. I don't represent the oil industry but I do represent you as a taxpayer . . ." continuing, "Gene, I'm not going to discredit this program by paying the company $1.23 per barrel more than it charged four months ago. We're making the market and we need the oil, to be sure, but you have got to be reasonable!" Well, Kohler and I expected this from past performance, but we were nevertheless awed by Hoffman's simple, concise reasoning and precise statements as he performed the role of a lion tamer. As Kohler later observed, "you don't have to have been a lion to be a lion tamer."

"If $2.23 is too high," Holman asked, "what *is* the price?" We countered that shipments to the alternative free market of the U.S. east coast would "net back" less than $1.50 f.o.b. Middle East. That is, $1.50, the "net back price," was calculated by deducting the amount of freight from the price charged per barrel of oil shipped from the Middle East to the U.S. east coast.

We reached an agreement to pay an interim price of $1.75, subject to further study. This savings of $0.48 per barrel, or nearly 20 percent, amounted to more than $120 million[14] by 1951. Moreover, our continuing price analysis made it possible for ECA to claim an additional $75 million based on the evidence that the oil companies were, in fact, charging a price of $1.43 per barrel f.o.b. on substantial shipments to the United States. The Hoffman–Holman confrontation inspired confidence that the Agency would survive to complete its mission—and, as always with strong leadership in such an Agency, some of the lambs began to act more like lions.

Kohler was indefatigable in preparing his own positions and expected no less from his staff.[15] This challenge of the major oil companies was an herculean undertaking. We were pitted not only against their management and supporting staffs but also against officials within ECA and other government agencies (including the State Department) whose support for the oil companies was of a more determined variety in many ways. The experience was simultaneously exhausting and exhilarating. What is clear to me in retrospect is that without the support of Kohler and Hoffman, our analyses would have come to naught in both oil and maritime insurance.

As relatively obscure public officials, we dared to face the fact that oil was priced by an oligopoly at excessive levels, and we proceeded to resolve the price problem by confrontation. The oil companies' claim of a "market price" met head on with ECA's refusal to pay what we regarded as excessive prices. Essentially, this was a test of credibility, with the result that the determination of Hoffman and Kohler finally prevailed because the oil companies felt they would lose and ECA must win.

Kohler's sense of professionalism and objectivity would not countenance any prejudice against oil or any other industry. It was a matter of right or wrong—a simple decision for a fiduciary of the public interest—and the right, when right, had to be backed by factual analysis fully documented and promptly delivered to sustain the positions that he and Hoffman were adhering to. After the first several months, Kohler's presence in the Agency became formidable. When he made up his mind, would-be adversaries among his peers preferred to go along rather than confront him and risk losing out by Hoffman's final decision. Kohler's peers rarely chose the latter course a second time.

---

[14] The merits of our position were underscored by the fact that ECA Middle East crude prices remained at or below $1.75 and did not rise to $2.23 until the mid-1960s. In subsequent years, officials of the major oil companies expressed their praise to me, with evident sincerity, for the ECA vigilance on prices. We can only speculate on what the consequences might have been on the pace (and magnitude) of European recovery at that time, but one high oil company official told me: "You kept us from killing the goose that laid the golden eggs for our European markets."

[15] As partial support, Mr. H. Morrison of our staff prepared what must have been one of the earliest large-scale empirical input-output analyses—really it was a version of what later came to be called a "process analysis model" —to enable us to analyze and counter industry (and agency) arguments on the "undesirable" effects our pricing policies might have on the patterns of world supplies and demands.

Cotton and Wheat: The Introduction of Statistical Acceptance Sampling

Although perhaps the subject of less intense pressures than we had encountered in oil and maritime insurance, other products were equally troublesome administratively, and called for imaginative responses. Wheat and cotton pricing was complex, largely because of the problems of ascertaining quality. How could ECA be reasonably certain that suppliers were shipping proper quality against the price billed? Many importers had a strong incentive to accept an under-quality shipment if the exporter would agree to deposit the excess payment (by ECA) to the importer's dollar account in Switzerland. Supplier's Certificate 100 and ECA Regulation I could not be relied on to prevent this abuse, especially when there was collusion between the importer and the exporter. How we proceeded can be sufficiently illustrated by reference to cotton shipment and financing.

After due consideration and a great deal of analysis and discussion, we hit on the idea of utilizing statistical sampling,[16] suitably adapted from the concepts of statistical quality control, which had received a good deal of acclaim as a result of their use by the military in World War II. Even after the technical and administrative details were worked out (with the help of the Department of Agriculture), however, we once again became cognizant of the need for top-level support. How, after all, could any government official survive the onslaught of Senate and House committees, whose chairmen were almost all from the cotton belt and who had cotton and wheat exporters as their very close friends? Kohler and I somehow managed to gain the confidence of the cotton and wheat trade and their acceptance of the new rules of the game: to ship the quality bought, and to price it right.[17] They rather welcomed the development of this new kind of quality-control scheme.

After the technical and administrative details were all worked out and cotton sampling was instituted, we received a call from Will Clayton, formerly Under Secretary of State, asking to see me at my convenience and informing me that he had come to Washington from Houston solely for this purpose. Clayton came directly to the point—ECA had stopped payment on a large cargo of cotton shipped by his firm, Anderson, Clayton and Co.—and he wanted to know the reasons for this action. I told him that we had ascertained that the cargo was priced for quality higher than actually shipped, or, "shipped shy," in the parlance of this trade.

Clayton acknowledged that this could well be the case. I took the liberty of explaining the new sampling procedures and quality controls along with the related documentation and "matching requirements." I asked him whether we could, in good conscience, have avoided

---

[16] Acknowledgment is due W. W. Cooper and D. Rosenblatt for bringing these developments to my attention, which, it may be recalled, was long before these ideas began to be utilized by accountants and auditors in other parts of their practice.

[17] Mr. Cook of Cook Industries, a leading cotton exporter, told me we had destroyed a long-time custom of "shipping shy."

this or some similar procedure, or whether there was a more effective way of protecting the public funds. He candidly replied that he would have done the same sort of thing in our position and congratulated us on the imaginative approach we had taken. We agreed on a substantial price reduction, shook hands, and payment was ordered.

This case is cited to show that the astute Will Clayton, as I believe most business managers would, preferred to compete in a clean market rather than in a dirty one.[18]

Audit and Control—Wider Implications

Problem solving arising out of audit and control was not confined to oil and insurance or cotton and wheat. The whole gamut of goods and services and business practices not only in the United States but elsewhere came under review and required knowledgable and firm, but nevertheless tactful, dealings in many different dimensions during the (approximately) three years of Kohler's controllership. Moreover, he knew how to build toward lasting effects. In fact, after he left, I, like others, could still feel the effects of his having been present during the program's formative stage. In fact, this feeling was almost palpably physical.

Six feet four inches in height, with a commanding appearance and resonant voice, Eric Kohler was neat and precise in speech and writing and possessed a tremendous capacity for work. His formula was to conceive the right thing

to do, whether popular or productive of powerful opposition, and then in his majestic style perfect the means of accomplishing the job to be done. He conceived an organization as a vehicle to get the job done, but he refused to be restricted by it. Rather, he felt compelled to exploit, and even to circumvent its jurisdictional compartments, whenever his sense of higher duty demanded.

I can best illustrate the "Kohler way" by our responses to some of the intricacies we frequently encountered. One example involved a very famous case. Our continuing past-audits revealed that two or three companies in Switzerland kept appearing on the ECA supplier's certificates as agents for shipments to Austria. Investigation revealed that the owners of the Swiss companies were directors of the Kreditanstalt, the Austrian bank holding company which controlled a large part of Austria's industry and commerce as well as banking. We did not have the proof, but it looked highly suspicious that Kreditanstalt directors were amassing personal fortunes in Swiss accounts by taking commissions via a Swiss agency on shipments of goods and equipment of millions of dollars to Austria paid for by ECA. The documentation of shipments appeared to be in compliance with ECA Regulation I and the supplier's certificate. Thus, the question involved whether what Austrians do was any of our business.

Kohler had already left the agency, but he had left his principles and his way of thinking with us. Following these principles, I had first to decide whether

---

[18]Senator Clark's investigative committee has been disclosing evidence that grain exporters in recent years may again be competing in a dirty market.

it was right to challenge this method of doing business. I decided it was right to do so, but since a foreign government was directly involved, diplomacy should be employed as an ally. Discipline by us, directed against this activity, might well have caused great embarrassment to the Austrian government, with the effect of undermining its credibility among its citizenry. The challenge was how to correct this situation immediately in the precarious context of the Austrian national elections then under way. The Communist Party was a serious contender at the polls. If these facts were exposed by them, the public scandal could well become the subject of election rhetoric with decided (perhaps decisive) advantages to them. In the latter case, the whole of Austria might then move irretrievably behind the Iron Curtain.

In considering how to proceed expediently, I had to take others into account. Only one other person in the agency had this information at that time.[19] On Thursday, at my invitation, Jim Cooley, ECA General Counsel, Mrs. Eleanor Dulles, the State Department's Austrian Desk Chief, and a CIA representative met in my office to be briefed. When they agreed that the matter ought to be further investigated, we discussed how it might best be done. I then outlined a plan: On Monday next, two representatives of the accounting firm of Haskins & Sells would meet me at Idlewild Airport to emplane for Vienna to be briefed by me *en route*. In the meantime, Mrs. Dulles would cable our Ambassador in Vienna to arrange a private meeting for me with Chancellor

Figl on Thursday. I would apprise the Chancellor of our findings and suggest that *his* office retain Haskins & Sells to conduct an investigation of the Swiss companies and the accounts of the directors of the bank, and thereafter take appropriate action.

The simplicity and speed of the plan appeared overoptimistic to my colleagues, but they agreed to it. A call to the managing partner of Haskins & Sells then set a meeting for me with him the next day in New York and he gave me the names of the two investigating accountants who could take a plane on Monday for Europe. In a call to Miss Shipley, Director of the State Department's Passport Division, I was assured that passports would be delivered to the two men on Monday at the New York Airport.

On Thursday in Vienna I met with Chancellor Figl and Foreign Minister Gruber. They readily, and indeed gratefully, agreed to my proposal that they conduct their own investigation under the supervision of the two accountants from Haskin & Sells. Figl saw the choice clearly of taking the risk of the investigation becoming public knowledge, but with credit for diligence, or of remaining passive and vulnerable to the possibility that the Communists would find out about it. In the latter event, they could be expected to explode the scandal on the Austrian voters still suffering from the economic hardships of war. By Figl's decision, the Austrian position was greatly strengthened in that the government was effectively dealing with its own scandal.[20] This result was achieved within one week of the inter-

---

[19] This was H. Morrison of our staff, who had brought the matter to my attention in the first place.

[20] Several years after this national election, the press reported some aspects of this case. I welcome this opportunity to report what happened and how it happened.

agency meeting in Washington. This was the Kohler way!

Summary and Conclusions

In this testimonial dedicated to a great American accountant, it is also fitting to try to memorialize something of what he accomplished in bringing his talents to bear as a public servant in the great, and perhaps decisive, endeavor that came to be known as the Marshall Plan. One way to measure his contribution, at least in part, is by reference to estimated dollar savings. The estimates prepared in my office indicate that crude oil costs were reduced by 20 percent, for an annual total approximating $40 million; grain and cotton costs were reduced by some 10 to 20 percent; and against the marine insurance premiums saved of $20 million, there were almost no offsetting losses on shipments. Assuming that all costs were reduced by 10 percent, the Controller's office might then lay claim to savings of $2.5 billion on the $25 billion program as a result of Kohler's "before" and "after" effects. This savings effectively increased the volume of shipments to Europe by 10 percent and avoided the necessity of asking Congress for still larger appropriations.

More important than the savings, perhaps, was the fact that ECA would probably not have survived much beyond the first year, or been allowed to operate as it did, if the Controller's office had not kept the program credible. This performance was critical to the continuing annual appropriations by Congress for the rapid recovery of Europe (and other parts of the world). If the program had been aborted by a less diligent administration, we can only speculate what would have been the fate of Western Europe and, indeed, the security of the United States.

In the three years of Kohler's tenure, 1948–1951, congressional committees and the GAO conducted no hearings or investigations, and, in fact, none appeared necessary regarding the prices paid in a program of some $25 billion. Full accountability was maintained and the GAO and congressional committee staffs were kept fully informed on all aspects of the vigilance that the Controller's office was seeking to maintain. Our internal vigilance of audits, analyses, and self-directed enforcement assured compliance with our policies and regulations on thousands of transactions involving hundreds of business firms and a dozen or more governments.

ECA was probably Kohler's largest assignment, whether measured in terms of money, multiplicity of transactions, international scope, or urgency. The remarkable fact is that Kohler's administration of this function was performed by a relatively small staff of no more than 100 to 150 persons. My part of the staff numbered 10 professionals to cover transactions involving some $6 billion annually.

I cannot claim that we were understaffed, although by most accepted standards we were overworked. Here, again, we must credit Kohler and Hoffman with establishing the pace and the style of work. The emphasis was on well-thought-out systems that maximized the use of staff and provided each professional with optimum conditions for creative work with no threats to its integrity. Following Kohler's style, each professional participated fully in the decision-making process. The morale of our office was gratifyingly high—sick leave was rarely taken and vacations were voluntarily deferred. Kohler's administration of staff would, in itself, make a useful study.

Some of the successor programs undertaken by the U.S. government for other parts of the world tried to proceed along similar lines. Their record of performance is mixed and, in some cases, there has been demonstrable failure. Whether these more recent programs were mismanaged or whether their lack of success was due to the nature of the problems must be left for others to decide. They might, however, conjecture on "what might have been" if Kohler and Hoffman had been present to imbue those programs and agencies with their integrity, practicality, and ingenuity as well as their dedication to achievement.

Finally, it should be noted that in the ECA days, our society had not reached maturity in appropriate recognition of the Controller's function in conserving and maximizing the use of public funds. This sad state prevails even today as the costs of federal, state, and local functions skyrocket to over $500 billion annually—about one-third of our gross national product—with mounting evidence of gross waste of public funds. The general public may not soon come to appreciate the contributions that the Eric Kohlers can make to its well-being. However, some progress in this direction may be achieved if the foregoing account serves as an inspiration to public servants to upgrade their performance.

I have tried to recount how two great men affected the course of administration of the Marshall Plan at a variety of critical junctures. In doing so, I have also recounted to myself the impact and lasting effects that these two men had on me. Working for, and with, Eric L. Kohler and Paul G. Hoffman, in any event, was a fulfillment of the highest caliber of public service as well as a training in doing the "impossible"— which, alas, others will hereafter be denied.

Appendix

As a memorial to the two men whose activities I have just described (partially) and also to enable each reader to appraise the scope of the undertaking in which they were engaged, I reproduce herewith the following statement from the Economic Cooperation Act of 1948:[21]

TITLE I

Sec. 101. This title may be cited as the "Economic Cooperation Act of 1948."

FINDINGS AND DECLARATION OF POLICY

Sec. 102 (a) Recognizing the intimate economic and other relationships between the United States and the nations of Europe, and recognizing that disruption following in the wake of war is not contained by national frontiers, the Congress finds that the existing situation in Europe endangers the establishment of a lasting peace, the general welfare and national interest of the United States, and the attainment of the objectives of the United Nations. The restoration or maintenance in European countries of principles of individual liberty, free institutions, and genuine independence rests largely upon the establishment of sound economic conditions, stable international economic relationships, and the achievement by the countries of Europe of a healthy economy independent of extraordinary outside assistance. The accomplishment of these objectives calls for a plan of European recovery, open to all such nations which cooperate in such plan, based upon a strong production effort, the expansion of foreign trade, the creation and maintenance of internal financial stability, and the development of economic cooperation, including all possible steps to establish and maintain equitable rates of exchange and to bring about the progressive elimination of trade barriers. Mindful of the advantages which the United States has enjoyed through the existence of a large domestic market with no internal trade barriers, and believing that similar advantages can accrue to the countries of Europe, it is declared to be the policy of the people of the United States to encourage these countries through a joint organization to exert sustained common efforts as set forth in the report of the Committee of European Economic Cooperation signed at Paris on September 22, 1947, which will speedily achieve that economic cooperation in Europe which is essential for lasting peace and prosperity. It is further declared to be the policy of the people of the United States to sustain and strengthen principles of individual liberty, free institutions, and genuine independence in Europe through assistance to those countries of Europe which participate in a joint recovery program based upon self-help and mutual cooperation: Provided, That no assistance to the participating countries herein contemplated shall seriously impair the economic stability of the United States. It is further declared to be the policy of the United States that continuity of assistance provided by the United States should, at all times, be dependent upon continuity of cooperation among countries participating in the program.

[21] Also known as the Foreign Assistance Act of 1948, 62nd Stat., 80th Congress, 2nd Session, Ch. 169, April 3, 1948.

Chapter 8

Impact of the Corporation Audits Division upon the U.S. General Accounting Office

Joseph Pois

Present Stature

The stature, recognition, and influence that the General Accounting Office presently has contrast sharply with the relatively pedestrian approach and limited credibility that characterized the earlier years of its existence. The primary factor in this impressive metamorphosis was the marked change in the manner in which the GAO conceptualized the scope of its audits and the way in which they are implemented. The self-initiated reviews of operational economy and efficiency and program effectiveness which have become the underlying motif in the functioning of the GAO have carried the office far beyond the centralized and rather mechanistic examinations of documents that initially marked its operations. The reviews for which the GAO uses the rubric "auditing" embrace, in the words of the Comptroller General, "not only examining accounting records and financial transactions and reports, but also checking for compliance with applicable laws and regulations; examining the efficiency and economy of operations; and reviewing the results of operations to evaluate whether desired results, including legislatively prescribed objectives, have been effectively achieved" (Comptroller General, 1975, p. 5).

The profound change in GAO is reflected in the leadership role which it enjoys in the public accounting profession. This represents a startling reversal from the aloofness, if not disdain, with which the profession regarded the GAO in its earlier days. The Government Corporation Control Act of 1945[1] was the watershed in vitalizing and professionalizing GAO's audit activities (Fenton, 1971, p. 88; Morse, 1975b p. 11).

Antecedents of the Corporation Control Act

Long before the 1945 enactments, the GAO had become increasingly conscious of its tenuous relationships with the federal corporations. In fact, Comptroller General McCarl, as early as 1928, expressed his concern over the use of such corporations. Referring to the U.S. Supreme Court decision in Skinner and Eddy Corporation v. McCarl,[2] he observed that Congress in creating these corporations surrendered legislative control over accounting for public money; and he earnestly recommended that "full and adequate provision be made for publicity in the financial transactions of such corporations by the requirement that they account through the General Accounting Office to the Congress for the expenditures of public money and that, with the exceptions stated in the law as being necessary for their operation, they be required to observe the sound principles stated in the law as of general application for the expenditure and accounting for public money"

(Comptroller General, 1928, p. 12). The following year, the Comptroller General lamented the fact that the Inland Waterways Corporation was an example "of an existing corporation in which the legislation creating it omitted to confer on the General Accounting Office jurisdiction to require an accounting to be rendered to it of receipts and expenditures" (Comptroller General, 1929, p. 12).

The sharp increase in government corporations during the economic downturn of the 1930s undoubtedly deepened GAO dismay over the special status enjoyed by this segment of the federal establishment. Fenton reports that of the 101 government corporations named in the Government Corporation Control Act as being subject to audit, 56 were created during the depression years of the 1930s and 16 were established between 1940 and 1943 (Fenton, 1971, p. 89).

Creation of the Reconstruction Finance Corporation in 1932, with its vast power to expend federal funds, impelled the Comptroller General to criticize the absence of any provision for an independent audit by the GAO (Comptroller General, 1932 p. 14). Interestingly enough, the audit which the GAO made of the RFC for the fiscal year 1945, following enactment of the Corporation Control Act, which resulted in a 10-

---

[1] This legislation (59 Stat. 597) was preceded by the George Act of February 24, 1945 (59 Stat. 5), which provided for the GAO to audit the financial transactions of all government corporations. The later legislation incorporated and extended greatly the provisions of the George Act.

[2] 275 US 1, the Court said: "Indeed, an important, if not the chief, reason for employing these incorporated agencies was to enable them to employ commercial methods and to conduct their operations with a freedom supposed to be inconsistent with accountability to the treasury under its established procedure of audit and control over the financial transactions of the United States."

volume report, was a milestone in the expansion of GAO's auditing sphere and in the profound recasting of its audit approach. Morse observes that "this audit concerned itself not only with major accounting deficiencies but also with problems encountered or observed with respect to RFC's general methods of operation, relationships with other Federal agencies, organizational structure, inadequacy of internal audit system, management of lending operations, management of trading and subsidy programs, and a host of other subjects" (Morse, 1975b, p. 15).

The Clash Between GAO and TVA

A bitter confrontation between the GAO and the Tennessee Valley Authority ensued when the GAO sought to audit the Authority in the same manner as it did regular governmental agencies. Eric Kohler, who was then serving as Comptroller of the TVA, proved to be a formidable adversary, and he manifestly relished the opportunity to challenge the audit competence and practices of GAO. The controversy continued even after McCarl, who had incurred Kohler's scorn, left and was ultimately succeeded by Lindsay C. Warren,[3] who sought to inject a broader perspective into the GAO and to abate the antagonisms that had developed between the GAO and the executive branch (see Brown, 1970; Mansfield, 1939; and Pritchett, 1943). The dispute reached a climax when, despite concessions made by the GAO

in the stance it had taken, "officials of the Corporation late in 1940 transmitted a memorandum to the General Accounting Office contending that by reasons of its corporate status and of provisions of Section 9(b) of its act, the Tennessee Valley Authority is wholly exempt from the Budget and Accounting Act and other statutes requiring accounting for public funds and hence exempt from the examination and settlement procedure under the Budget and Accounting Act (Comptroller General, 1941, p. 68). The issue was finally resolved in 1941 by congressional enactment of an amendment to the TVA Act, which legislation had been agreed upon by GAO and TVA and which was designed to "remove all differences of opinion on legal and procedural matters" (Brown, 1970, p. 22). Although the manner in which the dispute was resolved did not by any means represent a demeaning rebuff to the GAO, it can reasonably be surmised that the controversy had a salutary impact upon GAO from the standpoint of bringing out shortcomings in its approach to corporate audits.

Commercial versus Governmental Type of Audit

In negotiating with the Commodity Credit Corporation during the fiscal year 1943, the GAO agreed "that the regular governmental audit was not suitable to the capital fund operations of the Corporation" (Comptroller General, 1943, p. 6). At the same time, the GAO ex-

---

[3]After McCarl's tenure terminated in 1936, there was an interregnum until 1939, during which period the Assistant Comptroller General served as Acting Comptroller General. Fred H. Brown, appointed Comptroller General in 1939, occupied the post only until 1940, at which time Warren took over.

pressed doubts as to whether it was authorized to perform a commercial type of audit under the legislation then applicable to the CCC. The Comptroller General opined that one obstacle to using the governmental type of audit for the Commodity Credit Corporation was that "it is impractical, if not impossible, to assemble in one place the original vouchers and other original papers supporting the capital fund operations of the Corporation and still permit the Corporation to carry out the business responsibilities imposed upon it by the Congress." This observation reflected the fact that GAO audits, up to that time, had consisted primarily of a centralized review in Washington of documents transmitted by the respective government agency, a practice to which the TVA had taken strong exception. In fact, the GAO had undertaken pre-audits in which, prior to payment, it examined vouchers after they had been administratively approved.

In differentiating the "governmental type of audit" from the "commercial," the Comptroller General stated that the purpose of the former was that of determining "the validity of expenditures under appropriations made by the Congress, in the light of restrictions and limitations placed by the Congress generally upon the expenditure of appropriated moneys." It was viewed as part of a system to enforce the personal accountability of governmental officers authorizing or expending appropriated funds. The year 1945 was to afford the GAO a springboard for expanding its audit approach so that checking on accountability would be only one facet of its reviews of agency operations.

The Thrust for GAO Corporate Audits

The Comptroller General's efforts to get closer to the government corporations were encouraged by the enactment of legislation providing for GAO's audit of the financial transactions of the Commodity Credit Corporation beginning with the period July 1, 1944 (58 Stat. 106). It is very significant that this Act stipulated that the audits were to be made "in accordance with the principles applicable to commercial corporate transactions." In light of access difficulties which the GAO has sometimes encountered, it bears mention that the Act specifically gave the GAO representatives access to the corporation's papers, books, accounts, and property. The legislation also provided that the examination of the corporate records should be made at the place or places where such records were normally kept and that the corporation should retain custody of the documents "relating to its non-administrative transactions." The Comptroller General directed attention to the value of this act as a precedent for other corporations (Comptroller General, 1944, pp. 6-7).

There was increasing congressional concern over the proliferation of government corporations and the lack of effective control over their programs and operations. This culminated in the enactment of the Government Corporation Control Act of 1945, which one writer states "represented recognition by the Congress both of the need for a special type of government institution tailored to the requirements of business programs and for special types of controls over such institutions which would assure accountability without impairing essential flexibility" (Seidman, 1975, p. 89).

GAO Response to Its New Task

The Comptroller General recognized that the 1945 legislation for corporate audits had far-reaching implications, and expressed the view that the first step (the George Act) represented "the most forward-looking and outstanding measure in its field since the enactment of the Budget and Accounting Act in 1921" (Comptroller General, 1945, p. 3). The new legislation was the basis for the establishment of the Corporation Audits Division in the GAO. It is a commentary on the level of professionalism then extant in the GAO that the Comptroller General felt impelled to point out that the Division was "headed by a certified public accountant of long experience" (T. Coleman Andrews). As further evidence of the progress being made in strengthening GAO's technical capabilities, the Comptroller General went on to say: "The public accounting profession is cooperating splendidly in our efforts to build the finest aggregation of accounting talent within or without the Government."

The Professionalizing Impact of the Corporate Audit Program

These truly portentous steps in GAO's development had a profound impact which tends to be obscured by the fact that corporation audits are presently of limited significance in the totality of GAO's operations.[4] One highly significant effect was to bridge the gap between the GAO and the accounting profession. The poor image that the profession had of GAO was reflected in the fact that the American Institute's Committee on Governmental Accounting was criticized for not opposing the requirement of the Government Corporation Control Act that the audit of Government Corporations be made by the GAO. "Some members felt that we should insist on audits of federal Government corporations by independent certified public accountants" (quoted in Comptroller General, 1948, p. 19). In its 1947 annual report, the Institute's Committee on Governmental Accounting also observed: "Prior to 1945 relations between the General Accounting Office and the certified public accountants of the United States, as represented by the Institute, were impaired by lack of mutual understanding and confidence" (quoted in Comptroller General, 1948). It is not surprising, therefore, that in staffing the new division, the Comptroller General placed considerable emphasis upon the recruitment of certified public accountants. Although these efforts were hampered by the abnormal demands for qualified accountants within and without the government, there were factors conducive to GAO's mobilization of such talent. The cooperation of the accounting profession has already been mentioned; the experience of public accountants who had accepted assignments in federal agencies during

---

[4] The lower priority that GAO accords corporate audits is reflected in the fact that Comptroller General Staats initiated legislation that, effective July 1, 1974, changed the statutory requirement as to frequency of such audits from annual to "at least once in every three years" (88 Stat. 1962).

World War II undoubtedly helped to dispel the aloofness between governmental financial management and the profession. Most of the talent that had key roles in launching the new division bore the imprimatur of national accounting firms.[5] Furthermore, because of the backlog that faced the Division, the GAO was authorized to employ outside public accountants to supplement its own staff resources. The retention of national auditing firms also contributed to establishing good rapport between the profession and the GAO.

The effects of the thrust started by the Corporation Control Act impelled a British writer to observe: "The General Accounting Office has thus clearly placed itself in the hands of the accounting profession" (Normanton, 1966, p. 269).

The Impressive Accomplishments of the Corporation Audits Division

The corporation audits afforded GAO a vehicle for identifying shortcomings in the accounting of some corporations; specifically, Comptroller General Warren felt that in two cases (the Reconstruction Finance Corporation and the Federal Public Housing Authority) the conditions were such as to warrant special reports to the Congress (Comptroller General, 1947, p. 14). He inveighed against the inadequacies which the GAO audits had disclosed: "These unsatisfactory and deplorable conditions arose because the accounting requirements of

great and important undertakings of the Government either were not fully comprehended by their managers or ignored, neglected or regarded as having a relatively unimportant claim to attention, until the situation became very grave." At the same time, the Comptroller General bestowed accolades upon the accounting systems of the Tennessee Valley Authority, the Home Owners' Loan Corporation, and the Federal Deposit Insurance Corporation. The GAO had now entered a new arena and was in a position to flex its muscles with respect to professional matters of true moment.

The Comptroller General was required by the Corporation Control Act not only to include the prescribed financial statements in his report but also "such comments and information as may be deemed necessary to keep Congress informed of the operations and financial condition of the several corporations, together with such recommendation with respect thereto as the Comptroller General may deem advisable, including a report of any impairment of capital noted in the audit and recommendations for the return of such government capital or the payment of such dividends as, in his judgment, should be accomplished."[6] In citing the most important recommendations that he had made up to June 30, 1947, the Comptroller General included, among others, the following (Comptroller General, 1947):

1. That the corporations be required to pay interest to the United States Treasury on

---

[5] Fenton (1971) tells of "the early leaders" of the division.

[6] 31 U.S.C. 851. The act also called for a statement of sources and application of funds, which Morse (1975b, p. 21) points out "placed the financial reporting practices of the Federal corporations well in advance of those in private industry, where such a statement was not, at the time, a regular part of the financial statements which public accountants audited and expressed opinions on."

funds supplied by the Treasury, either as capital or as loans, at a rate equal to the interest cost to the Treasury of such funds.

2. That the corporations be restricted to borrowing from the United States Treasury only and not be permitted to borrow from the public.

3. That the corporations not be authorized to create subsidiary corporations or to provide the capital funds of other Government-owned corporations.

4. That corporations not be authorized to borrow funds from the U.S. Treasury for any use that does not contemplate recovery of the funds. (p. 15).

Manifestly, the GAO was now in a position to not only influence the financial management of government corporations but also to make significant inputs into congressional decision making with respect to these corporations.

Recognition Accorded GAO by the Profession

As one reads the remarks of the Comptroller General in the various annual reports that followed the enactment of the Government Corporation Control Act, he perceives not only an increasing tempo in the professionalization of the organization but also the steady consolidation of the advances that it was making both internally and in its relations with the profession. In his report for fiscal year 1948, the Comptroller General expressed the feeling that the Corporation Audits Division had "reached comparative maturity," and he further reported that the division was able to undertake all its audit assignments without calling on public accounting firms (Comptroller General, 1948, p. 18). By the end of the fiscal year, 54 of the Division's acccounting staff of 167 were certified public accountants.

The Comptroller General's comment that this ratio compared favorably with public accounting firms is indicative of the strong drive to place the Corporation Audits Division on a high professional level. It must have been a source of considerable gratification for Comptroller General Warren to be able to report that the American Institute's Committee on Governmental Accounting had stated that the new legislation had worked and that "the reports issued by the Corporation Audits Division have received wide and favorable attention" (Comptroller General, 1948, p. 19). The Institute's Committee also stated that relationships between GAO and the accounting profession had completely changed and that the profession had acquired a better understanding of the Comptroller General's problems.

By June 30, 1949, the 101 corporations originally included in GAO's mandate had decreased to 63, but the Comptroller General reported that the inactive and dissolved corporations were of such small size that the volume of regular audit work had diminished only slightly (Comptroller General, 1949, p. 30).

Organization-wide Impact of the Corporation Audits Division

The impressive accomplishments of the Corporation Audits Division in applying the commercial type of audit to the myriad government corporations injected the professional tone and breadth of perspective sorely needed by the GAO. The spillover effects of the Division's operations made for vital change in the totality of GAO's audit work. Site audits began to be the norm for GAO's audits, thereby breaking down the insularity that had inevitably militated against the effectiveness of GAO's audit efforts.

The ascendancy of the professional accountant meant that the legal staff was no longer the predominant professional group in the organization. The GAO had not only mobilized an imposing core of accounting talent but had demonstrated the capability to execute audit assignments of the most difficult nature. This inevitably engendered a much broader view of how GAO could meet the auditing needs of the federal establishment. Just about the time that the corporation audits program had achieved considerable momentum, the Comptroller General, together with the Secretary of the Treasury and the Director of the Bureau of the Budget, established the Joint Accounting Improvement Program (now known as the Joint Financial Management Improvement Program), which provided for collaborative effort among the three agencies directed toward the improvement of the government's accounting and financial reporting.

The Genesis of the Comprehensive Audit Concept

The activities in the corporate audit area gave rise to the concept of the "comprehensive audit." This concept played an unusually important part in the recasting of GAO's operations; its enunciation set in motion a process that culminated in the 1970 statutory legitimization of broad reviews. The ambiguity of the concept enabled the GAO to use it as a means for expanding the breadth and depth of its audit operations.

The Comptroller General stated that "an important element in this audit program is the appraisal of the methods employed in operating the accounting system and the effectiveness of internal control and related administrative practices in each agency" (Comptroller General, 1950, p. 40). At its inception, the comprehensive audit approach apparently was envisaged as being closely related to a commercial audit. The agencies initially selected for a comprehensive audit were, in the Comptroller General's words, "of a predominantly business or industrial type, and therefore lend themselves readily to the comprehensive audit approach" (Comptroller General, 1950, p. 41). This explains why the comprehensive audit program was assigned to the Corporation Audits Division. Once having espoused this concept, the GAO used it as a vehicle for the assertion and implementation of an auditing role that concerned itself increasingly with the managerial and program areas—so much so that in many instances the strictly financial facets were eclipsed by the more substantive aspects.

Budget and Accounting Procedures Act of 1950

The professional lift that the corporation audit program gave the GAO was buttressed by the Budget and Accounting Procedures Act of 1950.[7] In addition to other salient features, the Act provided statutory underpinning for GAO site audits and authorized the Comptroller General to require agencies to retain in whole or in part financial docu-

---

[7]The portion of the act of particular import to the GAO was designated as the Accounting and Auditing Act of 1950 (64 Stat. 834). The implications of this far-reaching legislation are discussed by Morse (1975a, p. 23).

ments that they had legally been required to submit to the GAO. Hence, the massive flow of documents into Washington for examination by the GAO was gradually to be terminated, and the "desk audit" was to be replaced by examinations made at the place or places where the accounts and other records are normally kept. Moreover, in determining the auditing procedures, the Comptroller General is required by the 1950 Act to "give due regard to generally accepted principles of auditing, including consideration of the effectiveness of accounting organizations and systems, internal audit and control, and related administrative practices of the respective agencies" (31 U.S.C. 67). Undoubtedly, a potent factor in the development that culminated in this legislation was the experience and the insights which the Corporation Audits Division afforded the GAO as to accepted audit practices.

Abolition of the Corporation Audits Division

It became GAO's goal to extend the comprehensive site audit programs to all agencies where practical. According to Comptroller General Warren, the techniques of auditing government corporations differed "but little from those employed in the comprehensive audit program. The chief difference is that, in the normal course of events, professional opinion is given as to the fairness of the financial statements of the corporations" (Comptroller General, 1952, p. 21). This afforded a rationale for discontinuing the corporation audit unit as a separate entity within the GAO. Early in 1952, the Corporation Audits Division was abolished and its functions transferred to

the newly created Division of Audits, which also absorbed the Audit Division, Postal Audit Division, and the Reconciliation and Clearance Division. Fenton states that the transfer was made while most of the initial comprehensive audits were still under way. These "and subsequent audits over the next several years were carried out by or under the supervision of men who had been associated with the Corporation Audits Division" (Fenton, 1971, p. 105).

Effect of Broader Audit Approach upon Primacy of the Accountant

By the time the Corporation Audits Division was absorbed by the Division of Audits, the professional accountant had assumed a pivotal role within the GAO. This had several effects. It injected into the organization a professional esprit de corps and staffed the agency with personnel possessing analytical competence and the capacity to deal with financial and other quantitative data in a meaningful manner. Still another effect of the ascendancy of the professional accountant in the GAO was that of gaining the support of the public accounting profession for the agency. Furthermore, the skill demonstrated in the corporation audits inevitably enhanced the stature which GAO had in the eyes of the Congress as well as the executive agencies.

But the very broad perspective currently reflected in GAO audits has meant the primacy of the professional accountant is no longer viable. The Comptroller General's emphasis upon the recruitment of a truly multidisciplinary staff recognizes that accounting skills, albeit still important and even inherent in an appropriate mix of requisite talents, can be regarded as only one of the disciplines essential for discharging GAO's mission as it is now broadly conceived. In fact, GAO will need to diversify its talents still further, and more of the key positions in the organization will have to be filled by other than professional accountants.

The GAO has turned completely with respect to its position in relation to the accounting profession. Initially, the office was held in low esteem by the profession; and it was the legal, rather than the accounting, staff which provided the technical leadership for the GAO. Then, the impressive improvements which had their inception in the accomplishments of the Corporation Audits Division, together with the attendant assumption of the leadership role by the accountant, firmly established GAO's stature within the accounting profession.

GAO's Leadership Role in Auditing

With the ascendancy of Comptroller General Staats, there was a stepped up momentum within GAO for expanding the horizons of governmental auditing. In enunciating the audit standards which GAO now espouses, Staats stated (Comptroller General, 1972):

This demand for information [about government programs] has widened the scope of governmental auditing so that such auditing no longer is a function concerned primarily with financial operations. Instead, governmental auditing now is also concerned with whether governmental organizations are achieving the purposes for which programs are authorized and funds are made available, are doing so economically and efficiently, and are complying with applicable laws and regulations. The standards contained in this statement were

developed to apply to audits of this wider scope.

GAO had been the prime mover in a highly significant effort in the auditing field which entailed collaboration with professional societies; representatives of federal agencies and state, county, and city governments; and public-interest groups. It took upon itself the task of promulgating standards that were to reach out beyond the federal government and "be applicable to all levels of government in the United States" (Comptroller General, 1972). The deference that the profession now accords GAO is reflected in the report which the American Institute's Committee on Relations with GAO prepared on the standards (Staats, 1976):

The members of this Committee agree with the philosophy and objectives advocated by the GAO in its standards and believe that the GAO's broadened definition of auditing is a logical and worthwhile continuation of the evolution and growth of the auditing discipline (p. 3).

Also exemplifying GAO's role as the driving force in the rethinking of governmental auditing are its influence in the creation of eleven intergovernmental audit forums and the project it undertook with the International City Management Association to demonstrate the application of broad-scope auditing at the local government level (Staats, 1976, pp. 4, 5). The thrust underlying these developments stems from the enhanced prestige which the GAO enjoys in connection with serving as a Congressional resource and as the auditor of the performance of federal departments and agencies.

The audit function as now conceived by the Comptroller General is characterized by a breadth that goes beyond what even the skillful and creative staff of the Corporation Audits Division envisaged. Yet it was this division that was the progenitor of a concept that was the vehicle for expanding the scope of GAO audits so as to embrace not only financial integ-rity and economy and efficiency of oper-ations but also program results. The pioneering efforts of the Corporation Audits Division made a major contribu-tion to the achievement of the stature, influence, and recognition presently associated with the GAO.

References

Brown, Richard E. 1970. *The GAO*. Knoxville, Tenn.: University of Tennessee Press.

Comptroller General of the United States. 1928. *Annual Report of the Comptroller General of the United States*. Washington, D.C.: General Accounting Office.

——. 1929. *Annual Report of the Comptroller General of the United States*. Washington, D. C.: General Accounting Office.

——. 1932. *Annual Report of the Comptroller General of the United States*. Washington, D.C.: General Accounting Office.

——. 1941. *Annual Report of the Comptroller General of the United States*. Washington, D.C.: General Accounting Office.

——. 1943. *Annual Report of the Comptroller General of the United States*. Washington, D.C.: General Accounting Office.

——. 1944. *Annual Report of the Comptroller General of the United States*. Washington, D.C.: General Accounting Office.

——. 1945. *Annual Report of the Comptroller General of the United States*. Washington, D.C.: General Accounting Office.

——. 1947. *Annual Report of the Comptroller General of the United States*. Washington, D.C.: General Accounting Office.

——. 1948. *Annual Report of the Comptroller General of the United States*. Washington, D.C.: General Accounting Office.

——. 1949. *Annual Report of the Comptroller General of the United States*. Washington, D.C.: General Accounting Office.

——. 1950. *Annual Report of the Comptroller General of the United States*. Washington, D.C.: General Accounting Office.

——. 1952. *Annual Report of the Comptroller General of the United States*. Washington, D.C.: General Accounting Office.

——. 1972. *Standards for Audit of Governmental Organizations, Programs, Activities, and Functions*. Washington, D.C.: General Accounting Office.

——. 1975. *Annual Report of the Comptroller General of the United States*. Washington, D.C.: General Accounting Office.

Fenton, John C. 1971. "The Corporation Audits Division—Its Legacy to the Seventies." *The GAO Review*, Summer.

Mansfield, Harvey C. 1939. *The Comptroller General*. New Haven, Conn.: Yale University Press.

Morse, Ellsworth H., Jr. 1975a. "The Accounting and Auditing Act of 1950—Its Current Significance to GAO." *The GAO Review*, Summer.

——. 1975b. "The Government Corporation Control Legislation of 1945." *The GAO Review*, Fall.

Normanton, E. L. 1966. *The Accountability and Audit of Governments.* New York: Frederick A. Praeger.

Pritchett, C. Herman. 1943. *The Tennessee Valley Authority.* Chapel Hill, N.C.: University of North Carolina Press.

Seidman, Harold. 1975. "Government-Sponsored Enterprise in the United States." in *The New Political Economy: The Public Use of the Private Sector,* New York: Macmillan Publishing Co., Inc.

Staats, Elmer B. 1976. "Govenmental Auditing—Yesterday, Today, and Tomorrow." *The GAO Review*, Spring.

Chapter 9

Turnaround at the GAO*

William W. Cooper and Walter F. Frese

Introduction

A remarkable accounting development of recent years is the emergence of the U.S. General Accounting Office as a recognized leader in the development of new practices and concepts in auditing. This is all the more remarkable in view of an early history (see the chapters by Pois and Stone) in which that agency had relied almost entirely on a weak and very limited concept of audits (i.e., "desk" or "voucher" audits and centralized account keeping for the federal government) as part of its attempt to exercise financial control. Accompanied by detailed prescriptions of forms and procedures and related regulations, that

effort at "accounting" had been a constant source of friction with the federal executive establishment. The story of how this change came about is the objective of this chapter. More precisely, it is one purpose of this chapter to describe some of the sources of this "turnaround at the GAO" from the standpoint of one of its participants.

To explain the many sources of this remarkable transformation would require a large and elaborate study. Here, however, we restrict ourselves to only one such "turning point"—a very important one—which is represented in the memorandum that is reproduced in Appendix B. Any reading of that memorandum, issued by Comptroller General

*Specific acknowledgment should be made of the numerous comments and suggestions from E. H. Morse, Jr., and Karney Brasfield, which contributed greatly to improving this chapter.

Lindsay Warren, on August 15, 1952, will show that its emphasis is on agency responsibility for accounting as (1) a tool for management and (2) a basis of accountability to others. This, as we shall see, was part of a series of developments that was moving the GAO from centralized accounting and voucher auditing as the focus for its own activities to another approach, which emphasized responsibility for accounting at the agency level accompanied by GAO site audits—with a very broad concept of auditing and a cooperative approach to formulating and stating accounting principles as guiding concepts for practices at the agency levels. Concomitantly, this was accompanied by further encouraging the individual agencies to develop their own accounting systems and related internal controls and audits as aids to management rather than as mere systems for legalistic record keeping at detailed clerical levels.[1]

Since this is a memorial volume to Eric L. Kohler, it is fitting to emphasize, at the outset, that he played a crucial role in bringing the memorandum of Appendix B into existence. It is also fitting to emphasize that this document represented a culmination of one set of developments while providing a platform from which new developments could be initiated that were pointed in the same direction. What these prior developments were and the direction in which they were pointed forms the main theme of this chapter. This includes the under-

lying philosophy and the kinds of interagency machinery that was utilized; for example, the machinery erected to coordinate the efforts of the GAO, the U.S. Treasury Department, and the U.S. Bureau of the Budget in a Joint Accounting Improvement Program that also involved other agencies of the federal government. What is clear now—and what was only a guiding principle at the time—is that the subsequent events referred to in the opening sentence of this introduction could not have occurred without these prior developments.

Background

This is not the place for a detailed and documented history of the development of accounting and auditing in the federal government. Such an effort would, in fact, take us back to the Constitutional Convention of 1789—and its prior history, too, since, as is well known, the U.S. Constitution itself deals with these issues. To supply needed perspective, however, we shall undertake a brief sketch of some of the major developments that preceded the Budget and Accounting Procedures Act of 1950 referred to in Comptroller General Warren's 1952 memorandum.[2]

For this synoptic historical review, we might commence with the Continental Congress, even before the United States of America was founded. In its resolution of April 1, 1776, the Continental

---

[1] See, for example, McEachren (1955, pp. 29-33) for a discussion of the improvements at agency levels which resulted from the developments we shall describe and which, as McEachren notes, "many commercial enterprises could well emulate."

[2] For a more detailed analysis of developments during this period, see the report of the Association of Government Accountants (1975, Chap. 1).

Congress established two important principles: (1) that no funds be withdrawn except on the basis of warrants, such funds to be entered on the books as charges to the persons receiving them, and (2) these persons should, within a reasonable time, provide a full accounting of all expenditures as a basis for adjustment and settlement of their accounts. In this same resolution the Continental Congress also established a "treasury office of accounts" and provided for the establishment of an "auditor general."[3] This approach, which linked auditing and accounting from a legal accountability standpoint, provided a guiding precedent for a long period thereafter.

When the U.S. Treasury Department was formed in 1789, the duties of advancing funds only under warrant and maintaining legal accountability controls were assigned to the Secretary. This was intended to implement the requirement in the U.S. Constitution "that no money shall be withdrawn from the Treasury except pursuant to appropriation made by law." Thus, in the phrases that were customarily used, "issuance only under warrant" was meant to provide a record that the Secretary had ascertained that the appropriation had actually been made by the Congress. "Legal accountability" was also required to establish that all pertinent legal requirements had been adhered to in the resulting expenditures.[4]

In 1894 the Dockery Act strengthened the centralized accounting and control functions of the Treasury Department, and also imposed on the Secretary of the Treasury the duty of supplying to the U.S. Congress an annual report on all receipts, expenditures, and balances. It further simplified the procedures of settlement and provided for a Comptroller of the Treasury to replace the several comptrollers in existence at that time.

Throughout the above developments, these "accounting functions" remained with the Treasury Department in the executive branch of the government. With passage of the Budget and Accounting Act of 1921, however, large portions of these responsibilities were transferred to the U.S. General Accounting Office, which was created by that act as an "independent" agency.[5] The Comptroller General, as head of this agency, was required to countersign all warrants issued by the Secretary of the Treasury. The Budget and Accounting Act also transferred from the Treasury to the General Accounting Office the "personal ledger accounts" of "accountable officers" and the responsibility for "audit and settlement" of all receipts and expenditures made by "accountable officers." Finally, the 1921 Budget and Accounting Act also gave authority to the Comptroller General to prescribe forms, systems, and procedures for administrative appropriation and fund accounting throughout the

[3] *Journals of Congress,* April 1, 1776, pp. 244-246.

[4] Acknowledgment is due T. Jack Gary, Jr., Director of Research for the first "Hoover Commission" Task Force on Budgeting and Accounting for allowing us access to his unpublished background memorandum, prepared with Irving Tenner, for the Accounting Policy Committee of the Fiscal, Budgeting and Accounting Project of the Commission ("Hoover Commission") on Organization of the Executive Branch of the Government.

[5] It was later identified by law as responsible only to Congress.

federal government and for the administrative examination of fiscal officers' accounts.

Thus, what had been functions of the executive branch were thereby transferred to an independent agency. In fact, the totality of these functions were split, since responsibility for preparing the annual report on receipts, expenditures, and balances remained in the Treasury. The Secretary remained the signer of warrants and also found it necessary to maintain his own accounting system as a basis for discharging his responsibilities. Finally, the Act provided for a completely new executive function in the form of a new agency, or rather an agency subunit, in the form of a Bureau of the Budget, located in the Treasury and responsible for the preparation of the executive budget under direction of the President.

The first Comptroller General, J. R. McCarl, proceeded almost immediately to set up an elaborate system of centralized bookkeeping controls to account for receipts, expenditures, and account balances. He viewed this as necessary not only as a basis for countersigning warrants and establishing legal accountability, but also as a basis for the audit and settlement of accounts of "accountable officers." In fact Comptroller General McCarl carried this to a point where his centralized system duplicated not only the system in the Treasury, but also the accounting system that the agencies of the executive branch had to maintain—for their own purposes of legal accountability—and this became the source of the frictions that were noted at the start of this chapter.

To further appreciate the source of these frictions, one needs to understand the way in which the Comptroller General exercised his authority to prescribe accounting forms, systems, and procedures. In the face of lack of authority by the executive branch, McCarl used his power as a basis for building up his own centralized accounting controls and the prescription of the forms, systems, and procedures for the various federal agencies. Indeed, the agency systems became primarily extensions of the GAO's centralized system of accounts, and the needs of the executive branch for an accounting that would be responsive to the requirements of their own management were almost totally disregarded. This created problems and frustrations at all levels of management responsibility in the executive branch.

At the central level, the Treasury Department and the Bureau of the Budget were without authority to require accounting recognition in the agencies of their needs for information in connection with various phases of their financial management responsibilities and in the development and execution of the budget.

Thus, Treasury lacked authority to develop an integrated accounting and reporting system that could tie the receipts and expenditures reflected in the agency accounts and related reports with those in the Treasury Department's own (overall) reports. This need was also ignored in GAO's approach to prescribing agency accounting systems, with the result that the receipts and expenditures in the budget summaries and other reports of the receipts and expenditures prepared by the Treasury from its own accounts were on a different basis from those reflected in agency accounts and reports. This situation also precluded development of basic improvements in the Treasury's central reporting function based on consolidation of its own and agency accounting results.

The Bureau of the Budget was also handicapped by its inability to obtain accounting support in the agencies for financial data required in various phases of BOB's own responsibilities in the administration of the budget. For example, GAO's prescribed accounting systems did not recognize the needs of the Bureau of the Budget for obtaining reports pertaining to the status of agency appropriations and related obligations and expenditures on a basis consistent with BOB's responsibilities in the apportionment process. As a consequence of this lack of coordination, the other executive agencies were saddled with the need for rendering two sets of monthly reports on the status of appropriations—one for the Budget Bureau and the other for the General Accounting Office. Even the latter process was rendered ineffective from a management viewpoint, however, by the fact that the accounting rules and procedures were prescribed by the GAO to fit into the requirements of the latter's own centralized system of accountability controls. As a result of these and other inconsistencies and gaps between accounting requirements prescribed by GAO and information needed by management at various levels in the development and execution of the budget, the accounting and budget functions at all levels in the executive branch functioned in a separate and uncoordinated manner.

In a fundamental sense the most serious aspect of the lack of coordination between accounting and budgeting was the resulting lack of incentive for agencies to develop the potential of accounting for providing meaningful information in their individual circumstances, and for controlling and evaluating program performance in relation to cost. This broader potential for accounting remained largely undeveloped owing to the labyrinth of paper work and detailed rules prescribed by the GAO to implement its own centralized system of legal accountability controls over receipts and expenditures. In addition, the overlapping and uncoordinated requirements of GAO and BOB that resulted from this approach focused primarily on controlling obligations and expenditures with prescribed allotment limits and periods so that, on the one hand, agency attention was diverted from program performance evaluation and direction and, on the other hand, no central leadership function emerged that could supply needed guidance in concepts and principles.

A number of attempts were made by the executive branch to transfer the authority of the Comptroller General to prescribe accounting forms, systems, and procedures into the Treasury Department or the Bureau of the Budget in the executive branch.[6] These efforts, vigorously resisted by the GAO, not only failed to get the required congressional support, but also resulted in contro-

[6] Under the Economy Act of June 30, 1932, President Hoover issued an executive order to transfer these powers and duties to the Bureau of the Budget, but because the House of Representatives adopted a resolution disapproving it, this executive order was never put into effect. On January 12, 1937, President Roosevelt transmitted to the Congress the report of the *President's Committee on Administrative Management* (the Brownlow committee), which recommended a restructuring in which the General Accounting Office would be restricted only to a post-audit function under a renamed General Auditing Office with authority and responsibility for accounting placed in the Treasury Department. At the same time, an opposing report by the Brookings Institution was filed by Senator Byrd for the Senate Select Committee to Investigate the Executive Agencies. After much debate (some of it acrimonious) nothing was done to modify the authority of the GAO along the lines of either proposal.

versies that added to the previously noted frictions between GAO and the executive agencies.

With the failure to obtain legislative authority to transfer responsibility for accounting requirements from the General Accounting Office to the executive branch, a noteworthy effort was made by the executive branch to deal with the problem, insofar as possible, by executive order. Efforts in this connection were started in 1940 by the newly formed "Division of Administrative Management" in the Bureau of the Budget, which was formed as part of the program to make the Bureau of the Budget a more constructive force in the management of executive branch operations. Working with staff from the Treasury, an executive order was developed (Executive Order 8512 issued August 5, 1940) which assigned responsibilities to the Secretary of the Treasury for developing an integrated accounting and reporting system within the executive branch, including provision for establishing principles and standards and uniform terminology for use by executive agencies and a system of financial reports required by the Director of the Bureau of the Budget for the information of the President. In a subsequent Executive Order (issued in March 1942), the concurrence of the Comptroller General was required in connection with the establishment of uniform terminology, classifications, principles, and standards. These efforts were not wholly successful, partly because Congress never provided sufficient funds for the Treasury to develop its intended control accounting and reporting functions, and partly because World War II interrupted these and other constructive efforts that had been started.

For the sake of perspective, it is worth noting that efforts at obtaining legislation that would transfer authority to prescribe accounting requirements from the Comptroller General to the Treasury as an agency in the executive branch were linked with similar efforts to transfer authority for controlling receipts and expenditures. Most of the opposition to these proposals was based on the conviction that control over receipts and expenditures from the point of view of legality through authority to settle accounts and claims ought to remain a function of an *independent agency*. The General Accounting Office possessed the requisite independence, and it was felt that the authority to prescribe accounting "forms, systems, and procedures" was necessary for fully effective implementation of these functions.[7]

Lindsay Warren and the Turnaround

Comptroller General McCarl's 15-year appointment terminated in 1936. Former U.S. Senator Fred Brown was the next appointed Comptroller General, but his tenure in this office lasted only for the brief period April 1939 to June 1940. From June 1936 to April 1939 and from

---

[7]Thus, the Brookings Institution study referred to in note 6 recommended that the accounting powers and responsibilities of the Office of Audit and Settlements (the new name proposed for the General Accounting Office in this report) should include preparation of comprehensive financial reports for the government as a whole and extension of its pre-audit activities to include advance decisions and direct settlements for the executive agency transactions.

June 1940 to November 1940 the job of Comptroller General was carried on by Richard N. Elliott, the Assistant Comptroller General, who served as the Acting Comptroller General during these periods. This brings us to the appointment of Lindsay C. Warren as the third Comptroller General of the United States and hence to the developments with which this chapter is mainly concerned.

While in Congress, Warren had been a staunch defender of the GAO. In fact, he had (so he felt) "saved the agency" against the recommendations of the "Brownlow committee,"[8] which would have taken away the agency's power to (1) control receipts and expenditures and (2) prescribe systems of accounts as reflected in the forms and record-keeping procedures of the various agencies. Nevertheless, as the newly appointed Comptroller General, Warren was willing to take a fresh view of the agency and its approaches to its responsibilities. This led to a series of interrelated changes which we may summarize in three major categories as follows: (1) A Joint Accounting Improvement Program was initiated with the GAO, the Treasury, and the Budget Bureau,[9] as well as the operating agencies that were also vitally interested in and affected by such developments. (2) Emphasis was placed on each agency's *individual* responsibility for developing and maintaining "ad-

equate" systems of accounting and internal control, including internal audit. (3) the GAO itself began to move from an emphasis on centralized accounting to an emphasis on auditing as its main way of contributing to improved functioning of the executive, on the one hand, and discharging its own responsibilities to Congress, on the other hand.[10]

These developments, as we shall observe, are all highly interdependent. That is, no one of them could have been effectively carried out without the others. Thus, if any one of them had failed, it is doubtful that the reversal of GAO's earlier approach could have been fully effected. Moreover, it is even more doubtful that the highly sophisticated (and innovative) auditing concepts and methods that GAO has now evolved would ever have materialized.

The Joint Accounting Improvement Program

For clarity, we shall deal with these developments one at a time as far as is possible. First, however, we observe a very important event which occurred with the passage of the Government Corporation Control Act on December 6, 1945. As discussed in the chapter by Pois, this resulted in the creation of the Corporation Audits Division of the

---

[8]This was the Committee on Administrative Management referred to in notes 6 and 7, which undertook its study of the organization of the accounting and auditing functions as only one part of its duties to study and recommend ways of improving the organization and management of the federal government. See, for example, Mansfield (1939).

[9]Under the recommendations of the Brownlow committee, the Bureau of the Budget moved from the Treasury Department into a newly created Executive Office of the President, where its functions were also broadened so that it could serve as the chief professional management staff for the President.

[10]This included movement away from centralized voucher auditing, with its legalistic focus, to a more modern concept which was ultimately to include audits at the site covering all aspects of management.

GAO, which, in turn, resulted in the Comptroller General's bringing into the GAO people with public accounting experiences and background. This staff brought with it a wholly new professional point of view and a new, and needed, set of competencies that were a key factor in enabling the GAO to move toward site auditing. This was helpful in other ways, too, as we shall see.

The professional type of audit performed by the Corporation Audits Division had potential for more than the activities of government corporations. It had great potential, too, for other GAO audits, by broadening the underlying concepts, which, when suitably adjusted, could also be extended to unincorporated agencies funded by appropriations. To accomplish this, however, it was necessary to secure very fundamental changes in the accounting systems and related systems of internal control of executive agencies, for without the latter an adequate basis for the subsequent GAO type audits would not have been available. To put the matter differently, existing systems, geared as they were to GAO's centralized system of legal accountability controls over receipts and expenditures of "accountable officers," would have proved to be completely inadequate as a basis for such audits.

A major overhaul of the government's accounting and control structure was clearly needed. This could presumably have been accomplished in a variety of ways. A cooperative approach between the executive agencies and GAO was elected, and this turned out to be fortunate in providing agency initiatives for the wanted improvements. This "bottoms-up" approach to agency improvements in accounting provided a great surge of new activity which was vitally important for all the other proposed developments.

It was desirable for GAO to provide leadership in the needed accounting developments. This it did in a "Joint Accounting Improvement Program" undertaken collaboratively with the Treasury and the Bureau of the Budget on a cooperative basis with the other agencies. To spearhead and coordinate these efforts, a new Accounting Systems Division was brought into being at the GAO and a series of other alterations in previous positions and practices were also begun.

The general nature of what was intended is set forth in the following testimony by Comptroller General Warren:[11]

On the day after the surrender of Japan, I called a meeting of my staff and told them the No. 1 problem in the General Accounting Office from that date was improvement of accounting in the Government. Because of the legal responsibilities and interests of the Treasury Department and the Bureau of the Budget from the standpoint of fiscal administration in the Government, I felt it was imperative to have their full participation in any such program. Because the day-to-day maintenance of accounting systems is the responsibility of the various administrative agencies their cooperation was just as important. Conversations were initiated by me with the Secretary of the Treasury, John W. Snyder, and the Director of the Bureau of the Budget, then James E. Webb;

---

[11] "To Improve Budgeting, Accounting and Auditing Methods of the Federal Government," Hearings Before the Senate Committee on Expenditures in the Executive Department on S. 2054 (February–March 1950). See also "The Accounting Systems Division in *The GAO Review*, Summer 1971.

and, as a result, we inaugurated in December 1947 what is known as the Joint Accounting Improvement Program.

In so doing, we recognized and later formalized in documents signed by all of us our complete agreement that

1. Current accounting and financial reporting are proper functions of the executive branch. Accounting systems prescribed by the Comptroller General should be in recognition of this as a fundamental principle.

2. Audit, independent of the executive branch, is an essential and proper function of the General Accounting Office. Properly designed accounting systems are a vital factor to the effectiveness of such independent audit.

3. Accounting systems should be developed as a cooperative undertaking as an essential to meeting the needs and responsibilities of both the executive and legislative branches of the Government.

We submitted our program to every agency of the Government. As I recall, without exception they enthusiastically endorsed it. They have all appointed representatives to work with the three top fiscal agencies to bring about needed accounting reforms. The program has been strongly endorsed by both the President and congressional committees, and we have kept the committees advised of progress. I want to mention here especially that great credit is due to this very committee for the suggestions given prior to setting up the program, for the support of the program, and for the participation in some of our work by staff members of the committee.

To spearhead the program, I set up in the General Accounting Office, in January 1948, an Accounting Systems Division to provide a small staff of leaders and technical advisers who could guide the agencies in the development of their accounting systems. To head up our work, we were fortunate in obtaining the services of Mr. Walter Frese, a certified public accountant, with experience in both the Budget and the Treasury as well as outside the Government.

Here we might explicitly note that items 1 and 2 in the preceding quotation settled the previously irritating jurisdictional issues by observing that (1) current accounting and financial reporting are proper functions of the executive branch of the government, while (2) audit—independent of the executive branch—is an essential and proper function of the General Accounting Office. This still left the possibility of overlapping functions in (a) the prescription of standards for federal government accounting as well as in (b) the development of the actual systems in all the detail necessary to meet each agency's needs and requirements.

We should recall at this point that these functions remained a GAO responsibility. Nevertheless, the way they were now to be discharged differed greatly from the approach that GAO had used in its earlier years. Thus, the Joint Accounting Improvement Program was, as already noted, undertaken by the GAO on a *cooperative* basis with the Budget Bureau and the Treasury Department. Also, to the maximum possible extent, emphasis was placed on each agency's responsibilities for developing its own accounting within very broad guidelines supplied by the GAO working under the cooperative arrangements of the Joint Accounting Improvement Program.

Of course, many agencies required help before they could reach a point where broad principles could provide adequate guidance. Provision for such help was to be supplied by the Accounting Systems Division, which quickly developed a philosophy which recognized that accounting should follow and service the needs of management in each agency and program. Although the need for continued review and evaluation of all programs was recognized by the Accounting Systems Division, there was also a recognition that no common yardstick was uniformly available for effecting the wanted evaluations—the kind of yardstick, for example, that "profit" is supposed to supply for private-sector activities.

These considerations caused the Accounting Systems Division to place primary emphasis on cooperative working relationships with various individual agencies. In this way, help and guidance could be supplied to each individual agency. At the same time, this close contact with individual agency practices and problems could provide a realistic basis for developing accounting principles and standards to be prescribed by the Comptroller General so that

> Consistent with known and determined needs this joint effort [the Joint Accounting Improvement Program] will develop a body of accounting principles, standards and terminology for accounting and financial reporting to be adhered to by all departments and agencies. Such developments [are] to be directed toward the goal of comparable and consistently maintained accounting processes and understandable [and] useful financial reports.[12]

Naturally this "bottoms-up" way of dealing with the agencies simultaneously aided them in developing accounting aids for their management at the same time that it provided a realistic basis to the Comptroller General for approval of individual agency accounting systems.

Although flexibility in meeting the needs of each agency and its program managers was to be emphasized, this had to be accomplished in a way that would also meet the needs of the Treasury and the Bureau of the Budget. The Joint Accounting Improvement Program was supposed to provide all of this while working toward raising the standards of government accounting practices. Coordination of the various viewpoints involved became a major responsibility of the Accounting Systems Division.

This Joint Accounting Improvement Program was formally launched by Comptroller General Warren with the letter to the heads of all government departments and agencies, which is included in Appendix A. Here attention might well be drawn to the importance that it accords the use of broad statements of accounting principles, in contrast to the detailed prescription of forms and procedures which GAO had utilized previously. Emphasis was on agency initiative, with explicit attention to linking the accounting function to agency management. Help, as well as leadership, was to be supplied by the Accounting Systems Division, together with the staff of the Treasury and the Bureau of the Budget. Finally, further reliance on the audit process by GAO was also noted as being dependent on progress in raising these accounting and managerial developments to sufficiently satisfactory levels.[13]

---

[12] Quoted from p. 3 of "Joint Program for Improving Accounting in the Federal Government," as issued on January 6, 1949, by Lindsay Warren, Comptroller General of the United States; John W. Snyder, Secretary of the Treasury; and James E. Webb, Director of the Bureau of the Budget.

[13] The Comptroller General's letter was followed, less than two months later, on January 6, 1949, by a comprehensive joint statement to all agencies by the Comptroller General, the Secretary of the Treasury, and the Director of the Bureau of the Budget. This statement, which had been developed by the staffs of the three agencies assigned to coordinate the joint program, provided (1) a general statement of policies and objectives, and (2) a summary of work areas on which work was being done or scheduled (see note 12). This document also provided the basis for initiating the annual agency progress reports, which then became an important way of providing information and guidance to the agencies as well as the staff of the Joint Accounting Improvement Program.

Implementation at GAO

Moving from general statements to specific implementations required action by the GAO as well as the agencies, and to this end Comptroller General Warren again took action, as indicated by the following letter:

July 14, 1949

Chiefs of [GAO] Divisions and Offices:

Sometime ago I asked the Chief of the Accounting Systems Division to prepare for me a brief memorandum outlining as specifically as possible what he conceived to be the logical effect of the joint program in terms of the organization and operations of the General Accounting Office. I asked him also to make such recommendations as he saw fit for the immediate changes which should be made to adjust the operations of the General Accounting Office to the program and to achieve all possible economies as quickly as possible, consistent with the proper exercise of the control and audit responsibilities of this Office. . . .
(Signed, Lindsay Warren Comptroller General of the United States)

The recommendations of the Accounting Systems Division were drastic, but they dramatized the turnaround which was intended at the GAO as well as indicating the progress that had been made in the agencies and the Treasury by means of the Joint Accounting Improvement Program. Their flavor is perhaps sufficiently indicated by the following excerpts:

1. The maintenance of the appropriation ledgers by the Accounting and Bookkeeping Division should be discontinued. . . .[14]
2. The maintenance of the Expenditure and Limitation Ledger by the Accounting and Bookkeeping Division should be discontinued.

3. The maintenance of the Receipt Ledgers by the Accounting and Bookkeeping Division should be discontinued. . . .
4. General Regulations No. 87 should be modified to dispense with the requirement that advance copies of the Schedule of Collections be sent to the General Accounting Office. . . .
5. The maintenance of the thousands of subsidiary trust fund accounts by the Accounting and Bookkeeping Division should be eliminated.
6. Maintenance of the so-called "General Ledger" maintained by the Accounting and Bookkeeping Division should be eliminated. . . .
7. The maintenance in the Accounting and Bookkeeping Division of the asset, liability and other accounts relating to the accounts of the Treasurer of the United States should be discontinued.
8. Arrangements should be worked out for transferring the function of reconciling and matching paid card checks with checks issued from the Reconciliation and Clearance Division to the Treasury Department as a necessary part of the internal control in the check payment procedure. . . .

As a corollary to these recommendations, the Accounting Systems Division memorandum included recommendations and proposed guidelines for uses of "site audits," with special emphasis on what was then referred to as "comprehensive audits." This was a concept that grew out of discussions between the Accounting Systems Division and the Corporation Audits Division. The term "comprehensive audit" was coined by Stephen B. Ives, Director of the Corporation Audits Division. He provided the following brief definition for the Accounting Systems Division memorandum:

The term "comprehensive audit" as used herein denotes a combination of the types of

---

[14]We are here omitting the detailed descriptions and explanations which accompanied each of these recommendations.

audit required by the Budget and Accounting Act and the Government Corporation Control Act; in other words, the verification of assets, liabilities, and operating results, combined with a voucher audit with power to take exceptions, aimed at the proper level, such power to be used with discretion.

Thus the "comprehensive audit" contemplated a very considerable broadening of GAO's audit function while providing a more effective and efficient basis for implementing GAO's traditional responsibilities for audit of receipts and expenditures from a legal accountability standpoint.

The Comptroller General's consideration of the recommendations and related comments he had received led to the following sequence of actions. By administrative order, dated October 19, 1949, the Comptroller General officially established the "Comprehensive Audit Program" in the General Accounting Office. This order provided a broadened definition for "comprehensive audit" and also provided that recommendations to the Comptroller General for agencies or programs to be assigned for comprehensive audit were to be developed jointly by the Accounting Systems Division, the Corporation Audits Division, and the Audit Division. Within a little over a month following the issuance of this administrative order, 12 major agencies or programs were assigned by the Comptroller General for comprehensive audit.

Against this background of a shift toward the comprehensive audit program, the Comptroller General next, on November 29, 1949, distributed a memorandum outlining the general policy decisions he had made on the basis of his consideration of the comments he had received on the recommendations of

the Accounting Systems Division. He stated that individual problems of detail would be considered in the light of these general policies as follows:

1. The General Accounting Office will place agencies of The Government on a comprehensive audit basis as and when it is determined to be feasible, advantageous, and otherwise permissible.
2. All operations in the General Accounting Office not essential to effective exercise of its audit and control responsibilities in the light of the comprehensive audit policy or otherwise, and which are not specifically required by law will be eliminated as rapidly as possible.
3. In the exercise of the control and audit responsibilities of the General Accounting Office, constant recognition will be given to an evaluation of internal control in the agencies, the Treasury Department, and in their relation to one another, as a basis for considering elimination or modification of present procedures of the General Accounting Office.
4. All Divisions will, as promptly as possible, submit to me recommendations for legislative changes deemed to be necessary or advisable in carrying out my policies. These recommendations must be submitted not later than December 15, 1949.

Based on these policies, and to the extent that existing law permitted, the Comptroller General took immediate action (on the same date) to discontinue the centralized bookkeeping operations, and related procedures along the lines already indicated. To make clear his intention of continuing even further along these lines, he also requested all division chiefs to provide him with recommendations for legislation that might be needed to do this.

To help provide a basis for orderly implementation of these changes in GAO operations, the Comptroller General also directed that a fact-finding survey be made of the organization and operations of the General Accounting Office for the dual purpose of (1) assuring the orderly implementation of the actions he had directed in connection with the discontinuance of centralized GAO bookkeeping and control operations and procedures, and (2) developing an analysis of the organization and operations of the General Accounting Office as a whole in the light of the general policies he had announced. Ted Westfall, then an Assistant Director of the Corporation Audits Division, was placed in charge of this survey, which became known as the "Westfall Survey."

Facts developed by this survey along with the legislative recommendations requested by the Comptroller General in the memorandum announcing his general policy decisions were considered in developing the legislation which became the Post Office Department Financial Control Act of 1950[15] and the Accounting and Auditing Act of 1950. The latter act is Title II of the Budget and Accounting Procedures Act of 1950.[16]

Impact on the Agencies

We can perhaps best highlight what was occurring and the consequences of this turnaround by quoting as follows from the history of the Federal Government Accountants Association (Association of Government Accountants, 1975)[17]:

> In 1948 there occurred two events, the impact of which on the modernizing of accounting for and auditing of appropriated funds paralleled that of the Government Corporation Control Act with respect to business type activities. The issuance of the report of the First Hoover Commission, appointed by President Truman pursuant to an Act of Congress approved July 7, 1947, brought to light the deplorable condition of the Federal Government's accounting methods and systems; the establishment of the Joint Accounting Improvement Program—later renamed the Joint Financial Management Improvement Program (JFMIP)—provided for the first time, an effective means of attacking and correcting the situation. Thus was ushered in the golden decade of accounting improvement in the Federal Government (pp. 9-10).

This golden age of accounting improvement was evidenced in a variety of ways, including a ground swell of accounting activity not only in the center but in the agencies as well. In informal as well as formal ways, this burst of creative activities made itself manifest.

As one case in point, we might mention the Federal Government Accountants' Association (now the Association of Government Accountants), which was founded in 1950. In January 1951, scarcely four months after its founding, the FGAA held its first full day's pro-

---

[15] In the case of the Post Office Department, the GAO had gone even further in keeping accounts as a basis for its control and auditing activities. (It kept, in the Postal Accounts Division, complete administrative accounts for the department.) Thus, separate legislation was considered necessary for the Post Office Department. Immediately following the enactment of the Post Office Financial Control Act of 1950, the Comptroller General transferred the operations and personnel of the GAO's Postal Accounts Division to the Post Office Department while he established the Postal Audit Division to audit the accounts and fiscal operations of the Post Office Department.

[16] See the discussion of this act in the chapter by Pois. See also the very important article by Morse (1975).

[17] See also Gary (1959).

gram (on the very relevant topic of "internal control") with more than 1000 persons in attendance. Nor was this burst of activity merely a passing fad. Now a well-established organization, further fleshed out by a chapter structure, the Association of Government Accountants continues as a constructive force in government accounting which has attracted the talents of outstanding individuals, including Eric Kohler, who "gave unstintingly of his talents in FGAA's early years" (Association of Government Accountants, 1975, p. 44), as acknowledged in its certificate of recognition to him in 1961.

Enactment of the Budget and Accounting Procedures Act provided the Comptroller General with the legal authority he needed to proceed along the lines indicated in the preceding section. Confirmation of the results of his prior actions now being abundantly in evidence, the Comptroller General proceeded to utilize this new authority. Within a little over a month he issued an order abolishing the Accounting and Bookkeeping Division in the GAO, and along with it he abolished the maintenance of something like 500,000 ledger accounts. He also moved increasingly in the direction of reorganizing GAO's audit activities around the "comprehensive" on-site approaches. And he undertook other actions as well.

As a result of these (and related) developments, a congressional committee[18] was subsequently able to report as follows:

The General Accounting Office does not keep books for the Government. At one time it did keep numerous ledger accounts and other records relating to appropriations, receipts, public-debt transactions, expenditures, and accountability of Government fiscal officers. Also, at one time, the Office maintained, pursuant to law, the administrative appropriation and fund accounts and other accounting records of the Post Office Department.

This kind of job, however, is not done any longer. The keeping of detailed accounting records was discontinued as a result of changes authorized or directed in the Budget and Accounting Procedures Act and the Post Office Financial Control Act, both enacted in 1950. The somewhat anomalous function of maintaining accounts for the Post Office Department was discontinued by the General Accounting Office after the Post Office Department Financial Control Act placed this responsibility in the Post Office Department where it belonged.

Since enactment of the Budget and Accounting Procedures Act of 1950, the General Accounting Office has placed greatly increased emphasis on its comprehensive audit program, both in the civil agencies and in the defense agencies of the Government. This type of audit requires professional accounting and auditing personnel, with the result that since 1950 there has been an increase in the number of higher grade personnel in the General Accounting Office. However, this increase has been more than offset by a decrease in lower grade personnel. As a result, the General Accounting Office has been able to realize significant personnel savings. At June 30, 1950, the General Accounting Office had 5,083 employees engaged in accounting, auditing, and investigative activities. Based on 1957 salary rates, for comparative purposes, the annual salary costs of these employees was $22,766,000. At June 30, 1957, there were 3,007 employees engaged in the same activities at an annual salary cost of $17,250,000. The reduction of 2,076 employees included 798 who were transferred to the Post Office Department in November 1950. The net

---

[18] House of Representatives Subcommittee on Manpower Utilization of the Committee on Post Office and Civil Service, August 7, 1958, pp. 11–12.

reduction of 1,278 employees, exclusive of the 798 transferred to the Post Office Department, represents an approximate annual savings in salary costs to the General Accounting Office of $3,364,000.

Of course, far more was involved than simplifications and improvements at the GAO itself. The practices of the entire federal executive establishment were also to be affected in a manner that is indicated by the following guiding principles set forth in the same memorandum from the Accounting Systems Division which was referred to in the preceding section.[19]

1. The individual operating agencies of the Government are the key points for effectuation of real control over the financial operations of the Government. Accordingly, the joint program, and the exercise of your [i.e., the Comptroller General's] responsibilities for prescribing systems, must be directed at providing effective controls in the agencies, and, as a consequence, in the whole system of accounting in the Government. The joint program states in this respect that the keeping of proper records and exercise of proper control at that point (i.e., in each agency) are the foundation on which the entire system of accounting and reporting in the Government must rest.
2. The consolidation and necessary integration of accounting processes for the Government as a whole will be accomplished with the proper integration of accounting practices of the individual agencies with the accounting of the Treasury Department. The "linking together" of agency and Treasury accounting systems will provide "internal controls" in the accounting for the Executive Branch as a whole and will enable the Treasury Department to develop, on the basis of its own and agency accounting

results, composite financial statements for the Government as a whole.
3. The control and audit procedures of the General Accounting Office should be adjusted to the effectiveness of accounting and internal control in the agencies and in the Treasury Department. This will result in the maintenance of control by the General Accounting Office on a broader and more effective base through the prescribing of accounting systems requirements, systems inspections, and "comprehensive audits" of accounting records, including those of the Treasury Department.

Development of Principles and Standards

We have already mentioned the two-fold advantages of the "bottoms-up" approach which the GAO's Accounting Systems Division continued to employ. On the one hand, it provided maximum assistance to the individual agencies in developing accounting systems in the light of their own problems and management needs. On the other hand, it provided a realistic basis for the evolution of accounting standards and principles by the Comptroller General in collaboration with other agencies (and congressional committees) in the Joint Accounting Improvement Program.

The first of these developments was soon proceeding at a pace that made it necessary to turn increasing attention to the latter. In fact, Eric Kohler, who had closely observed these matters (as a continuing adviser to the Accounting

---

[19] See also the report cited in note 18, which deals with this topic in detail, with generally favorable comments for the GAO and the Joint Accounting Improvement Program. The Bureau of the Budget, however, is urged in the summary recommendations to "further accelerate its efforts under the joint program" while again noting (p. 13) the need for the bureau to provide more leadership by the establishment for this purpose of a new staff office under an assistant director.

Systems Division), believed, about 1951, that there was a real need and opportunity at about this time for consolidation of results already attained, in preparation for further progress. These needs and opportunities could best be served, he believed, by a clear and succinct statement from the Comptroller General to the top management in each agency which (1) summarized the basic thinking that had already evolved and (2) pointed the direction for further progress.

The memorandum of August 15, 1952, from the Comptroller General to the heads of all departments and establishments, as included in Appendix B, emerged from these considerations in a collaborative endeavor between Eric Kohler and the staff of the Accounting Systems Division. This document has since provided a continuing framework for subsequent activities at the GAO. In fact, Karney Brasfield, who had joined the Accounting Systems Division in January 1952, was able to turn his full attention to developing the GAO's Accounting Principles Memorandum No. 1 (see the chapter by Brasfield in this volume). This is the first of a series of such memos seeking to state general principles as guides for federal government accounting. Hence, it is of interest to observe that the Comptroller General's November 26, 1952, letter of transmittal specifically mentions the August 15, 1952, memorandum of Appendix B, together with the other developments we have been discussing, as follows (Comptroller General, 1952):

From the beginning of the [Joint Accounting Improvement] Program the development of accounting principles and standards has been approached as an evolutionary process. Many of the basic ideas, such as agency responsibility for the development of systems designed to meet their specific needs, were set forth in initial releases under the joint program and were subsequently incorporated in the Budget and Accounting Procedures Act of 1950 as a matter of law. My communication of August 15, 1952, to heads of departments and agencies titled *The Contribution of Accounting to Better Management* also covered some of the broader aspects of the underlying philosophy of the program.

We may appropriately close this section by observing that the accounting-oriented developments enunciated in this first GAO statement of accounting principles (Comptroller General, 1952) were consistent with what was then happening at the forefront of private enterprise accounting—as in the various statements of accounting principles which Kohler also coauthored with others in the American Accounting Association—with its emphasis on costs and accrual accounting while allowing for exceptions in individual agency practices where the latter were individually noted and justified.[20] We may also note that fundamentals of this approach have continued to serve as a basis for the subsequent statements of principles issued by the GAO as a guide for federal agencies and, of course, this also opened the way for the developments in the new GAO-type audits that we shall note in the next section. It is in this sense, then, that the developments we have been dis-

---

[20] Kohler's activities as Controller of the Marshall Plan, as described by Nakasian in his chapter, also provided a model of what could be accomplished along the lines indicated in Appendix B and, of course, all of the personnel in the Accounting Systems Division, and others, too, utilized the occasion of his presence in Washington for numerous exchanges and consultations which he freely—indeed eagerly—contributed.

cussing culminated in the memorandum of Appendix B, which also served as a platform for further developments pointed in the same directions.

On-site Auditing and Subsequent Developments

Proceeding along the paths we have been examining in our discussion of this turnaround, the Comptroller General was in a position to switch GAO's emphasis to a full deployment of on-site audits as a way of evaluating and contributing to the improvement of operations in federal agencies. In fact, the second portion of the 1950 Act (i.e., the Accounting and Auditing Act of 1950) also cleared the way for this approach to auditing in virtually all federal agencies (see Morse, 1975).

The wide variety and complexity of federal programs and agencies, ranging from the relatively simple expenditure control problems of an agency such as the SEC and extending to the complex imponderables of the Department of Defense, strongly militates against any simple reduction to single overall measures of efficiency and/or effectiveness. This, too, suggests the use of auditing as a more flexible approach than was possible under the previous centralized accounting approach. It also suggests an innovative use of audits in order to comprehend the wide-ranging nature of the programs that are encountered in going from one federal agency to another, as the GAO now does.

Since the emphasis was now to be on management, it became essential to develop a strategy that would bring together planning, budgeting, and ac-counting for simultaneous consideration at the topmost levels of management in each particular agency and/or program. The way to do this had been cleared by the document in Appendix B and the actions to which it was related. There remained, however, the task of developing the corresponding auditing concepts and procedures with which to meet these requirements. This was a real challenge, since the practices of commercial auditing—or audit practices in other parts of governmental and/or nonprofit enterprises—provided very little in the way of precedent.

Instead of attempting to describe all the developments in auditing that were undertaken at the GAO, we simply observe that they ultimately produced what we may refer to as "GAO-Type Audits." Some salient differences between this audit approach and those of the usual "attest" variety may help to clarify what is involved. First, the usual commercial attest audit is built around the concept of verifying the representations of management. In fact, by and large, it is confined mainly to the financial statement representations of management—as when an auditor issues (or fails to issue) an unqualified certificate attesting to the validity of the financial statements prepared by the management of the company under examination. In contrast, GAO-Type Audits are characteristically representations of the auditors with, possibly, an accompanying response by agency management. Concomitantly, it is the GAO rather than the agency's management that selects the area and the nature of the audit to be performed, and hence it is the GAO that assumes responsibility for this selection (perhaps under congressional directive) as well as the way in which the audit is conducted.[21]

The latter kind of approach carries with it portents for other developments of auditing as a tool of management evaluation and control. Unlike the attest audit, the GAO-Type Audit now extends to the audit of *all* phases of management and is not confined only to special aspects of an agency's financial transactions and reports.[22] This includes not only management's "efficiency" in the use of resources but also its "effectiveness" in terms of management's ability to (1) state and (2) accomplish its objectives in various programs. Finally, it even extends to such issues as the "propriety" of these objectives and the methods used to secure them.

In the preceding section we indicated some parts of the role that Eric Kohler played in modernizing and improving GAO's approaches to accounting. Kohler played an important role in these audit developments as well. This is perhaps best indicated by the following testimonial prepared (at our request) by E. H. Morse, who was himself one of the leaders in these developments:[23]

Note on the Support of Eric Kohler for the GAO Audit Program

With the adoption of the comprehensive audit program by Comptroller General Warren in 1949, it became incumbent on the top audit officials to prepare appropriate policy guidance for the use of the GAO auditors who were going to be expected to carry out this program.

At this stage the experience in this type of auditing in GAO was quite limited and what there was was based on that accumulated in the Corporation Audits Division. Officials and staff members of this division were assigned responsibility for carrying out this program which involved an extension of the principles and procedures of commercial-type auditing beyond the Government corporations to the unincorporated agencies on a gradual basis. With the creation of the staff position of director of audits in 1951 a staff was assembled to work with the director of audits in developing policies and procedures and exercising appropriate leadership to carry out this program. An early assignment (which fell to me) was to prepare a manual. This project was started immediately and with the abolition of the then existing four audit divisions and their consolidation into a new Division of Audits early in 1952 this project became one of high priority.

In looking for ideas and concepts to include in such a manual for which there was no precedent either in GAO or anywhere else, one of the published works that we consulted was Eric Kohler's book "Auditing," originally published in 1947. This work was one of the best that we encountered for our purposes since it placed more emphasis on analyzing and interpreting what the accountants were recording than most published books. We did not copy anything from the book, but the philosophy of the Kohler text was absorbed along with other ideas in preparing the GAO Comprehensive Audit Manual.

After we had made some progress in drafting the manual, we invited Eric Kohler to review it and provide any comments and suggestions that he thought were warranted. The only documentation of this assistance is a letter dated August 17, 1953, to Robert L. Long, who was then the Director of Audits, transmitting notes and suggestions on several of the chapters in the manual. These suggestions were considered but most important was the Kohler philosophy re-

---

[21] This selection coincides with the way in which some companies utilize their internal audits, and hence it is to be understood that we are referring above only to the kind of attest audit that is presently associated with external (CPA-type) audits. See, for example, Churchill et al. (1976).

[22] Further background on these types of audits and how they relate to commercial-type audits are examined in the chapter by Brasfield.

[23] On the leadership role of E. H. Morse see also Brasfield in the introductory section of the next chapter.

flected in one paragraph of the letter which is quoted below.

"I am much impressed with the thoroughness and good quality of your coverage. You have emphasized quite properly the need on the part of the auditor for the development of what the engineers have been calling for a good many years 'value judgments.' With this, as I believe you know from my book, I am in complete agreement. The auditor is a measurer of operating competence. In obtaining figures, breakdowns of figures, and reclassifications of figures, and in uncovering errors of principle and procedure the auditor is dealing with the deadwood of the past—the end-products of good, bad, and indifferent decisions which accounts reflect. But these alone are interpretable in limited and very formal ways. It is what is behind the figures that counts—the design, management, and output of an operation for which the figures afford what has come to be regarded (in the business world anyway) as the leading (and best available) clues."

This philosophy is still an integral part of the GAO audit philosophy. The main difference in practice is, however, that much of our work in the 1970s goes directly to management performance from the standpoint of efficiency, economy and effectiveness without necessarily getting involved in what the accounting records display.

Internal Auditing

A very important part of the GAO audit policy is to promote strong internal auditing in the Federal departments and agencies. The basis of this policy is to promote strong systems of internal management control and to promote the idea that strong internal audit systems make it possible for GAO to concentrate on other management problem areas that the internal auditors cannot effectively cope with and also to focus on problems of the kind that the Congress is more likely to be interested in.

In 1957 the General Accounting Office completed and published a statement of internal audit principles and concepts for the guidance of all Federal agencies. The purpose of this statement was to let all agencies know what we expected in the way of internal audit systems

and to provide guidance on how they should organize their systems. Another purpose was to provide GAO's auditors with the basic framework against which to review the effectiveness of such systems.

Eric Kohler was also a strong believer in strong internal audit systems as indicated by paragraph 3 of Comptroller General Warren's August 15, 1952, statement on the contribution of accounting to better management to which Mr. Kohler contributed materially.

The GAO statement has been revised twice since 1957. The first such revision occurred in 1968 and at that time Mr. Kohler offered his services to us in reviewing our drafts and making suggestions for improvement. His assistance on this project was very helpful in enabling us to produce as clearly worded a statement on the subject as has ever been produced. He was a stickler for clear and unequivocal use of the English language and the suggestions that he made to us along these lines were vigorous and useful and were for the most part accepted.

Consulting Role

Mr. Kohler continued his endorsement of the GAO type of auditing from time to time although he was not further involved in any of our specific projects. He did serve on Comptroller General Staats' Consultant Panel for several years beginning in 1966 and frequently expressed his support of the type of audit work that GAO was doing whenever the subject came up. (Signed E. H. Morse, Jr., Assistant Comptroller General, April 15, 1977)

Conclusion

The concepts and procedures involved in such GAO-Type Audits are still in a process of evolution. In the chapter by Brasfield, which follows, this evolution is discussed and related to events subsequent to those discussed in the present chapter. As will be seen in the following chapter, accounting alone is no longer a sufficient basis for audits and evaluations under the expanded GAO concept of auditing. Nevertheless, the developments we have been discussing have been of basic importance in directing accounting to performance based budgeting and away from its almost exclusive emphasis on legality of receipts and expenditures.

Throughout this chapter we have stressed the importance of providing incentives at the agency levels for developing systems suited to the needs of their management while also stressing the need for leadership and unifying principles such as were supplied by means of the Joint Accounting Improvement Program. At the agency level this led, for instance, to the development of adequate property records and systems of internal controls, which, in turn, are evidently vital to reliance on any type of external post-audit procedures. On a government-wide basis, these developments have resulted in a movement toward "accrual accounting" as a basis of transaction control and analysis and away from a predominant reliance on the "commitment obligations basis," which almost inevitably diverted attention from the transactions associated with program performance and toward paper work and the legalisms associated with detailed expenditure controls. This also accelerated a related evolution toward a coordinated cost-based accounting in the budgeting and programming agencies.

All of the above, and more, continues as part of the developments needed for an integrated approach to accounting and budgeting which is suited to the needs of each agency and its program managers. The unifying principles and standard terminology which also continue to evolve from the developments described in this chapter are, of course, meant to be useful to program managers. They are also intended to provide a meaningful and easily understood basis of communication for the persons to whom these managers are (or should be) accountable. Such then are the continuing fruits of the turnaround at the GAO which we have tried to describe in this chapter.

In closing, it is fitting to again note the importance of the document in Appendix B, which Eric Kohler helped to draft. It can be regarded as a plateau which served to cap one set of these developments while providing a staging area for the others.

Appendix A

**COMPTROLLER GENERAL OF THE UNITED STATES
WASHINGTON 25**

B-45109   October 20, 1948

COPY OF LETTER SENT BY THE COMPTROLLER GENERAL
  OF THE UNITED STATES
TO THE HEADS OF ALL GOVERNMENT DEPARTMENTS AND AGENCIES

This will acquaint you with a broad program which is under
way in the General Accounting Office, with active participation
by the Bureau of the Budget and the Treasury Department, for improving accounting in the Federal Government. I am writing you
and the heads of other agencies to enlist your cooperation.

The program contemplates the full development of sound accounting within each agency, as a working arm of management, in
terms of financial information and control. At the same time it
envisions an integrated pattern of accounting and financial reporting for the Government as a whole responsive to executive
and legislative needs. Balanced recognition will be given to the
need for a flexible basis for accounting development within
agencies in the light of varying types of operations and management problems and to overall fiscal, reporting, and audit responsibilities. The accounting and reporting principles, standards
and basic procedures established will take into consideration the
various areas of responsibility involved, the elimination of overlapping operations and paper work, and the fuller application of
efficient methods and techniques in accounting operations throughout the Government.

While significant progress has been made in improving Government accounting and financial reporting in particular areas, it
is my conviction that improvements of this nature can contribute
far more if conceived and developed as part of an interrelated
program. It seems clear to me that the combined efforts of all
concerned are essential to the success of a program of this
nature.

As the initial step, I requested and obtained from the Secretary of the Treasury and the Director of the Bureau of the Budget
their assurances of full cooperation with me in the joint development and execution of the program from the standpoint of their
responsibilities, needs, and fundamental interests. To spearhead

this program, in the light of my responsibilities dealing with the prescribing of accounting systems, I created in my Office the Accounting Systems Division. Working arrangements are in effect between that Division and the staffs of the Bureau of the Budget and the Treasury Department.

It is now desired to effect definite arrangements for the active participation of all agencies of the Government in the further planning and developmental work to be done. It is the purpose of this letter to advise you, in general, of proposed courses of action to enable you to make specific plans for the participation of your agency.

First, I wish to deal with the concept of my responsibility in the prescribing of accounting systems. I believe this function should be exercised so as to provide all possible encouragement to the agencies to exercise their own initiative and responsibility in the solution of their accounting problems. In line with this, it will be my objective, as the program progresses, to prescribe requirements largely in terms of standards, principles, and basic forms, procedures and terminology. A framework will thus be provided for development and approval of accounting systems, consistent with sound principles, fitted to agency needs and integrated with the central accounting and reporting facilities.

This approach depends upon on accounting organization in each agency capable of and responsible for dealing with accounting from the standpoint of operating factors and, within the framework of prescribed requirements, molding a system to the particular needs involved. There is required a linking of the accounting function to a sufficiently high level of agency management to bring it close, on a day to day basis, to management considerations as they evolve, and appropriate coordination of the accounting function with internal control and budgetary responsibilities. With such an organization, each agency will be able to contribute to the general program through constructive proposals affecting accounting requirements both in their internal application and in relation to the general pattern of accounting.

The Accounting Systems Division is being staffed with a limited, but carefully selected group of qualified accountants and technicians to take the lead in formulating basic requirements, to review accounting forms, systems, and procedures as the basis for my approval when appropriate, and to provide technical assistance and guidance to agencies. Their efforts will be supplemented by appropriate participation by the staffs of the Treasury Department and the Bureau of the Budget. As soon as staff facilities permit, a program of constructive review and appraisal of agency accounting systems will be instituted, from the viewpoints of harmony with the general standards, principles and requirements, and development within the agency's own area of responsibility.

I regard the active participation of the Treasury Department as of great importance to this undertaking. That Department has a vital interest in the results to be achieved in terms of fulfilling its fiscal responsibilities and providing current financial information regarding the operations of the Government as a whole based on integration of accounting results. The Accounting Systems Division will participate with the Fiscal Service of the Treasury Department in developing the full potentiality of Treasury accounting and reporting. This work will be an important factor in determining requirements for agency accounting systems.

One of the prime requisites of accounting in the Government is to develop reliable information and control in connection with the formulation, enactment, and execution of the financial program of the Government. Therefore, the active participation of the Bureau of the Budget is important to the development of accounting requirements in proper relation to improved budget administration. Staff members of the Bureau of the Budget who are working actively with representatives of the Accounting Systems Division will contribute further to the program by providing consulting assistance in connection with management problems which are related to accounting development. With participation of the Bureau improvements in accounting will go hand in hand with improvement in budget processes.

I should like to mention the relationship of this entire program to the audit and control responsibilities of my Office. It is fundamental that external audit programs must be developed in balanced relationship with internal control considerations. Hence, General Accounting Office audit and control methods will be under continuous review in the light of increased effectiveness of the accounting systems of the Government. The potentialities inherent in the review and appraisal of accounting systems in actual operation and in audits at the site of operations will be developed as an integral part of this program. The whole program should result in savings of paper work and elimination of overlapping in accounting operations.

It is obvious that a program of this magnitude cannot be entirely accomplished within a short period. It must be approached as an evolutionary process rather than by making drastic changes that might overtax existing facilities and disrupt the present continuity of accounting and reporting operations. We will build in the direction of the ultimate goal starting with those principles, systems, and procedures embodied in the present structure of accounting which analysis demonstrates to be sound. Immediate improvements, in the right direction, will be effected even though they fall short of ultimate objectives. On the other hand, there will be no disposition to deal recklessly with established concepts merely in the interest of change. While the purpose will be the accomplishment of all possible improvements within the framework of present law, recommendations for changes in legislation or new legislation will be developed in connection with specific situations when found to be necessary to insure the application of sound accounting or audit principles and procedures.

The ultimate effect of the program upon which we have embarked will be to give not only the Executive Branch, but the Congress, much better information as to the operations of the Government and means of control of its financial affairs. I regard it as inherent in my responsibility to the Congress to see that the accounting requirements and machinery of the Government make their full contribution to intelligent and informed legislative considerations. Appropriate liaison will be maintained with Congressional committees.

Illustrative of the evolutionary nature of the approach are several phases of the program scheduled for early development. The results of joint studies already made in connection with the administrative examination of fiscal officers' accounts are being developed in the light of this program. The recommendations growing out of the joint study of property accounting are likewise being considered as a part of its immediate and longer range phases. Attention is being given to eliminating the overlapping reporting requirements of Budget-Treasury Regulation No. 1 and General Regulations No. 100, to provide immediate improvements and as a preliminary step to working out with the agencies more fundamental improvements in reporting based on accounting records. Likewise, General Regulations No. 100 is being studied for modification in the direction of greater flexibility in agency accounting pending further and more far reaching development of basic requirements. In the meantime it is hoped that agencies will exercise initiative in developing for consideration of the General Accounting Office desirable modifications in existing accounting systems or requirements.

In order to provide effective and continuing participation by your agency, I will appreciate your appointing someone to represent you and the viewpoints of your organization in this program. Working arrangements will be established whereby your representative, in conjunction with representatives of other agencies will collaborate with the Treasury Department, Bureau of the Budget, and General Accounting Office. I do not mean to imply that contacts should be restricted to such representative since obviously it will be necessary to reach many points within some agencies for the satisfactory solution of accounting problems. I believe, however, that in addition to taking care of the cooperative arrangements and major contacts, your representative should be able to perform an important function in seeing that due recognition within the agency is given to the consideration of its entire accounting situation and that the best accounting talent of the agency is utilized for this purpose. It is also contemplated that agency representatives will be called upon to join with my staff in special studies of various phases of the problem.

The views in this letter are shared by the Secretary of the Treasury and the Director of the Bureau of the Budget and I speak for them equally with myself on the subject. I look forward to the participation of your agency in the program and will appreciate your comments and the early designation of your representative in order that such participation may be effected as soon as possible.

Sincerely yours,

(signed)   *Lindsay C. Warren*

Comptroller General
of the United States

Appendix B

COMPTROLLER GENERAL OF THE UNITED STATES
WASHINGTON 25

August 15, 1952

TO: Heads of Departments and Establishments

SUBJECT: The Contribution of Accounting to Better Management

One of the most important aspects of the Joint Accounting Improvement Program is to improve the service which accounting renders to management. Now that our cooperative work with the agencies has been under way for some time, we believe it is timely to bring together in one place some of the basic thinking which has evolved. The added responsibilities placed upon heads of agencies by the Congress in the Budget and Accounting Procedures Act of 1950, along with the continued improvements in accounting and related endeavors which the Congress and the President can properly expect under such Act, further emphasize the importance of crystallizing these broad concepts. The statement set forth below has been prepared with these thoughts in mind.

THE ROLE OF ACCOUNTING IN MANAGEMENT

Every administrator in the Federal Government has an individual responsibility for the economical attainment of the authorized objectives of his agency. Effective accounting plays a vital part in the discharge of this responsibility.

1. ACCOUNTING   Accounting furnishes a framework which can be
   A PART OF   fitted to assignments of responsibility by
   MANAGEMENT   management for specific areas of activity. At
                   the same time, it supplies a basis of reporting
                   as one element by which the success of the oper-
                   ation can be judged. Decisions regarding future
operations are made with greater confidence by management and the Congress where it can be demonstrated through accounting results that past performance has been consistent with planned programs and within established financial limits.

2. EFFECTIVE   The head of each agency is responsible under the
   ACCOUNTING   law for the accounting methods followed within
   A RESPON-   his organization. Although he ordinarily dele-
   SIBILITY OF gates this authority and assigns full responsi-
   MANAGEMENT   bility for accounting to a professionally
                qualified subordinate, the ultimate responsibil-
                ity remains in his hands. He should personally
                participate from time to time in formulating ac-
counting policies and in reviewing the effectiveness of the results
produced by the accounting processes. Such a relationship is the
best assurance that accounting will continue to give full recognition to management needs and will always be correlated with assignments of responsibility within the agency. At the same time, the
administrator should satisfy himself that acceptable accounting
standards applicable to his operations, based on the best professional practices and the standards supplied by the Comptroller
General, are being observed. To this end it is essential that
the accounting viewpoint be represented in the establishment of
general policies of the organization and other top-management
decisions.

3. INTERNAL   Internal controls essential to good management--to
   CONTROL   which accounting can so effectively contribute--
                require a carefully planned organizational struc-
                ture, well-defined operating policies and
                procedures, clear delegations of duties to sub-
ordinates, competent personnel, and a strong internal audit program.
A broadly constituted internal audit program provides the administrator and his subordinates not only with the auditor's findings
on financial transactions but also with objective views of the
manner in which policies and procedures, whatever their nature,
have been carried out along with recommendations for improvements.
Prompt action on such reports is, of course, a necessary step in
the functioning of the system of internal control.

4. EMPHASIS ON Every expenditure in its primary form is best
   COST AS   conceived as a direct cost of some essential,
   BASIS FOR   planned activity. Furnishing important measures
   EVALUATING   of performance, costs deserve the unremitting
   RESULTS   attention of administrators. To facilitate
                comparison as well as control, the classifica-
                tion of planned and actual expenditures must
                follow a like pattern. It should be the aim of

management to continuously strive to improve both quantitative
and qualitative measurements of performance.

5. BASIS FOR   Costs of approved programs can best be kept
   EXPENDITURE   within legal as well as administratively im-
   CONTROL   posed limits if the individual in charge of
                      each activity is made responsible for the costs
                      to be incurred thereunder. Under such a plan a
                      cost in every instance is the result of an in-
dividual decision. It is important, therefore, that (within limits
fixed by higher authority) whatever the device employed to limit
costs it should be under the direct control of the individual who
has been charged with the duty of making such decisions. This
necessity becomes even more apparent when it is recognized that
informal decisions as to plans for future expenditures are likely
to be more important than actions which can at once be reduced
to conventional documents such as contracts and purchase orders.
Indeed such documents are usually no more than the formalized
portion of a much larger program of expenditure. The control of
expenditures thus becomes a matter of individual responsibility
rather than of formal recordkeeping. Successful financial control
requires clearly defined authorizations and limitations under
which responsible persons can be held accountable.

6. NEED FOR   Accounting results are conveyed to management
   INFORMATIVE   through reports; to be of maximum value they
   FINANCIAL   must be rendered promptly. The content and ar-
   REPORTS   rangement of reports for internal purposes should
                      be designed to serve the objective of keeping
                      management currently informed and should be re-
                      lated to the assignments of management responsi-
bility within the organization. Management has the obligation to
review them to see that financial operations, including the effect
of decisions made by management, have been properly reflected. In
addition to management, the Congress and the public are entitled
to financial reports which fully disclose the operations of individual agencies and the Government as a whole.

7. NEED FOR   Emphasis has been placed by the Congress on the
   CONTINUED   continued orderly improvement of accounting and
   IMPROVEMENTS   an adequate framework to make this possible has
                      been provided in the Budget and Accounting Proce-
                      dures Act of 1950 and other laws.

Because of the importance of accounting to management, improvements
in accounting processes in Federal Government agencies warrant the
full support of top management.

We are fully aware that in the vast operations of the Federal
Government there is no single set of generalizations, no matter
how broad, which will fit all circumstances. However, we believe
your review of existing practices in the light of the concepts
contained in the above statement would be worthwhile. The magnitude of Federal expenditures makes it more important than ever
that we seek every reasonable means of obtaining full value for
each taxpayer's dollar spent. One means is to develop and utilize
accounting to the maximum extent in terms of the contribution
which it can make to better management.

The Secretary of the Treasury and the Director of the Bureau
of the Budget join me in urging that you review this statement with
key members of your staff.

Your comments on the concepts contained in the statement set
forth above and any suggestions for increasing the effectiveness
of the Joint Accounting Improvement Program are invited.

(signed) *Lindsay C. Warren*

Comptroller General
of the United States

References

Association of Government Accountants. 1975. "Accounting and Auditing in the Federal Government Prior to 1950," in *The First Twenty-five Years of the Federal Government Accountants Association*. Washington, D.C.: Association of Government Accountants.

Churchill, Neil C., W. W. Cooper, J. G. San Miguel, V. Govindarajan, and J. Pond. 1977. "Developments in Comprehensive Auditing and Suggestions for Further Research," in *Symposium on Auditing Research*, II. Urbana, Ill.: University of Illinois Department of Accountancy.

Comptroller General of the United States. 1952. Letter accompanying the transmittal of *Statement of Accounting Principles and Standards for Guidance of Executive Agencies in the Federal Government*. Washington, D.C.: General Accounting Office, November 26.

Gary, T. Jack, Jr. 1959. "Improvement in Federal Accounting: Past Accomplishments and Future Challenges." *The Federal Accountant*, 9(2), December.

Mansfield, H. 1939. *The Comptroller General*. New Haven, Conn.: Yale University Press.

McEachren, J. W. 1955. "Accounting Reform in Washington." *The Journal of Accountancy*, 100(3), September.

Morse, E. H. 1975. "The Accounting and Auditing Act of 1950—Its Current Significance to GAO." *The GAO Review*, Summer.

Chapter 10

Development of GAO Auditing Standards and Their Relevance to the Practice of Public Accounting

Karney A. Brasfield

Introduction

This chapter assumes a familiarity with the chapters by Pois and Cooper-Frese which appear elsewhere in the volume. Pois, it may be recalled, credited the Corporation Audits Division of GAO with the introduction of a professional or, more precisely, a professional analytic viewpoint with an emphasis on objectivity and a familiarity with audits, as found in the practices of U.S. public accountancy in the 1940s. Cooper and Frese described the decentralization of accounting from the GAO with an accompanying emphasis on agency responsibility for the development of adequate systems of accountability.

These developments, which occurred under Comptroller General Lindsay Warren (Weitzel, 1977), opened the way toward the present GAO emphasis on

auditing and, in the process, opened the way to new and expanded uses of the audit process as a tool to provide information for legislative and oversight endeavors of the Congress.

The purpose of this chapter is to carry on from the Pois and Cooper-Frese chapters to examine the characteristics of present GAO audit practices and concepts. In particular, we perceive the continuing evolution in audit practices and concepts to stem from two sources:

1. Explicit expression by the Congress of the need for improved means of evaluating and controlling today's massive and sophisticated Federal programs, beginning with the unprecedentedly large "Great Society Programs" of the Lyndon B. Johnson era.
2. The imaginative responses and innovative initiatives of GAO under the leadership of Comptroller General Elmer B. Staats (1966) and Assistant Comptroller General Ellsworth

H. Morse (technical) in (a) broadening the scope and characteristics of the audit approaches utilized, and (b) expanding and improving the analytic capabilities of GAO's professional staff.

My perceptions and opinions are those of an observer of the evolution in GAO activities during a period when I was a participant in the practice of public accounting. The selection of events and my assessment of their significance are intended as an illustrative rather than a documented chronicle of developments. The extensive italicizing[1] of the quotations we shall use are intended to emphasize points (sometimes subtly phrased) for readers not already familiar with the developments at issue.

Finally, I should say that forces underlying the developments we shall describe are complex in their interaction. Thus, for instance, I have referred to the Great Society Programs beginning in the LBJ era as one source of those developments. The Vietnam war also raged throughout most of the period of Johnson's presidency, and it would be surprising if the huge defense expenditures this engendered did not also motivate some of the concerns arising in this period.

Returning to the events we shall chronicle, we start in the next section with some of the historical antecedents that also played a part in these developments.

GAO's Statutory Base for Audits of Governmental Activities

Among its basic provisions the Budget and Accounting Act of 1921 directed the Comptroller General to investigate *"all matters* relating to the receipt, disbursement, and *application of public funds"* and, in regular and special reports to the Congress, to "make recommendations looking to greater *economy or efficiency* in public expenditures."

In the years between 1921 and the present, Congress has reiterated and specifically dealt with GAO's mandate in many different laws. In general, these enactments seem to signify a growing concern by Congress with ways to enhance its knowledge and control of ever-expanding federal activities rather than a recognition of a need for increased GAO authority. However certain points focused upon in specific enactments, such as we shall now observe, are milestones in the evolution of audit concepts and practices.

The Government Corporation Control Act of 1945 extended GAO's authority to cover federal activities employing the corporate form. However, of greater importance for our purpose was the recognition by Comptroller General Warren during this period of the need to modernize GAO's approach in carrying out its audit function and the seminal contribution made by the professionals assembled in the Corporation Audits Division, as discussed by Pois in his chapter.

Similarly, the Accounting and Auditing Act of 1950 defined the accountability of executive agencies and laid the foundation for modernization of audit approaches, as detailed in the Cooper-Frese chapter. Further, Section 206 of the Legislative Reorganization Act of

---

[1] *All* italicizing in what follows is supplied by the author of this chapter and is not part of the original statement being cited.

1946, reiterated Congress's intention that the Comptroller General make expenditure analyses to determine *"whether public funds have been economically and efficiently administered and expended."*

Beginning at about this point, the audit coverage of GAO, inspired by the staff of the Corporation Audits Division, was significantly addressed to how executive branch programs were being carried out. This began to supply a management focus in contrast to the audit of documents and the settlement of disbursing officers accounts in earlier years. It was in this period that the term "comprehensive audit" was developed to characterize *"an audit to determine how well the agency or activity had discharged its financial responsibilities"* (Comptroller General, 1953, p. 16). Under this approach, "financial responsibilities" came to be viewed in a rather broad sense—essentially to mean the effectiveness, efficiency, and economy in a stewardship or management sense.

It is also to be noted that GAO, beginning with the leadership of Comptroller General Lindsay Warren, became particulary conscious of opportunities to render assistance to Congress on specific problems and areas of federal activity. Many reports covering such activities are recited in the annual reports of Comptroller Generals Lindsay Warren and Jospeh Campbell during this period, say, 1945 to 1965. But the forward thrust in audit practices and concepts that distinguish GAO today was yet to come.[2]

Initial Recognition of the Audit of Program Results as a Concept

Two concurrent forces of change that had their beginning in late 1967 can be identified as landmarks in the evolution of GAO audit practices and concepts. One was initiated with the Economic Opportunity Amendments of 1967. The other was the action by Comptroller General Staats to broaden the scope of GAO's work and its staff capabilities.

When it enacted Section 201 of the Economic Opportunity Amendments of 1967, Congress took a positive step in defining the kind of information it sought. Under this legislation, the Comptroller General was "required to make an investigation in sufficient depth of *programs and activities* financed in whole or in part under the Economic Opportunity Act of 1964, to determine the efficiency of the administration of such programs and activities by OEO and by local public and private agencies, and *the extent to which such programs and activities achieve the objectives set forth in the Act"* (Comptroller General, 1968. p. 120).

This new congressional assignment to GAO was reported upon at some length (pp. 68–83) in the Comptroller General's 1969 annual report. A number of significant points which relate, almost prophetically, to the subsequent evolution of auditing concepts in the GAO are identified in the introductory paragraphs of that report (Comptroller General, 1969):

---

[2]The current legislative mandate for the review of federal programs and activities is contained in Section 204 of the Legislative Reorganization Act of 1970 as amended by Section 702(a) of the Congressional Budget and Impoundment Control Act of 1974.

The statutory direction to make this investigation did not add greatly to the authority vested in the Comptroller General to review, investigate, and appraise performance of the programs and activities authorized by the act. The assignment made by Title II, however, was, at least in degree, *considerably greater in scope than the audit work normally performed* by the General Accounting Office. The *unique and unprecedented character of this examination* lies in the direction contained in paragraph. . . .

. . . There we were directed to *formulate judgments* as to the extent to which OEO's antipoverty *programs are achieving the objectives* set forth in the act. This task was an extremely complex and difficult one. *The methods of evaluating social programs* such as these *and the indicators of progress or accomplishment are not well developed or understood.* We recognize that, as *the scope of governmental programs increases,* the *Congress is recurrently confronted with the necessity of appraising accomplishments* that cannot be measured in terms of dollars expended or in terms of such tangible yardsticks as the number of miles of road built or pieces of mail delivered. We recognize that *it is essential that efforts be made to develop new yardsticks of effectiveness to meet the needs of the Congress.*

Fortunately, at about the same time the Comptroller General had decided to (1) embark on a program to augment his staff with talent drawn from persons trained and experienced in a wide range of disciplines in addition to accounting and law, and (2) develop a systems analysis capability, initially by establishing a small specialized staff and later by extensive training efforts designed to equip a major portion of GAO's audit staff with the basic concepts of systems analysis. These initiatives by the Comptroller General paralleled the adoption of PPBS (planning–programming–budgeting system) in the executive branch as an improved technique for defining goals, determining alternatives, and selecting programs.[3]

In subsequent sections we present some observations concerning the developments in GAO audit practices and concepts which have evolved from the forces identified above. One way to highlight these developments is by means of comparison and contrast with relevant activities in the public accounting practices of CPA's during the period.[4] *Inter alia,* this will also enable us to examine some of the reasons why the review of economy and efficiency of operations and effectiveness in achieving program results has *not* been similarly developed by the public accounting profession.

Development, Scope, and Application of Audit Standards

In the publication *Standards for Audit of Governmental Organizations, Programs, Activities and Functions* (Comptroller General, 1972), the following definition appears:

1. The *term "audit"* may be used to describe not only work done by accountants in examining financial reports but also work done in reviewing (a) *compliance with applicable laws and regulations,* (b) *efficiency and economy of operations,* and (c) *effectiveness in achieving program results* (p. 3).

To bring this into perspective, we may compare this statement with the *Codification of Auditing Standards and Proce-*

---

[3]Part 3, Hearings Before Senate Committee on Government Operation, March 26, 1968.

[4]No attempt is made in this discussion to cover developments in internal auditing.

dures (American Institute of Certified Public Accountants, 1972), which contains the following sentence in the foreword: *This statement is not intended to apply to the function of independent auditors insofar as they relate to tax practice and management services.*" Thus, as illustrated above, the GAO standards use the term "audit" to describe a much wider scope of activities. As opposed to including a review of efficiency and economy of operations and effectiveness in achieving program results, the AICPA standards are restricted essentially to the "attest function," that is, the function of audit for the purpose of expressing an opinion on financial statements issued by management.

In developing its standards, GAO capitalized on—and for practical purposes adopted—the standards of the public accounting profession for their general standards (training and proficiency, independence, and due care) and standards of field work. And, while adopting the accounting profession's standards for financial reporting—with somewhat greater emphasis on disclosure of relevant background information—including issuance of appropriate opinions, GAO standards for reporting on other "audit" activities refer to such elements as findings, conclusions, and recommendations. Thus, its view of the audit process is one in which the resulting report is issued by GAO. It is not confined to a process pointed toward attestation of a report prepared by the management of an executive agency.

There are similarities as well as differences, of course. Indeed, the basic

authority for prescribing auditing standards, or at least the way it has been implemented to date, is not essentially different for the Comptroller General and the public accounting profession, in that both are based on general acceptance. For example, the Comptroller General relied upon leadership and persuasion in issuing the 1972 *Standards for Audit of Governmental Organizations, Programs, Activities and Functions* and cites no statutory authority. Adoption of the standards by the executive branch relies upon authority vested in the Office of Management and Budget as the President's representative. In this way the Comptroller General and the AICPA have proceeded in a very similar manner, since the latter's *Codification of Auditing Standards and Procedures* also depends significantly on persuasion, but to a degree on the companion ethical standards of the profession.

There are, however, very substantial differences in application. The Comptroller General does have statutory authority and responsibility for prescribing *accounting principles.*[5] In contrast, in the private world, this authority is gained essentially by acceptance and in fact is shared by many elements, including the FASB and regulatory agencies of government, such as the SEC. Notwithstanding current review and expression of interest by congressional committees, such as hearings held by the Moss and Metcalf committees, there is substantial reason to believe the consensus is that, with hard-won evolutionary improvements, accounting principles and financial reporting standards can best be

---

[5]The Accounting and Auditing Act of 1950 (64 Stat. 834).

developed by the private sector with participation and a degree of oversight by government.

Accounting principles and related financial reporting are vital elements in the work of the independent auditor in the private world. He has a pervasive responsibility to assure readers of public company reports that his attest function results in management reporting that adheres to Generally Accepted Accounting Principles. However, specific applications can be highly controversial, and in today's litigious environment the resulting litigation is a substantial burden.

A further illustration, but of lesser significance, occurs in the audit of state and local governments. There is no single body of authoritative literature, with MFOA/NCGA, AICPA and FASB each contributing authoritative viewpoints on pieces of the total.

The Comptroller General does not have comparable problems. The accounting principles that serve as the basis for financial reporting by federal agencies are generally not controversial, and he has clear authority to prescribe them.

Another example of differences in the application of auditing standards is important. In the private world, the development of Generally Accepted Auditing Standards has historically been the province of the profession, through pronouncements of its representative body the AICPA. However, in recent years the courts, and it seems almost everyone else, have not hesitated to disavow the viewpoint of the profession on its responsibility to discover fraud. The resultant controversies and possible penalties, both civil and criminal, can be devastating. The Comptroller General has great interest from a systems and inter-

nal control viewpoint in the prevention and detection of fraud, but the primary responsibility rests in the executive agency involved. In any event, there is no known precedent of sanctions being applied to the federal auditor for failure to detect fraud.

Some Reasons for Differences

Turning from this brief portrayal of differences, we next consider some of the reasons for these differences in private and governmental practices.

One reason is that, imperfect as such indicators may be, the private world does have accepted measures of performance, such as liquidity, return on invested capital, and earnings per share, which do not generally exist for governmental activities. Further, the GAO has a defined audience, the Congress. Diverse though it may be in its interests and concerns, the Congress has demonstrated and indeed has formally expressed its desire for *information on performance* with a degree of coherence and relative preciseness that presently has no counterpart in the private world. However, some may argue that if the public accounting profession developed a way to report on, say, the efficiency and economy of corporate operations, then lenders, directors, and/or stockholders would eventually demand it. Witness the current thrust for audit committees made up of outside directors. In any case, neither legislative directive nor market incentive seems to be compelling such developments at present, except, possibly, in parts of the internal audit function. (See footnote 4.)

We observed earlier the difference

between the GAO's own report of the results of an audit and the audit by a CPA in private practice, which is customarily pointed toward attestation (i. e., the expression of an opinion) concerning one or more parts of a report by management. There are also differences in the selection of an area for audit as well as the scope and character of the audit to be undertaken. The CPA in private practice responds to a client request and must reach agreement on the nature and scope of the audit undertaken. The GAO has clear authority as well as responsibility to undertake audits on its own initiative. Its limitations are its resources, and GAO management exercises a skillful and disciplined approach in selectively determining and monitoring the audits it undertakes. However, as contrasted with public accounting practice, GAO is not required to obtain the approval of the management of the entity to be audited. Nor, with minor exceptions, does the cost of the audit impinge upon the resources of the entity being audited, except for such support as may be required to provide information through supplying data, time devoted to interviews, and so on.

There is also no competitive market mechanism directly related to GAO decisions similar to that which is faced by the public accountant in the public or the private world. Costs versus benefits are reckoned by the GAO rather than the management of the entity being audited. The savings from recommendations reported by GAO are persuasive, but, because of the relatively vast amounts of dollars involved in most federal programs, it would be difficult to challenge GAO's costs versus the benefits in any case. However, audits of

economy and efficiency of operations and achievement of program objectives are time-consuming and the conclusions may be highly subjective and frequently controversial. It also remains to be demonstrated that the full scope of the GAO standards can reasonably be applied in smaller units of government by the public accounting profession or perhaps others. And there is a question whether elected officials of such units will deem it practical to cope with the opportunities that such audits may provide for adversaries to pursue partisan advantage derived from the audit reports.

In concluding this section, we may observe that the GAO authority and the environment in which it operates are much more conducive to experimentation and development of new approaches to auditing than much of the rest of the world—in either government or industry. Further, the relative stability of direction (15-year tenure of the Comptroller General) and a year-to-year availability of resources are important advantages. In short, the GAO has the advantage of being a manageable entity from the viewpoint of size and the ability of its leadership to have an impact in carrying out longer-range objectives through continuity. Whether, in fact, this situation will continue remains to be seen, of course, but the accomplishments of GAO under its present leadership are impressive.

Problems and Prospects for Future Extensions

There are a number of inhibiting factors that would face the public accounting profession in undertaking reviews of economy and efficiency of operations and program achievements in the world of public corporations under standards involving broadly defined scope and public reporting practices. For the most part, other than economic considerations (fees of public accountants), these inhibiting factors are not applicable to the same extent to reviews of governmental activities by either the GAO or CPAs. We have already mentioned some reasons, such as the availability of a variety of "overall" measures by means of which private-enterprise activities can be more easily evaluated. There are other reasons as well.

First would be the question of the audience. Corporate management can and does engage CPA firms and numerous others to provide consulting services through specifically stipulated engagements. Each such engagement is essentially unique as to scope and resources to be applied.[6] These engagements are not designed to meet a broadly defined and universally applicable scope, such as efficiency and economy of operations or achievement of program objectives. Further, there are no criteria for dissemination of reports rendered as urged by the GAO standards for reports on audits in the public sector.

In public accounting practice the foregoing activities would typically be described as consulting engagements or management advisory services. Many would be called "audits" under GAO terminology. There are, of course, generally observed standards for competence and quality, but not for scope. Issues of audit independence and third-party accountability are not normally

relevant, and identifying stockholders and the public (including regulatory agencies) as the audience would probably be regarded as a serious and unacceptable transgression of corporate management prerogatives.

Some regulatory bodies responsible for setting rates are currently undertaking inquiries that involve efficiency and economy (e.g., in constructing utility plants such as the Alaska pipeline and North Anna Nuclear Plant of the Virginia Electric and Power Company). From time to time the Department of Defense has made somewhat comparable surveys of contractors, sometimes identified as "should cost" studies. Some of such inquiries have involved engagements with public accounting firms, but again the scope and reporting have been unique for each engagement rather than conforming to generally applicable standards. Typically, these could be identified as consulting rather than audit engagements.

Questions of credibility and legal liability would certainly arise and the latter would probably necessitate new bodies of law for such extensions to public accounting practice. For example, if a CPA firm publicly reported that a new product (program) of its audit client was either unsuccessful (or successful), it might well be interpreted as condemnation (or as endorsement) of the product. Similar issues would arise if a CPA firm reported that the product was being carefully manufactured and tested to meet quality standards but that the capability of the company to service the product was ill-planned, undercapitalized, or otherwise not effective.

Any assessment of future prospects

---

[6]Trade and industry groups generate similar engagements and these, too, take a variety of forms.

must take into account that the leadership of the accounting profession has become preoccupied with the awesome and vital problems associated with civil suits and the behavior of regulatory agencies in a period in which fraud and illegal activities in public companies has received much attention. In my view this has been a limiting factor in pursuing developments in the private world that would parallel the expansion of audit scope in the government world. In fact— other than an early orientation report for CPAs—what has been done to date to examine the application of these developments in some detail even in the public sector has been undertaken, for the most part, by the management advisory services segment of the profession (AICPA, 1973).

It is not surprising for the management advisory services segment of the accounting profession to display great interest and leadership in pursuing the review of efficiency and economy of operations and effectiveness in achieving program results in both the public and private sectors. It is in the MAS segment of large public accounting firms where we are most likely to find a concentration of those versed in disciplines other than accounting and auditing.

As we observed earlier, in keeping with its definition of audit, the GAO leadership has wisely chosen to extend the range of disciplines available in its staff. This has been accomplished and the staff has been integrated in pursuing the audit function to a degree which does not easily come about in public accounting, because of the dominance of the attest function as opposed to the consulting function. The expertise (gained through experience) required in applying the many rules and conventions embraced by the attest audit undoubtedly continues to dominate. This is further reinforced in these firms by the traditional imprimatur of competence vesting in the CPA title, which does not have the same significance in MAS activities. This is not to say that public accounting firms do not utilize a multidisciplinary approach in many audit endeavors (e.g., applications of statistical sampling and techniques for auditing computer maintained records). Similarly, it is not unusual for a firm to put together an audit–MAS team to carry out a particular engagement. However, there is traditionally an organizational recognition in the profession of audit, tax, and MAS as separate functions, and this, too, creates barriers that carry over even into the organization and activities of AICPA.

Conclusions

We have tried to trace developments at GAO against a backdrop of preparatory activities described in the chapters by Pois and Cooper-Frese. Briefly, we described a series of important developments in audit practice stemming from (1) congressional needs for oversight and evaluation of the massive social legislative programs beginning in the Lyndon Johnson era, and (2) initiatives begun about the same time by the GAO under Comptroller General Staats.

After describing these developments and contrasting them with present public accounting (CPA) practices, we undertook to identify major reasons for the differences as we observed them. Finally, we attempted to assess some of the likely prospects and problems that might be encountered in extending these new developments in private sector (CPA) practices.

In a world that never stands still, it would seem prudent for the public accounting profession to consider such possible extensions. A ready route for doing so in a way that could also render an important public service is available through a variety of public-sector applications. This could provide a learning experience and possibly also an opportunity to advance the state of the art of auditing. Thoughtful efforts and innovative experiments might then be assessed en route to the possibility of expanding these activities into a variety of new private-sector applications for the audit function. Challenges abound, of course, but the opportunities seem inviting. They are inviting enough, I think, to make the endeavor worthwhile.

References

American Institute of Certified Public Accountants. 1972. *Codification of Auditing Standards and Procedures.* New York: The American Institute of Certified Public Accountants, Inc.

——. 1973. *Auditing Standards Established by the GAO—Their Meaning and Significance for CPAs.* New York: The American Institute of Certified Public Accountants, Inc.

Comptroller General of the United States. 1953. *Annual Report of the Comptroller General of the United States.* Washington, D.C.: General Accounting Office.

——. 1968. *Annual Report of the Comptroller General of the United States.* Washington, D.C.: General Accounting Office.

——. 1969. *Annual Report of the Comptroller General of the United States.* Washington, D.C.: General Accounting Office.

——. 1972. *Standards for Audit of Governmental Organizations, Programs, Activities and Functions.* Washington D.C.: Government Printing Office

Weitzel, Frank H. 1977. "Lindsay Carter Warren: Comptroller General of the United States, 1940-1954." *The GAO Review,* 12(2), Spring.

Part IV

The Present

Chapter 11

Financial-Statement Principles That Are Useful for Security Analysis*

Myron J. Gordon

Introduction

It has been said that corporate financial statements serve a variety of purposes. This chapter, however, is concerned with only one of them, providing information that is useful to investors for deciding whether to buy, sell, or hold the common shares of a corporation.

We, therefore, are concerned with two questions. One is: What do investors want to know for the purpose of making such investment decisions? The other question is: How useful are the alternative bases of income determination and asset valuation that are or may be used in financial-statement preparation for obtaining the desired information? More precisely, we shall compare the usefulness of net present value, historical cost, replacement cost, and general price-level adjusted cost as bases for income determination and asset valuation in providing information for investment decisions.

Valuation of a Share

In finance, we represent an investor as maximizing the utility of his or her wealth one period hence. This depends on the person's personality and on the mean, variance, and perhaps other para-

*This chapter is an extension of "Accounting Principles that Serve the Information Needs of Investors," presented at the Symposium on Decision Making in Business of the Netherlands School of Business, Breukelen, Holland, August 27, 1976. It has benefited considerably from the comments on an earlier draft by W. W. Cooper, Yuji Ijiri, and Joshua Ronen. They, of course, bear no responsibility for any errors that remain.

meters of his wealth one period hence. The change in an investor's utility with his investment in a share depends on the risk–return attributes of the share. Nonetheless, for our purposes, we may look on the investor as being concerned only with the price and value of the share.[1] He knows the price, and he estimates the value.

A reasonable representation of the estimate is the expected value of the dividend for the coming period plus the price at the end of the period discounted at a rate appropriate to the risk of the sum. Visualizing the repetition of this valuation process in each succeeding period, it can be seen that the value of a share is the expected values of the future stream of dividends discounted at a rate appropriate to their risk, or

$$V = \sum_{t=1}^{\infty} D_t/(1+k)^t$$

where D_t is the expected value of the dividend in period t and k is the discount rate.

The process of share valuation may therefore be represented as the direct estimation of V by one means or another, the estimation of k and the future D_t for a share, or the estimation of future earnings and other variables that enter into the determination of D_t and k.

Investors' Information Needs

One solution to the information problem open to the accountant is to give the investor exactly what he wants to know—the value of the firm's common stock. The post-World War II literature on this subject began with a monograph by Sidney Alexander which had the limited objective of contrasting what accountants do in measuring income and wealth with what economists do or at least write about with regard to the measurement of these variables[2] (Alexander, 1950). This monograph was followed by a number of articles and books which proposed and to some extent discussed the implementation of net present value as a basis of measurement in preparing financial statements.

The formidable problems in estimating net present value have led some writers to qualify the objective and propose that value in some limited purpose be the basis of measurement (e.g., value in liquidation or "exit value").[3] However, the value figure that investors want is the net present value of the expected future cash flows in the expected employment of the firm's assets and not in one of the numerous alternative uses that are not contemplated or at best are most unlikely to take place.

Such efforts at avoiding the problem of estimating value are understandable. What is required is the estimation of the

---

[1] The value of a share as distinct from its price is the investor's estimate of its price one period hence discounted to the present. Under fairly weak assumptions, the investor maximizes his utility by maximizing his wealth (i.e., the value of his shares).

[2] In practice, economists commonly use a cost basis of measurement, as in the national income and wealth accounts.

[3] Recently, the leading advocates of some variation on value as a basis of measurement in accounting have been R. J. Chambers (1966) and R. R. Sterling (1970).

firm's dividends over all future time and arriving at a discount rate appropriate to their risk. Given a solution to this problem so that we have a determination (estimate is a better word) of the value of the firm at the start and end of the period, the measurement of income is an easy task. As of the start of a period, the expected income for the period is simply the product of the value at the start of the period and the discount rate used to arrive at the value, or Vk. However, the realized income or holding-period return during a period is the dividend plus the change in value. As I have pointed out elsewhere, realized income is the dividend plus the change in the present value of expected future income (Gordon, 1967; Gordon and Shillinglaw, 1974, chap. 10). The latter figure is determined by the change in the expected future dividends and the change in the discount rate over the period.

There is no denying that security analysts want to know the value of a share, the yield at which it is selling, their product (which is the expected income on the share), and, most of all, what the realized holding-period return on the share will be for the coming period. It does not follow, however, that security analysts want accountants to devote their time and energy to the estimation of these quantities through the use of net present value as a basis of measurement in preparing financial statements. I am not even sure that the academics who have been advocating variations on net present value as a basis of reporting would, in the last analysis, support its adoption.

The investment decisions of investors reflect in one form or another a comparison of a share's price and their estimate of its value. Furthermore, the investors estimate of a firm's value *should* be arrived at in the manner just described or by methods consistent with that process if anything like rational decisions and a rational allocation of resources is to occur. Investors and the security analysts who advise them use wide range of information sources in reaching judgments on a share's value. Practically all of them make some use, for better or worse, of the financial statements prepared by accountants. Would these analysts look with favor on the substitution of one more judgment, that of an accountant, for the information accountants provide under a cost basis of valuation? My reading of the evidence is that the answer to this question is no. The answer is correct unless it can be shown that accountants have talents or access to resources that would make their value estimates more accurate than those currently being produced.

Furthermore, given the penchant for objectivity and accuracy for which accountants are justly famous, the figure they would arrive at should be obvious. The finance literature on security valuation and capital-market efficiency has found evidence to support the conclusion that all the publicly available information with regard to the value of a share is fully reflected in its price with little or no lag.[4] Accordingly, in the absence of inside information, the best estimate of the value of a share is its price. I will not go into the problems an accountant would face if his estimate of a corporation's value were based on

---

[4] For a statement of the theory and review of the literature on the subject, see E. F. Fama (1970).

inside information that the management had not itself made public. Therefore, accountants required to use net present value as the basis of measurement in financial reporting might be well advised and would be reasonably expected to use market price for the value of a company.[5] I hope we will all agree that accountants should not abandon what they are now providing investors through corporate financial statements and provide instead a piece of information that the investor can obtain more rapidly by buying the morning newspaper.

Capital–Market Efficiency

Before taking up alternative cost bases of measurement, it may be desirable to consider a more recent and perhaps more serious challenge to the traditional practice of accountants than the proposal that cost should be replaced with value as the basis of financial reporting. I refer to the theoretical and empirical research on capital-market efficiency. A necessary condition for capital-market efficiency is that share prices fully reflect all available information at all times.

Capital markets are said to be efficient with regard to publicly available information if the following conditions are satisfied. First, there is no objective rule for analyzing past prices, published financial statements, or other publicly available information by which an investor can earn risk-adjusted returns superior to what can be earned without the benefit of the information. Also, no person whose performance is a matter of public record (e.g., mutual-fund managers) can consistently earn superior returns, regardless of how he or she uses the information. The evidence to refute these two propositions is at best very weak, and we shall assume that they are true.

There is no question that money is made on the basis of inside information. However, the extent to which this takes place, which is the important question, is extremely difficult to ascertain. Hopefully, it is relatively small.

A consequence of capital-market efficiency with regard to public information is that an investor need not search out and analyze the publicly available information for the purpose of discovering over- or underpriced shares. She or he need not even be concerned with the risk-return attributes of individual shares for the purpose of putting together a portfolio that efficiently satisfies his risk-return preferences. All that he need do is put together a well-diversified portfolio of shares, measure its expected return and risk, and lever up or down to satisfy his preferences between risk and return. Furthermore, all this requires no reference to corporate financial statements, if the expected return and risk of a share are measured under the rules commonly used to implement capital-asset pricing theory (CAPT).[6]

---

[5] Security analysts would certainly welcome management forecasts of future cash flows and perhaps management views with regard to their risk. However, this is quite different from the statements provided by the firm's independent accountants. For a proposal along these lines, see Cooper, Dopuch, and Keller (1968).

[6] In practically all the tests of CAPT, the past data on holding-period return are used to arrive at expected return and risk. Since past holding-period returns are completely determined by price and dividends, no reference to financial-statement data was involved in measuring expected return for these tests of the theory. Hopefully, security analysts go beyond the average realized holding-period return in estimating what a share will earn.

Does it follow that corporate financial statements serve no useful purpose as far as investors are concerned—and therefore that this chapter can be brought to a close right now? I believe that the answer is no. Although each investor may not gain by trying to make abnormal profits on the market, it is fortunate that enough of them try so as to make prices fully reflect all available information. Lorie and Hamilton (1973) made the point as follows:

There is a curious paradox. In order for the hypothesis to be true, it is necessary for many investors to disbelieve it. That is, market prices will promptly and fully reflect what is knowable about the companies whose shares are traded only if investors seek to earn superior returns, make conscientious and competent efforts to learn about the companies whose securities are traded, and analyze relevant information promptly and perceptively. If that effort were abandoned, the efficiency of the market would diminish rapidly (p. 98).

Although the search for abnormal returns serves a socially useful purpose, may we question the usefulness of financial statements for the search process? Capital-market efficiency is not consistent with a systematic lag in the response of stock prices to financial statement information. Otherwise, abnormal returns could be systematically earned on publicly available information. Does it follow that financial statements have no informational content? Do stock prices fail to respond in any meaningful way to financial-statement information at the time it is made public? Are share prices independent of how income is defined for financial reporting? It is now widely believed that the answers to such questions as these are yes.

There is a considerable body of empirical evidence which provides very strong support for the following proposition. If we take the earnings and other data presently provided by financial statements and incorporate them in a share-price model that is designed to explain the expected value and the variability of a firm's future dividends, the model explains a good deal of the price variation among shares.[7] In other words, a good deal of information that is fully reflected in share prices at each point in time is financial-statement information or is incorporated in financial statements.

It should also be noted that the phrase "fully reflected in share prices" does not mean that share prices *accurately* reflect all available information. Since we have no way of knowing what a share's price should be at any point in time, we cannot say whether or not the price accurately reflects the information. All we can say is that there is no known way of acting on the information to consistently make money on future price changes. The failure of cross-section models to fully explain the variation in price among shares is due to some combination of the following reasons: (1) the models do not incorporate all relevant information, financial statement or otherwise; (2) share prices do not *accurately* reflect all available information at each point in time; and (3) the financial statements contain information that is not accurate.

What are the implications of these propositions for the behavior of share

---

[7] See, for example, the empirical material in Gordon (1962). See also Whippern (1966). Any number of other pieces of empirical research could be cited.

prices over time? First and foremost, share prices move from one period to the next so that, subject to some error, they maintain a consistent relation with the information contained in financial statements.[8] Second, this consistency is achieved by analysts who obtain information between the dates that financial statements are published and interpret that information in terms of its impact on financial statements. Third, insofar as the information leads to the over- or undervalutation of a share, publication of the financial statements will lead to the further adjustment of prices. This correction of share prices on the basis of published financial statements means that there will be no consistent relation between the change in earnings from one financial statement to the next and the change in share price at the time a financial statement is published.

One further point should be noted. It was acknowledged that no one can consistently make money on the analysis of financial-statement information. However, the consistency between share prices and financial-statement information means that with regard to each share price–time period event, *the analysts who correctly predict and interpret the financial statement and other information more often than not dominate those who fail to do so.* Otherwise, there would be no correlation between share prices and the information.

What conclusions may we draw from these observations with regard to the use of financial statements in security analysis? First, any investor may safely proceed on the assumption that security analysis is not worth the effort, because a large enough number of analysts do a good enough job analyzing the publicly available information to keep the markets efficient. Second, we can be sure that if everyone turned to throwing darts in order to pick stocks, capital markets would become inefficient and the analysis of available information would become quite profitable. Third, we can also be sure that our busy analysts are able to make share prices fully reflect the information in financial statements by the time the statements are published because the statements are prepared. The statements are a framework for the analysis of the interim information, and the statements are a source of information for the further adjustment of share prices.

A recent book by Dyckman, Downes, and Magee (1975) provides a comprehensive review and analysis of the recent literature on the implications of capital market efficiency for accounting. What I do not understand about the book is the sense of apprehension about the consequences of financial market efficiency conveyed by the final chapter. Far from casting doubt on the usefulness or relevance of financial statements, this literature would seem to confirm the previous findings. Ball and Brown (1968) found that an individual could profit from learning a corporation's income sometime before it was publicly announced. Beaver (1968), May (1971), and others have found that investors react to earnings reports in the sense that volume is greater and price variation is greater at the time earnings are reported

---

[8]This is true only as long as the investor has no reason to believe that the financial statements are misrepresenting the firm.

than at other times. Beaver, Kettler, and Scholes (1970) confirmed that financial statement data can be interpreted to convey information on the risk of a corporation. Another empirical finding is that stock valuation is independent of differences in income when the difference is due to the simultaneous use of different measurement rules by different firms and when the information required to put all firms on the same measurement rule is publicly available. Some commentators consider such results grounds for questioning the usefulness of financial statements, and they are consoled by conflicting evidence on these questions (Dyckman, Downes, and Magee, 1975, pp. 27–30). However, like Beaver (1973), I would be more disturbed if I believed the conflicting evidence reflected anything but the informational content of different accounting methods.

Confusion on the relation between accounting and capital market efficiency may be due to the fact that capital-market efficiency as the term has been used in the literature has a serious limitation that is not adequately recognized. A game may be fair without being interesting or socially useful. Whether or not financial statements and their "quality" make the work of security analysts more interesting need not concern us. On the social usefulness of financial statements, assume that investors are not only denied the information contained in financial statements but are also denied the information used to predict the data in such statements. The only information available to investors is dividend and price data. In all likelihood, capital markets would still be efficient in the sense that analysis of this information would be of no benefit in finding over- and underpriced shares. In fact, capital markets would be more efficient without financial statements insofar as there is any possibility that the analysis of the data contained therein aids in the discovery of over- or underpriced shares.

Although capital markets would be efficient with regard to publicly available information, they would be inefficient with regard to the information that is potentially available. With share prices reflecting only past prices and dividends, corporate managements might well take advantage of the enhanced informational content of the dividend to manage invesvestor expectations. Consequently, anyone who had the data contained in corporate financial statements could consistently make abnormal profits.

An undesirable social consequence of restricted information is the misallocation of resources due to the greater departure in share prices from the prices that reflect all potentially available information. Perhaps an even more undesirable social consequence would be a higher cost of capital (risk premium) on average, as a result of the greater investor uncertainty about future stock prices. Of course, price stability in the short run would be enhanced with information limited to the management-controlled dividend.

Perhaps the most striking thing about the recent literature on capital-market efficiency and accounting and the related literature on information theory and accounting is how little they have advanced empirical research in the area. We always knew that the efficiency of capital markets in allocating funds among firms and in reducing the risk-premium component of the cost of capital depends on the quality of the information provided to investors. However, capital-market theory and information theory tell us very little in response to two questions: What is the information that is incorporated in share prices? How does one go about improving the quality of information contained in financial statements? Unfortunately, comparative analysis of alternative approaches to financial reporting must still rely on the far-from-satisfactory methods of research that existed prior to the advent of this body of literature. Its primary empirical contribution has been to confirm the proposition that the information contained in financial statements is used to predict a firm's future dividends and price so that this information and share prices are related.

Cost–Based Financial Information

Recall that a share's value is the expected values of the future cash flows or dividends that the share will pay discounted at a rate appropriate to their risk. Therefore, the questions we face may be posed as follows. Do financial statements based on cost provide information that is useful in forecasting the expected values and variability of a share's future dividends? Can we compare and choose among the alternative cost bases of valuation for this purpose? Let us first consider the rationale for cost-based financial statements.

Assume that for the last five years an historical cost corporation's financial structure has been constant, it has earned a return of r on its common equity, and it has retained the fraction b of its income. If these relations are expected to hold in the future and if last year's earnings per share were Y, next year's dividend is expected to be $(1 - b)\, Y\, (1 + br)$ and the dividend is expected to grow thereafter at the rate br. There is, therefore, a causal relation between financial statement data and the dividend, and one may reasonably be used to forecast the other.

In fact, few if any firms present the orderly stable picture just described. Assume instead that we have a firm with a history over the last five years described in Table 11–1. For our purposes it will be adequate to consider only the return on common data. Should we characterize the firm as having a return on common equal to the 12 percent average over the five years? Do the last two years represent an aberration that should be ignored or at least heavily discounted? Do these two years repre-

TABLE 11–1

Selected Five-Year Historical Data for a Hypothetical Company

	1971	1972	1973	1974	1975
Earnings	$2.40	$0.92	$3.69	$6.68	$6.54
Dividend	$1.60	$1.00	$1.00	$1.60	$1.80
SOYCEBV[a]	$30.00	$30.80	$30.72	$33.41	$38.49
Return on common stock	8%	3%	12%	20%	17%
Retention rate	33%	-9%	73%	74%	72%

[a]Start-of-year book value of the common equity.

sent a new level of performance or points on an upward trend? The accountant who prepared the statements from which these data were derived has no special qualifications for answering these questions and should not attempt to do so. Each analyst must find his or her own answer, using whatever additional sources of information he considers useful, including the judgments of other analysts and additional financial statement information. The answer to this and related questions such as the inferences that may be drawn from past data on the firm's dividend, debt, and investment policy are the basis for the analyst's estimation of the parameters of the firm's future dividends or surrogates such as next year's price or earnings.

It is, of course, true that the past record of dividends, earnings, and financial structure do not tell what the future holds for a company. However, the past is the only source of information we have for predicting the future. The past may well contain other useful information, but few security analysts would be willing to reach a conclusion on a security without the information contained in the corporation's financial statements.

In examining historical data, the analyst might reasonably put the reasons for fluctuations in the company's return on common in three categories. One is changes in financial policy. Another is changes in sales volume and cost price spread for the firm's products. The third, sometimes called noise or extraordinary events, is illustrated by a gain or loss from the liquidation of a capital asset or the write-up or write-down of inventory due to a change in its cost over the accounting period.

The analyst would like to have the noise, that is, the income attributed to these nonrecurring events, filtered out if they are strictly nonrecurring and have no information content for predicting the future. Since no one can be sure that a particular event is purely random, the analyst would prefer to have the gain or loss associated with such events shown separately and reach his or her own judgment on their predictive value.

However, these extraordinary events are not the sole or even the most important problem facing the security analyst. Changes in financial policy and in operating profit over time complicate arriving at the rate of return and dividend policy that are the best estimates of what will happen. The data in Table 11-1 and related financial-statement information are also used to estimate the variability and risk of a firm's dividend expectation. The causal relation or at least association between cost-based financial statement data and the mean and variance of future dividend growth is evidenced by the empirical research referenced in the previous section.

Historical and Replacement Cost

Let us now compare the merits of historical and replacement cost as bases of income determination and asset valuation. The difference between them may be stated both briefly and roughly as follows.[9] With replacement cost, revenue

[9]For a precise comparative statement of the measurement rules under historical-cost and replacement accounting, see Gordon (1953). For another and more detailed comparison of the two methods of measurement in the same spirit as the analysis that follows, see Revsine (1973).

is charged with the inventory and depreciable assets consumed in generating the revenue at their current market price. Inventory and net plant accounts are written up or down to replacement cost with the offsetting credit made directly to a subaccount of net worth. Historical cost charges against revenue the actual cost of the assets consumed, and it thereby recognizes as profit the difference between actual and current cost. The replacement cost of the assets appear in the accounts as the assets are replaced, and the difference between actual and replacement cost of the assets consumed may be said to go to net worth through the income account.

Assume now an economy in which the prices of various products and the price level in general fluctuate from one period to the next. They are uncertain, but the best estimate of any price or the price level 1, 2, . . ., n periods hence is the current price or price level. In short, we do not have an inflationary environment.

In this uncertain but noninflationary environment, the inventory profit (difference between actual and current cost of goods sold), which is included in historical cost earnings, is a legitimate component of realized nominal earnings. It is also true that the best estimate of its amount in any future period is zero, and the informational content of the earnings record for predicting future earnings is improved if the noise is suppressed or if the inventory profit is so identified in the accounts.

Unfortunately, it is not clear that the plant profit (difference between current and historical cost of the depreciation charge) should be treated in the same way as inventory profit. First, the replacement cost of the depreciable assets consumed is quite difficult to measure.

Second, the plant profit during a year is a complex function of the cumulative movement in prices over many past years and not just the change in price over the current year. Third, future plant profits are correlated with their past values, and the plant profit will go to zero very gradually over time as the existing plant becomes fully depreciated. It follows that eliminating from the income account or separately reporting the plant profit may not have the same informational content as the corresponding treatment of a firm's inventory profit. Doing so may add more problems than it eliminates.

The conclusion I reach is that in a noninflationary environment, historical cost is to be preferred to replacement cost. The benefits of the latter are provided by separately reporting inventory profit. Historical cost also avoids the problems of measuring the depreciation charge at replacement cost, problems that are not trivial and provide little if any compensating benefits.

Let us now recognize the world in which we are currently living. There has been positive inflation on average over a considerable period of time, so that there is a large gap between the historical and current cost of the depreciable assets of most firms. Furthermore, the best estimate of a product's price and the general price level 1, 2, . . ., n periods hence would incorporate price growth at some rate.

Under historical cost, past earnings figures include inventory profits that are, on average, positive and fluctuate over a wide range. It appears that average rate of change and the variability of the change in the price level are positively correlated (Gordon and Halpern, 1976). Hence, the higher the rate of inflation, the greater its variability, and the greater the noise due to inventory profits in historical-cost statements. Separately reporting this element of profit allows the determination of how operating profit and the operating return on common have varied with inflation over time. It also allows a more accurate estimation of the inventory and operating component of profit in the future insofar as past experience is a basis for predicting the future. For those who believe that inventory profits in an inflationary environment are not a component of true profits, replacement-cost accounting for inventory is preferable. However, either course of action provides the analyst with the information she or he requires to forecast a firm's future profits without inventory profits or with inventory profits, assuming some rate of growth in the price level.[10]

The difference between the actual and replacement-cost depreciation charge will depend materially on the extent of the inflation over the past 10 to 25 years. If the inflation has been great, the difference between historical and replacement-cost depreciation will be large. In his projections for the future the security analyst may well be interested in the difference between the two figures. Both figures cannot be obtained from the financial statements when the accounts are kept only at historical cost. On the other hand, they both can be obtained under replacement-cost accounting, since it requires that historical-cost data be

presented as well. Although the replacement-cost determination of the depreciation charge and the net plant account is subject to a considerable margin of error, the error may well be small enough in relation to the amount involved to make the data useful.

A question of great interest to the security analyst is the rate of return the firm will earn on future investment. Return on book, what the firm is earning on its existing assets or common equity, is of limited value for this purpose, but it is of some value. This extrapolation is certainly more useful if the return on book is based on replacement cost in an inflationary environment. Furthermore, the error in the measurement of replacement cost is unlikely to impair the usefulness of the extrapolation as much as the ad hoc adjustment of return on book data based on historical cost.[11]

The conclusion which follows from these observations is that when there has been considerable inflation and the inflation is expected to continue in the future, there is some advantage in using replacement cost as the basis of income determination and asset valuation. This advantage is eliminated or at least substantially reduced, however, if historical-cost statements present as supplementary information the replacement cost of the depreciation charge and net plant account and the amount of inventory profit in earnings.[12]

---

[10]This appears also to be the position taken in Edwards and Bell (1961). It is restated in Edwards (1975).

[11]The assumption is that historical-cost return will be in error because of changes in the inflation rate from one period to the next. In addition, it may be argued that the desire of firms to maintain a real rate of growth makes historical-cost rates of profit and payout unreliable predictors.

[12]Therefore, the U.S. Securities and Exchange Commission should be commended for requiring the supplementary reporting of replacement-cost inventories and plant assets (SEC Amendment to Regulation S-X, adopted March 24, 1976).

General Price–Level Adjusted Cost

The departure from historical cost financial statements that has received the greatest attention from both academic accountants and organizations of practicing accountants in North America has been general price-level adjusted historical cost (GPLAC). The considerable attention devoted to specifying exact rules for implementing the principle makes any summary description of it extremely difficult. What follows will be a gross simplification' that ignores, among other things, the problems posed by intra-period price-level changes.[13]

Assume that the inventory at the start of the year and the inventory at the end of the year were both acquired on those dates. The start-of-year inventory is multiplied by the ratio of the end-of-year to start-of-year values for a general price-level index, and the price-level adjusted inventory is carried to cost of goods sold. Under replacement cost a specific index is used. Hence, this basis of measurement departs from current or replacement cost in that the inventory profit is eliminated from the income statement only insofar as the prices of the items in inventory move proportionately with the general price level.

With regard to the plant account, assume that at the start of the year the historical cost of each item has been multiplied by the ratio of general price index for the start of year to the price index at the time the item of plant was acquired. The account is then multiplied by the ratio of the end-of-year to start-of-year values for the general price index.

This figure is then allocated between the depreciation charge for the year and the end-of-year balance of the plant on the basis of the fraction of the plant consumed during the year. Hence, both the charge and the balance in the account represent the general price-level adjusted historical cost instead of the historical or replacement cost of the respective quantities.

The same procedure is applied to the ownership equity account. That is, the amount invested and retained in each past year is multiplied by the ratio of the general price index at the start of the year to the year of the addition to the net worth account. The ownership equity at the end of the year is the income (less dividends), as calculated above, plus the start-of-year equity price level adjusted to the end of the year. For a corporation with monetary assets equal to its liabilities, the GPLAC assets sum to the GPLAC net worth with each calculated independently.

Turning to the monetary accounts, there is no price-level adjustment to the net monetary or net debt position. The consequence is that the GPLAC adjustment to the net worth account is greater than the GPLAC adjustment to the real assets if the company has a net monetary position and the opposite if the company has a net debt position. This difference is eliminated by carrying the gain or loss on the net debt or monetary position due to the change in the price level to the current period's income statement.

These ideas are illustrated in Table 11–2. Assume that a firm with a piece of

---

[13] For a more detailed and precise description of the practice recommended, see Financial Accounting Standards Board (1974).

real estate that cost $100 at the start of the year is subject to a 10 percent depreciation rate and is financed by $40 of debt at 8 percent interest and $60 of common equity. The rental revenue is $18, the interest charge is $3.20, and if the general price level rose by 25 percent, the depreciation charge is $12.50. The end-of-year net book value of the building is price-level-adjusted to ($90) (1.25) = $112.50. The debt account is unchanged, and the ownership equity is price-level-adjusted up to $75.00. Finally, there is a $10.00 gain on the company's net debt position (because the net debt has not been price level adjusted), which when added to the $2.30 income after depreciation and interest results in a net income of $12.30. Adding this to the net worth, and recog-

nizing that the firm's cash flow from operations was $14.80, reconciles the income statement and balance sheet.

The distinguishing feature and chief argument advanced in favor of GPLAC statements is that the consequences of relative price movements are recognized as income and the consequences of changes in the general price level are excluded from income. Under replacement cost, the distinction is between operating income and capital gains due to changes in the level of asset prices. GPLAC, like historical cost, makes no such distinction. Income includes capital gains as realized through sale as well as operating income, but the capital gains attributed to the change in the general price level are eliminated.

GPLAC also has the great practical

TABLE 11–2

Illustrative Derivation of GPLAC Financial Statements

Building		Debt		Ownership Equity	
Bal. $100.00			$40.00 Bal.		$60.00 Bal.
(3) 25.00					15.00 (3)

Cash		Allowance for Depreciation		Income Statement	
(1) $18.00	$3.20 (2)		$12.50 (4)	(2) $ 3.20	$18.00 (1)
				(4) 12.50	10.00 (3)

(1) Rental revenue
(2) Interest charge
(3) Recognition of price-level change
(4) Depreciation expense

advantage over replacement cost of eliminating the problem of measuring the replacement cost of the plant assets, since the adjustment to all accounts is on the basis of a generally accepted price index. Under replacement-cost measurement it would be theoretically wrong to use a general price index on the plant account, but for most practical purposes the error would not be serious in an inflationary environment.

Perhaps the most serious theoretical and practical problem associated with GPLAC statements is the treatment of gains or losses on the firm's net monetary or debt position. Under replacement-cost measurement, they are carried to the net worth account directly and thereby excluded from operating income. Under GPLAC they reach the net worth account by way of the income statement. The chief argument for GPLAC statements is that they merely extend historical cost to an inflationary environment. However, the fundamental principles of historical cost are the going-concern principle and the realization principle, and the GPLAC treatment of the firm's net debt or monetary position violates both these principles.

Under GPLAC the price-level adjustment to a firm's assets is offset by a credit to net worth insofar as the assets are equity-financed and by a credit to income insofar as they are debt-financed (Table 11–2). Income is realized as a consequence of the increased purchasing power invested in the firm's assets. Clearly, income is realized without a

sale having taken place. The going-concern principle would suggest that, at best, income is realized when the firm's debt position is reduced. However, GPLAC does not even require a turnover in the asset or the debt to realize income on an increase in cost.[14] The implicit assumption is that the firm is liquidated at the end of each period.

It should be noted that the realization principle also creates difficulties for replacement cost. Although carrying the gain or loss on the net debt (monetary) position to income is a violation of the principle, carrying such a gain or loss directly to net worth also violates the principle. With replacement-cost valuation, the distinction between realized and unrealized capital gains or losses is eliminated. All capital gains and losses are excluded from income—at least operating income. The question whether they should be excluded from income or reported as income separate from operating income remains. The issue is important for matters such as the income tax, but for the prediction of future income, it is of no consequence how the holding gains reach the net worth account as long as they are reported separately from operating income.

The previous discussion of GPLAC statements is all by way of background. Our interest in them here is not for the purpose of "correctly" measuring income and balance sheet quantities. The abandonment of long-established accounting principles does not trouble us if the usefulness of the financial state-

---

[14] Ijiri provides a way out of this contradiction through an alternative rationale for GPLAC statements. "Instead of interpreting price-level statements as being prepared under the same set of accounting principles and expressed in a different unit, we may interpret them as statements expressed in the *same* measurement unit as in conventional statements but prepared under a set of accounting principles *different* from those used in conventional statements." See Ijiri (1976, p. 228).

ments for the prediction of future income is thereby improved. The evidence has not been favorable. There have been considerable complaints that the methods employed are complicated and the statements are hard to understand and interpret. Empirical findings on the consequences of GPLAC statements have not increased confidence in them (Davidson and Weil, 1975).

Two attributes of GPLAC statements would seem to impair their usefulness for prediction apart from their complexity. One is the previously discussed recognition of a gain or loss on the change in the real value of the firm's net debt position. The other is the elimination of a fraction of inventory profit from income that depends on the relation between the specific and general price index. The corresponding treatment of the plant account is of no great consequence. My conclusion is that GPLAC statements are materially inferior to their historical- and replacement-cost alternatives for the prediction of future income by security analysts. The empirical work by Davidson and Weil (1975) would seem to support this conclusion.

Conclusions

The conclusions reached in the preceding pages contrast sharply with much of the literature on the comparative merits of alternative measurement rules for financial statements in an inflationary environment. It may therefore be advisable to make clear the differences and to provide an explanation for them.

Our major conclusions are that in an inflationary environment (1) the security analyst is better served by replacement- or current-cost financial statements than

by historical-cost statements; and (2) this information advantage largely disappears if replacement-cost data are provided as supplementary information to historical-cost statements.

By contrast, the literature on financial statements in an inflationary environment can be characterized as follows. First, the dominant idea raised is that the continued use of historical cost in financial accounting seriously threatens the satisfactory functioning of the economic system. Second, apart from occasional academic works on the subject, such as my paper and the book by Edwards and Bell (1961), there has been little interest in replacement-cost statements or information prior to the pronouncement on the subject by the Securities Exchange Commission.

Third, public accountants, as represented by the American Institute of Certified Public Accountants and the Canadian Institute of Chartered Accountants, have devoted practically all their efforts to exploring the use of general price-level adjusted historical-cost statements. Finally, corporate financial officers who represent the views of the managements of their corporations are simply unhappy. Their views as reflected in the pronouncements of the officers and committees of the Financial Executives Institute are that (1) historical-cost statements in an inflationary environment are intolerable, and (2) any of the proposed alternatives to historical cost, including GPLAC, are unsatisfactory.

My explanation for the contrast between the conclusions reached here and the sharply different positions just stated is quite simple. This chapter has been concerned with the informational content of financial statements for security analysis. The concern expressed in the literature referred to above has been with the distribution of income consequences of the statements. The dire consequences of historical-cost statements that are complained about are paying taxes, dividends, and wages on the basis of historical-cost income. The concern is with inadequate after-tax earnings from the viewpoint of meeting the capital requirements of industry and protecting investors from expropriation through inflation.[15] The legitimacy of these fears and the effectiveness of income measurement as a means of influencing income determination and avoiding the calamities feared are beyond our scope here.

It may, nonetheless, be noted that this concern with the distribution of income is an explanation for the unhappiness expressed by financial executives in response to the concrete proposals for changing the rules of measurement. The inadequacy of the accounting rules proposed may not be the sole reason for their rejection. Financial executives may well want the freedom to adjust for inflation when profits are high and not do so when profits are low. Any precise set of rules which denies them this freedom is unsatisfactory, particularly if the rules do not even reduce taxable income and thereby increase real income. The continuing examination of GPLAC statements by public accounting organizations in North America and their failure to take any action may be the most sensible way for them to deal with the conflicting forces that operate on them.

---

[15] See Klaassen (1977) for interview-derived support for this conclusion (p. 17). This may help explain the difference between what the Financial Accounting Standards Board does and what W. H. Beaver (1973) proposes they do.

References

Alexander, Sidney S. 1950. "Income Measurement in a Dynamic Economy," in *Five Monographs on Business Income.* New York: American Institute of Accountants.

Ball, R., and P. Brown. 1968. "An Empirical Evaluation of Accounting Income Numbers." *Journal of Accounting Research,* Autumn.

Beaver, W. 1968. "The Information Content of Annual Earnings Announcements," in Empirical Research in Accounting: Selected Studies 1968, Supplement to the *Journal of Accounting Research.*

——. 1973. "What Should Be the Objectives of the FASB?" *Journal of Accountancy,* August.

——, T. P. Kettler, and M. Scholes. 1970. "The Association Between Market Determined and Accounting Determined Risk Measures." *Accounting Review,* October.

Chambers, R. J. 1966. *Accounting Evaluation and Economic Behavior.* Englewood Cliffs, N.J.: Prentice-Hall, Inc.

Cooper, W. W., N. Dopuch, and T. F. Keller. 1968. "Budgetary Disclosure and Other Suggestions for Improving Accounting Reports." *Accounting Review,* October.

Davidson, S., and R. L. Weil. 1975. "Inflation Accounting for Utilities." *Financial Analysts Journal,* May/June.

Dyckman, T. R., D. H. Downes, and R. P. Magee. 1975. *Efficient Capital Markets and Accounting: A Critical Analysis.* Englewood Cliffs, N.J.: Prentice-Hall, Inc.

Edwards, E. O. 1975. "The State of Current Value Accounting." *Accounting Review,* April.

——, and P. W. Bell. 1961. *The Theory and Measurement of Business Income.* Berkeley, Calif.: University of California Press.

Fama, E. F. 1970. "Efficient Capital Markets: A Review of Theory and Empirical Work." *Journal of Finance,* May.

Financial Accounting Standards Board. 1974. *Financial Reporting in Units of General Purchase Power.* Stamford, Conn.: Financial Accounting Standards Board.

Gordon, M. J. 1953. "The Valuation of Accounts at Current Cost." *Accounting Review,* July.

——. 1962. *The Investment Financing and Valuation of the Corporation.* Homewood, Ill.: Richard D. Irwin, Inc.

——. 1967. "An Economist's View of Profit Measurement," in *Profits in the Modern Economy.* Minneapolis, Minn.: University of Minnesota Press.

——, and Paul Halpern. 1976. "Bond Share Yield Spreads Under Uncertain Inflation." *American Economic Review*, September.

——, and G. Shillinglaw. 1974. *Accounting: a Management Approach,* 5th ed. Homewood, Ill.: Richard D. Irwin, Inc.

Ijiri, Yuji. 1976. "The Price-Level Restatement and Its Dual Interpretation." *Accounting Review*, 51, April.

Klaassen. January 1977. "Current Replacement Value Accounting in Western Europe (especially Great Britain, the Netherlands, and Western Germany)." Netherlands: Free University.

Lorie, J., and M. Hamilton. 1973. *The Stock Market: Theories and Evidence.* Homewood, Ill.: Richard D. Irwin, Inc.

May, R. 1971. "The Influence of Quarterly Earnings Announcements on Investor Decisions as Reflected in Common Stock Price Changes," in *Empirical Research in Accounting: Selected Studies 1971*, Supplement to the *Journal of Accounting Research.*

Revsine, Lawrence. 1973. *Replacement Cost Accounting.* Englewood Cliffs, N.J.: Prentice-Hall, Inc.

Sterling, R. R. 1970. *Theory of the Measurement of Enterprise Income.* Lawrence, Kans.: University Press of Kansas.

Whippern, R. F. 1966. "Financial Structure and the Value of the Firm." *Journal of Finance*, 21, December.

Part V

The Future

Chapter 12

Accounting and Accountability Relations

William W. Cooper and Yuji Ijiri

Background: Accounting and Accountability Relations

Accountants are now supposed to be expert in many things. This includes expertise in the valuation of assets, say, which they share with others such as economists and/or engineers. It also includes expertise in organizing information systems or even the organization of organizations, which accountants share with computer information specialists, say, and organization theorists or management consultants.

This still leaves unstated, however, the central function which accountants perform and which distinguishes them from others whose expertise criss-crosses the practices (and responsibilities) of accountants in many different ways. Here we shall argue that this central theme is "accountability" and that the distinguishing characteristic of accountants lies in their expertise in detecting and determining "accountability relations" and how they should be serviced for a satisfactory functioning of modern society.

We do not mean to argue that this special expertise (and responsibility) is only of recent origin, or that it has emerged only from the complex and confusing issues occasioned by change—including the change relations[1]—which are so much a part of modern society. It is, rather, of ancient origin, at least as far as the emergence of the "modern

---

[1]See especially the discussion of methodological (as distinct from substantive) change in Charnes and Cooper (1968); see also Toffler (1970).

world" is concerned. Indeed, this issue of accountability relations is the central rationale for the idea of double-entry bookkeeping (i.e., the debit and credit system) which emerged with the beginnings of modern (as distinct from medieval) society sometime during the fifteenth century. This double-entry approach, in fact, distinguishes modern accounting from all of its (single-entry) predecessors whenever it takes a fully articulated (systems) form.

To state this matter differently, we may observe that single-entry accounting—or indeed even "no-entry" accounting—may have been and, in fact, still can do equally well for keeping track of transactions and their consequences as long as there is no "accountability to others." A familiar illustrative example is the record-keeping systems of a purely personal character, such as most of us maintain, say, for our households or our personal checking accounts. Note, however, that although single-entry may suffice for the latter, it is not up to the requirements of the bank, which must account to each of us—and to others, too—for our assets (e.g., our deposits) and our liabilities (e.g., loans outstanding), which the bank's management has commingled with the assets and liabilities of others.

Accountability Relations

Turning from the immediately practical to the ultimately philosophical, we may usefully recall John Dewey's discussion of the concept of a "transaction" in his seminal but now largely forgotten book, *The Public and Its Problems* (Dewey, 1927). Starting with an "action," such as an "exchange" between two persons, Dewey proceeds to focus on the "trans"—or "transcendent"—portion of this action. It is the latter, the effects on others (who are not immediate parties to the action), he observes, which gives rise to "governments" and their attendant regulations as one mode of protection. Indeed, this is the gist of the argument in his book as to how a "public" and its "government" are joined together to form a "state," in which all can coexist in the presence of a multiplicity of such *trans*actions.

Dewey sees regulation, particularly regulation by government, as the one means of reaction. We may, however, also suppose that there are other possibilities—many of which remain to be discovered and/or developed. In any event, we shall want to focus on accountability and its attendant possibilities for self-regulation as one such alternative.

With this in mind, we may, therefore, say that one part of what we need in the way of a more formal characterization is now at hand. In particular, accountability relations arise, with their attendant needs for accounting, whenever a transaction occurs, or is about to occur—since, as we have just observed, this means that third-party interests over and beyond those of the parties immediately involved in the exchange are likely to be affected.

What about the parties who are *immediately* involved in the proposed or completed action? We shall assert that accountability relations may also be present from this quarter as well. There is no question that this is the case when the two individuals occupy relations of sub- and superordination and/or relations of delegator and delegatee. To date at least, these kinds of accountability relations have provided the mainstream of day-to-day functioning for accountants dealing with accountability relations. These have extended from the functionings of managerial accounting of a special-study variety all the way to the routine reports that form the backbone of most internal cost, budgeting, or financial accounting systems.

It is quite possible that such "other person" accountability needs are also present in transaction relations between the immediately acting parties. Consider, for instance, the very cornerstone of the theory with which Adam Smith reversed some 2000 years of previous philosophical thinking when he published his *Wealth of Nations* in 1776. It had always been argued, at least since Aristotle, that if one party gained, the other must lose (in exactly equal amount) in any exchange, free or otherwise. Smith, we may recall, had the acumen to ask why the second party would enter into such an exchange. Proceeding from this basis, he argued that an exchange would occur (in the absence of force or fraud) only if *both* parties gained. Control of force and fraud being relegated to governments, all other aspects of regulation could be eliminated and the remaining parts of any transaction left solely to the control processes of freely functioning markets. No other functions of accountability remained to be resolved.

As we have already observed, the presence of third-party effects does give rise to accountability relations, across as well as within organizations,

even when these effects do not enter into the considerations of the two exchanging persons. This "trans"-actional aspect of such jointly advantageous exchanges was, for the most part, omitted from Smith's considerations. Nevertheless, it is part of the accountant's job to identify such relations of accountability, which may need to be serviced, not only when omitted from the considerations of philosophers and/or economists but also when omitted from the considerations of those who are paying for the accountant's services.

Now we return to another omitted part of Smith's very basic proposition. Granted that an exchange will occur only when both parties gain, we may also ask how much each has gained. Then we can go on to ask whether the fact of (perhaps) vastly unequal gain may raise any issue of accountability. This we can recognize is a much less developed area than the transaction area—with its attendant externalities— but it is an equally old and important area in which issues of accountability relations may require identification and satisfaction. For instance, this has long been present in the recognition at equity of such issues as a possible realization of "unconscionable profits" by one or more parties to an exchange, perhaps even a "free exchange," when issues of unequal knowledge arising from a possible fiduciary relation are involved.[2] For another instance, it was the basis of a possible problem in ethics which ancient philosophers[3] (such as Aristotle) had in

---

[2] Actually, this has now been moved from the status of a doctrine in equity to a doctrine in law in situations such as the "disclose or abstain" rule arising from the Texas Gulf Sulphur case under SEC rulings. See, for example, the discussion of what Borden (1977) refers to as the "canon of a new ethic."

[3] Including those concerned with similar reasonings for church, as well as state, on issues such as "just price" and a "fair day's work."

mind and which were swept away, along with everything else they had to say on the subject of exchange, when Adam Smith reformulated what they had also been saying about the necessity of actual loss in the presence of actual gain in *any* exchange. In any event, this area of accountability concern is likely to become increasingly important in the complex and rapidly changing relations that will undoubtedly continue to be distinguishing marks of our society. Hence, we would be unwise to omit issues such as these from the areas of accountability that require attention even in a market-oriented society.

Gathering all of the above together, we shall now say that accountability relations are involved whenever third-party effects, as in a transaction, are potentially present. They are also involved when issues of propriety (legal or otherwise) can appear between transactors as well as when issues of efficiency or effectiveness are involved in the discharge of one person's responsibility to another. The latter (i.e., issues of accountability for efficiency and effectiveness) are the ones that are normally encountered in the design of ordinary accounting systems. Effectiveness (i.e., ability to state and accomplish objectives) presently receives somewhat more emphasis in the design of internal (as compared to external) reporting systems, but we shall also allow for possible future expansions toward external reporting in this dimension of accounting. Efficiency, on the other hand, is concerned with ratios or differences of benefits and costs in whatever activities are undertaken and hence focuses only on one dimension of management that may need to be related to other dimensions for adequate accountability. Relations between efficiency and effectiveness are common in internal reporting systems, as when budgeted and actual revenues are simultaneously reported for purposes of comparison or when standard costs or quantities, say, are used to determine whether efficiency was achieved at the expense of effectiveness, or vice versa. Finally, a variety of devices, ranging from internal to external audits and other such devices, are used to determine propriety not only of objectives but also the methods utilized to attain these objectives, as well as the integrity, or validity, of the reports that others must rely on for their perceptions of efficiency, effectiveness, and propriety.

All of these considerations, and more, are of concern for the issues of accountability—and accountability relations—which we shall be addressing in the sections that follow.

Servicing Accountability Relations

As should be apparent, the preceding discussion does not restrict accounting to accountability relations in ordinary managerial contexts. It also does not restrict it either to the older "stewardship" function of accounting or to newer functions, such as providing information for decision making by managers. It does retain, however, the key concept of performance measurement, which is common to both the stewardship and informational functions of accounting, while (possibly) extending them to new dimensions and new audiences as well.

In order to explore the significance of these remarks it will be prudent for us to start with the familiar framework of internal management reporting systems.[4] Therefore, let us consider a manager whose department produces two types of products from two machines. One unit of product 1 requires 3 hours of operation by machine 1 and 5 hours of operation by machine 2, while one unit of product 2 requires 2 hours of operation by machine 1 only. On any "working day," machine 1 may not be operated for more than 12 hours, while machine 2 may not be operated for more than 10 hours. The department carries no inventories, since all its products can be sold in the market immediately. Each unit of product 1 produced earns $1 and each unit of product 2, when produced, earns $0.5 in contributions to overhead and profit.

If we let x_1 be the number of units of product 1 produced during a day and x_2 the number of units of product 2, we may state the problem in a linear programming form:

$$\text{Maximize } x_1 + 0.5x_2 \qquad (1)$$

$$\text{subject to} \quad 3x_1 + 2x_2 \leqslant 12$$

$$5x_1 \qquad \leqslant 10$$

$$x_1, x_2 \geqslant 0$$

The maximum contribution margin is obtained, while satisfying all constraints, when $x_1 = 2$ and $x_2 = 3$, with a resulting contribution margin of $3.5, as can be readily verified by solving this linear programming problem.

Let us now assume that the example described above maintains for a 20-working-day reporting interval and consider the problem from the viewpoint of accountability. Here we shall assume

only a two-way relation, in which the manager of this activity is accountable to his or her superior on all pertinent aspects of performance. The superior, however, is interested primarily in the earnings contribution margin from this department's operation. Therefore, he specifically instructs this manager that the contribution margin, perhaps specified numerically, represents a goal that the manager should try to improve.

It follows now, in a relatively obvious way, that one of the key items of disclosure that is absolutely essential in this accountability relationship between the manager and his superior is the amount of contribution margin that has been earned. This is needed to show the extent to which the explicitly prescribed goal is achieved, and thus some such measure of performance is needed as an indispensable part of accountability statements.

A relatively easy and complete way to satisfy this accountability need is by means of the relation $\pi = x_1 + 0.5x_2$, for whatever values are assigned to x_1 and x_2. The value of π, the contribution margin, should therefore be routinely reported, but the other details, such as the values of x_1 and x_2, may need to be provided only as particular occasions may warrant—for example, for supplementary information when something out of the ordinary is to be explained. The latter (i.e., the values of x_1 and x_2) become matters of "accounting judgment," so to speak, as to when and how they should be reported. Provisionally, we may assume that the relation of accountability may be satisfied if x_1 and x_2

[4]We are here focusing on profit-making enterprises. For an alternative, but complementary, approach which emphasizes *auditing* in a *governmental* (including nationalized industry) context, see the excellent discussion in "Public Accountability and Audit: A Reconnaissance" by E. Leslie Normanton in Smith and Hague (1971).

TABLE 12-1

Accountability Statement

Accountor: F. A. Smith, Assembly Shop Manager (signed)
Accountee: J. R. Jones, Factory Manager
Period: Month ending February 28, 197_

Goal Achievements

Contribution margin earned	$60
Operating hour constraint observed	
Machine 1	100%
Machine 2	95%

are reported only in special situations. No such liberty attends the reporting of π, however, which should be built into the routine of the regular reporting system if the accountability relation is to be serviced in a satisfactory manner.

We have now observed a distinction between regular and special reports and the need for servicing the latter as a special accountability relation when the occasion arises. Nor is this all. In addition to contribution margins, there may be other goals that are imposed upon the accountor. We may also distinguish between active goals, such as the contribution margin which is to be actively pursued, and passive goals, which take the form of constraints that should be complied with. If the superior in the preceding example is concerned, for instance, with the operating-hour constraints on machines 1 and 2 due to, for example, an agreement with labor unions or because of matters relating to machine maintenance, then whether or not these constraints were violated should also be a part of performance measurement. It may take the form of a "0 or 1 report" (i.e., whether or not the constraints were violated), or it may be serviced in further detail by reporting the amount and the proportion of the time during which the violations occur.

This is to say that the way in which the accountability relation should be serviced alters from the previous example, and now the statements should include a report on $\pi = x_1 + 0.5x_2$ and whether or not the two constraints $3x_1 + 2x_2 \leqslant 12$ and $5x_1 \leqslant 10$ were complied with.[5]

A simple form of such an accountability statement might appear as in Table 12-1, assuming that during the month February 197- this shop earned total contribution margins of $60 during the 20 days of operation. During this period, also, the machine-hour constraint for machine 1 was honored completely, but in the case of machine 2, this was done only 95 percent of the total operating days. Thus, this statement supplies the requisite information on the active goal as well as the passive goals but without further details, such as the amounts produced or the exact

---

[5]The other two constraints, $x_1 \geqslant 0$ and $x_2 \geqslant 0$, are natural constraints that cannot be violated under normal circumstances and hence they would lie outside the accountability reports.

TABLE 12-2

Accountability Statement
Accountor: F. A. Smith, Assembly Shop Manager (signed)
Accountee: J. R. Jones, Factory Manager
Accountant: K. C. Brown, Factory Controller (signed)
Period: Month ending February 28, 197_

Goal Achievements	
Contribution margin earned	$60
Operating hour constraint observed	
Machine 1	100%
Machine 2	95%

occasions when constraint violations occurred.

Note that there are four key elements in this accountability statement. It states the names of the accountor and the accountee, the period for which accounting is done, and the performance measure. Note, in particular, the identification of the accountee, which appears in this accountability statement because here the accountability relationship is a two-party relationship. Its aim is to discharge a specific responsibility for accountability laid by the accountee upon the accountor. We call special attention to this fact since, unless the accountability charges are identical, or unless there are special circumstances to warrant it, the use of the same data in an accountability statement addressed to a different accountee may not be warranted even when, so to speak, the "facts" are the same as we have already indicated.[6]

Role of the Accountant

For many purposes of accountability, the direct kind of communication from accountor to accountee is satisfactory. In other circumstances, it may be desirable to add a specialist in preparing such reports, not only because of the burden of the work but also because the attention of a professional specialist in satisfying the relations of accountability is required.

As a simple example, we shall imagine that such an accountant is brought into the picture described above so that the report in Table 12-1 gives way to the one shown in Table 12-2. Note that the presence of the accountant's signature signals the presence of a new participant, who now assumes responsibility for preparing this report (and perhaps others) which will satisfy the needs of *both* accountor and accountee.[7] Indeed, the

---

[6]There may, of course, be situations where an accountor issues a *general* accountability statement addressed to the public in general. (Such a general accountability statement may occur when the accountor wishes to have all potential accountability charges for a certain area of his activities discharged once and for all.) Even in this case, however, the accountees should be so identified, because it indicates that the statement was prepared with this broad, unspecified audience in mind.

[7]In many systems the signatures of all three parties—accountor, accountee, and accountant, is required (e.g., within prescribed periods of time) to indicate that all relevant persons are satisfied with the report.

TABLE 12-3

Accountability Statement		
Accountor: F. A. Smith, Assembly Shop Manager (signed)		
Accountee: J. R. Jones, Factory Manager		
Accountant: K. C. Brown, Factory Controller (signed)		
Period: Month ending February 28, 197_		
Goal Achievements	*Actual*	*Optimum*
Contribution margin earned	$60	$70
Operating hour constraints observed		
Machine 1	100%	100%
Machine 2	95%	100%

accountant may also go beyond the indicated reporting relation when, for instance, she or he ascertains that other relations of accountability are to be served. In other cases, this kind of action may be proscribed for particular activities, but the accountant is nevertheless responsible for maintaining records and reports in a form that is potentially available for such services as when auditors, say, or others in the accounting process, deem it necessary to utilize the indicated data in servicing the needs of others.

Extending the Service

Locating and servicing accountability relations—or at least maintaining an adequate basis for doing so—provides one dimension of the accounting function. But there are others. It is the responsibility of an accountant in a situation such as the one we are studying to exercise his or her knowledge as a member of the accounting profession, to extend the kinds of reports that might be supplied. A case in point is the utilization of standards and/or budgets—or other such devices—to improve the usefulness of reports to accountor and/or accountee.

For example, in the linear programming case above, it may be very useful for the accountee to know that the maximum contribution margin that can be expected of the accountor is $3.5 (attained at $x_1 = 2$, $x_2 = 3$). Actual performance may then be compared with this optimum result as shown in Table 12-3, for an assumed 20 operating days.

Such a standard based on an optimum solution is not always available, in which case the accountant must consider [8] other possibilities. For instance, one very important and commonly used basis for comparison involves actual performance in the previous period. The importance of the last period's result is evidenced by the fact that financial statements are normally presented in a comparative form showing this year's results, indicating whether performance is improving

---

[8]That is, this is a responsibility that may reasonably be assigned to him, either explicitly or implicitly.

or worsening. To put the matter differently, the accountant in our accountability relation trio is responsible for knowing that this is a common accounting practice and that he is also responsible for ascertaining whether such prior period comparisons will help to service this situation as well.

The idea of between-period comparisons may be extended toward the future, too, or even to indicating forecasted performance for the coming period in its own right. This extension raises additional questions and provides further insight into the nature of accountability. Is the accountor to be held accountable for actions that he has not yet taken? The answer must clearly depend on the possible consequences of the pending actions and the kinds of accountability relations that are likely to be effected. For instance, even at the level of the very simple two-person relation we are presently considering, the following considerations would appear to be decisive in most circumstances.

1. *Preventive actions by the accountee.* If the forecasted performance is grossly inadequate from the accountee's standpoint, he may wish to take remedial action. If the accountability relationship originated in a delegation of authority, the accountee may now wish to review the planned action with the accountor and, if not satisfied with the accountor's proposed plan, may wish to take the delegated authority back from the accountor. If the accountability relationship originates in a contract, it may stipulate the accountee's right to intervene in order to influence or alter planned actions under certain conditions, and, of course, legal and other means may also be available to prevent the occurrence of potentially damaging results.

2. *Protecting the accountor.* Informing the accountee of likely consequences from the accountor's action may also benefit the accountor. Thus, if the forecasted performance, as reported, is considered to be inadequate by the accountee, he or she is given a chance to react to it with possibly less serious consequences to all (including the accountor) than an after-the-fact report might suggest. Furthermore, these serious consequences might be averted entirely if the accountee is informed in advance in a way that might enable him to alter other circumstances (e.g., through the actions of others) that might interfere with effective execution of the proposed plans.

3. *Setting standards.* Forecasted performance, when accepted by the accountee either explicitly (by his action of approval) or implicitly (by his lack of corrective action) then becomes a standard. Both the accountor and the accountee agree, explicitly or implicitly, to evaluate the actual performance in relation to the forecasted performance. The variance between the actual and the forecasted performance may then be used as one measure of effectiveness for the accountor's subsequent performance. Conversely, when the plan (or forecast) has been accepted and signed by all concerned, the accountor has a reasonable basis, attested to by a third party, the accountant, as to how to appraise his own effectiveness by reference to plans versus actuals, as in Table 12–4, where we have emphasized the distinction between active versus passive goals by providing a relatively complete picture for the former (embodied in the contribution margins) and only a partial picture for the latter as embodied in the machine hour constraints.

Goal Programming—Impact Analysis

We now go one step further and bring the accountant further into the picture by allowing him or her to operate "on his own" as a full-scale professional. In particular, we may expect him to observe the need for attending to third-party impact (accountability) needs while still staying within the bounds of

TABLE 12–4

Accountability Statement			
Accountor: F. A. Smith, Assembly Shop Manager (signed)			
Accountee: J. R. Jones, Factory Manager (signed)			
Accountant: K. C. Brown, Factory Controller (signed)			
Period: Month ending February 28, 197_			
Goal Achievements:	*Last Month*	*This Month*	*Next Month*
Contribution margin earned			
Projected	$50	$70	$50
Actual	$55	$60	–
Operating hour constraints observed			
Machine 1	100%	100%	100%
Machine 2	95%	95%	100%

customary internal management reports in the following manner. We shall assume that the accountant-controller referred to in the reports discussed in preceding sections is cognizant of the likelihood that forces are present in society which point to the need for accommodating pressures— e.g., environmentalists concerned with reducing this firm's particulate emissions and that, at the same time, other groups are concerned with increasing its employment of "minorities."

First, this accountant-controller observes that the interests of these two groups are not necessarily consistent and they may also not be compatible with the firm's present production processes and capacities—for example, as reflected in the particular activity modeled above (1) in linear programming form. Second, he observes that anticipatory action is in order which may be of immediate interest to the managers who he is presently servicing, and that this same action may also be of use when the interests of these additional groups— environmentalists and minorities—may need to be serviced by the planning and reporting processes.

Bearing these considerations in mind, we may assume that this accountant draws on his knowledge of recent professional developments and formulates the following goal programming model[9] to be used in place of (1):

$$\text{minimize } u = \delta_1^+ + \delta_1^- + \delta_2^+ + \delta_2^- + \delta_3^+ + \delta_3^-$$

subject to: (2)

$$12 \geqslant 3x_1 + 4y_1 + 2x_2 + 2y_2$$

$$10 \geqslant 5x_1 + 5y_1$$

$$6 = x_1 + 2y_1 \qquad -\delta_1^+ + \delta_1^-$$

$$3.5 = x_1 + y_1 + \tfrac{1}{2}x_1 + \tfrac{1}{4}y_2 \quad -\delta_2^+ + \delta_2^-$$

$$5 = \qquad\qquad\qquad 5y_2 \quad -\delta_3^+ + \delta_3^-$$

[9]See, for example, Cooper and Ijiri (1976) for further discussions of goal programming and its possible uses to accommodate conflicting (possibly contradictory) interests in a management-planning accountability system.

with all variables constrained to be non-negative. Here the first two constraints are associated with machine capacities (per day) as before [see model (1)]. The new variables, y_1 and y_2, however, represent alternative processes for producing the same products as before. The other three constraints are "goal constraints."

The first of these goal constraints,

$$6 = x_1 + 2y_1 - \delta_1^+ + \delta_1^-$$

is associated with increasing the amount of minority employment. The goal is 6 hours of such employment, with x_1 contributing 1 such hour per unit utilization and y_1 contributing 2 such hours per unit utilization. Evidently, the latter is twice as effective in this constraint as the former. On the other hand, the process associated with y_1 utilizes the 12 hours available from machine 1 at a greater clip than the process associated with x_1. See the coefficients associated with x_1 and y_1 in the first constraint in (2). This is because the labor associated with y_1 is less skilled than the more experienced labor associated with x_1.

The second goal constraint,

$$3.5 = x_1 + y_1 + \frac{1}{2}x_2 + \frac{1}{4}y_2 - \delta_2^+ + \delta_2^-$$

is directed to the contribution margin, where \$3.5 is the maximal possible contribution margin available, as was discussed in connection with (1). Observe that x_1 and y_1 each contributes at the rate of \$1 per unit utilization. This means that the use of the processes associated with x_1 and y_1, respectively, are distinguished only by their behavior in the other constraints (as already

noted) and not in the "contribution-margin goal constraint."

Turning to the alternative processes associated with x_2 and y_2, however, we note that the former provides \$1/2 per unit utilization toward the contribution margin, as before,[10] whereas the latter (i.e., y_2) contributes only at the rate of \$1/4 per unit utilization. On the other hand, only the latter contributes anything to the environmental (reduction in emission) goal constraint, which is the last constraint shown in (2),

$$5 = 5y_2 - \delta_3^+ + \delta_3^-$$

The problem now is to balance this all out, as is done in the model above via the objective in (2):

$$\min u = \delta_1^+ + \delta_1^- + \delta_2^+ + \delta_2^- + \delta_3^+ + \delta_3^-$$

These $i = 1, 2, 3$ values for δ_i^+ and $\delta_i^- \geqslant 0$ represent deviations above and below the goals, respectively, in each of the preceding goal constraints. Hence, the objective is to minimize the sum of these deviations, which is accomplished by the following program:

$$x_1 = 0, \quad y_1 = 2, \quad x_2 = 1, \quad y_2 = 1 \qquad (3)$$

for which

$$\delta_1^- = 2, \quad \delta_2^- = 0.75 \qquad (4)$$

and all *other* δ_i^+ and $\delta_i^- = 0$.

As is readily confirmed, this means that minority employment will be $\delta_1^- = 2$ hours *below* the indicated goal with the program given in (3). The latter value (i.e., $\delta_1^- = 2$), which results from

---

[10]Compare the discussion for linear programming model (1).

the minimum deviation program in (3), is accompanied also by $\delta_2^- = \$0.75$ in (4), which is the amount below the \$3.50 maximum possible contribution margin that will then be attained. Finally, all other δ_i^+, $\delta_i^- = 0$, so that, in particular, $\delta_3^+ = \delta_3^- = 0$, which means that the environmental (reduction in emissions) goal will be attained exactly.

There are a variety of additional considerations which the accountant-controller can usefully bring to the attention of the interested managers, and one possible way to do this is shown in Table 12-5. Stripping away all ancillary information, we observe that the planned deviations, which are all below goals, are shown in the row labeled "Planned deviation." These planned deviations total to the amount (2.75) shown on the right under the heading "Total MEUNITS" (which are managerial evaluation units). The important point to be brought to management's attention here is that these units are all equally weighted. See the notes at the bottom of the table.

If for no other reason than that experimentation pointed toward accommodating the outside-the-firm interests associated with these goals, it may be desirable to explore how the model might respond to different systems of weights. However, we shall not undertake that task here. Instead, we shall focus on other information which is also pertinent to these goals. This information, obtained from the "dual" problem to (2), is summarized in Part II of Table 12-5 in a way that is pointed to

possible facilities alterations (cf. Cooper and Ijiri, 1976). Observe, for instance, that if the capacity of the first machine is increased by 1 hour, the contribution margin (as oriented toward this particular goal) will be incremented by \$0.25.[11] No contribution to the indicated minority employment goal, however, will be obtained from the increment in this machine's capacity.

This is in direct contrast to what will be obtained (at best) from incrementing the capacity of the second machine by 1 hour. In the latter case, a 0.4-hour improvement in minority employment will be experienced *without* any improvement in the contribution margin goal.

Finally, if *both* machines are each incremented by 1 hour in their respective capacities there will be a \$0.25 improvement in the contribution margin and a 0.4-hour improvement in the minority employment picture. In total, there will then be an improvement of 0.65 MEUNIT in the measure of overall goal attainment,

$$(2.75) + 0.65 = (2.10)$$

which means that in this system of equal weights, we will now lie a total of only (2.10) units *below* all goals.[12]

In our analysis we have focused on altering machine capacities by providing an accounting information system that enables management to readily assess possible goal consequences. We could, of course, have gone in exactly the opposite direction and arranged a system

---

[11] This does not allow for the cost of the indicated 1-hour increment to machine capacity.

[12] Recall that the δ_i^+ values are associated with deviations *above* the goals indicated in (2), while the δ_i^- are associated with deviations *below* these same goals.

TABLE 12-5

Proposed Accountability Statement for Plans to Goal Comparisons

Accountor: F. A. Smith, Assembly Shop Manager
Accountee: J. R. Jones, Factory Manager
Accountant: K. C. Brown, Factory Controller (signed)

PART I: Operating Programs

	Income Statement ($)	Employment Statement (MOWHRS)[a]		Environment Statement (TONS)	Total MEUNITS[b]
Goals	Contribution Margin 3.50	Minority: 6	Other ...	−5	0
P R O G R A M S	Sales ...	2	...	−1	0
	Costs ...	2	...	−4	0
	Profit 2.75	4	...	−5	0
Planned deviation[c]	(0.75)	(2)	...	0	(2.75)

PART II: Goal-Impact-Evaluation Analysis for New Investment Alternatives

Facility to Be Incremented[d] (Hours)	Impact per Unit Facility Increment			Total MEUNITS[b]
	Profit ($)	Employment (MOWHRS)[a]	Environment (TONS)	
M_1	0.25	...		0.25
M_2		0.40 ...		0.40
M_1 and M_2	0.25	0.40 ...		0.65

[a]MOWHRS, man or woman hours.
[b]MEUNITS, Management evaluation units, all weighted at one unit per unit deviation from each goal.
[c]These planned deviations are optimal—that is, they deviate from the goals indicated at the head of each column to the minimum possible extent—under the conditions indicated by the model, with all goal deviations being equally weighted in the resulting sum.
[d]M_1, first machine; M_2, second machine.

in which management might assess the facilities processing consequences by altering each of the indicated goals. The latter will certainly be necessary if these reports are used, say, as a basis of negotiation with these outside groups or others for the purpose of planned accommodations to their possible reactions. On the other hand, it has seemed most prudent here to start and stay close to present management experience and requirements before essaying wider-ranging exercises in anticipation of what may ultimately be required to service the accountability requirements of such additional groups.

This, in any event, is what we have done here. Hence, we may close this section by observing that only the accountant has signed the report in Table 12-5. That is, unlike the reports in the preceding sections, this is his or her recommended new addition to the reporting system. After this first step has been accepted by management, it may then become part of the accountant's task to extend the experiments further in ways that can ultimately make it possible to accommodate the requirements of others along lines such as those we have just indicated.

Other Extensions—The Role of the Auditor

We have now indicated how a professional accountant can (and should) relate to the scientific research community in his or her relations to management and management accountability.

We have also indicated how he might service present relations in ways that can help prepare management for dealing with the issues of accountability to wider audiences. Since our focus is on internal accountability processes, we can only allow limited scope to our accountant in addressing the issue of wider audiences if we want management to maintain final authority—and responsibility—for such decisions.

There is another route that we might pursue, however, which also bears on the issue of identifying and servicing the accountability relations that are present at various junctures. This is the route of the relation of the auditor (both internal and external auditor) to the accountant. The former (i.e., the internal auditor) has begun to experiment with uses of auditing in a variety of ways to increase its utility to management (see, e.g., Churchill et al., 1977). These may ultimately extend to consideration of the accountability relations that need to be served, of course, but for the moment one must concede that there is very little in the way of experimentation with audit reports or findings directed to such ends in the field of internal auditing.

The same is true in the area of external auditing where, *a fortiori*, one would expect responses to the auditor's responsibility for identifying and servicing all of its client's accountability relations to be of paramount importance. Partly in response to the numerous lawsuits of recent years and partly, perhaps, because of the institutional arrangements it is utilizing,[13] the public accounting profession seems to be

---

[13]This criticism has been made in perhaps its strongest form in the Metcalf Committee Report. See U.S. Congress (1976).

moving in almost the opposite direction. Thus, the Financial Accounting Standards Board, for instance, would narrow accounting responsibility (i.e., financial reporting responsibility) only to the information needs of claimants who appear (or who might appear) on the right-hand side of the customary balance sheet. Thus, under *Objectives of Financial Statements of Business Enterprises,* (Financial Accounting Standards Board, 1976), the opening statements are as follows:

Financial statements of business enterprises should provide information, within the limits of financial accounting, that is useful to present and potential investors and creditors in making rational investment and credit decisions. Financial statements should be comprehensible to investors and creditors who have a reasonable understanding of business and economic activities and financial accounting and who are willing to spend the time and effort needed to study financial statements (p. 3).

Furthermore, the Commission on Auditor's Responsibilities[14] of the American Institute of Certified Public Accountants observes:[15]

The core of the Commission's recommendations is a modification of the present notion that the audit is confined to a specific set of annual financial statements of a corporation. Instead, the independent audit should be viewed as a function that provides assurances over a period of time on corporate management's accountability *to users of financial information.* [Italics supplied.]

On the other hand, there are at least "straws in the wind" which may be indicating that it will soon be blowing from a different quarter. We have already observed some of the extensions of internal audit beyond the limits of financial audit only. These extensions are also occurring in the U.S. General Accounting Office, which has also done a great deal of experimenting with its published audit reports, which are now directed to a great variety of audiences—and accountability relations.[16]

More recently, the AICPA itself has released a report, *The Measurement of Corporate Social Performance,* by its Committee on Social Measurement, which opens with the following statement (AICPA, 1977b, p. 3):

Every business action, if traced with sufficient care, will be found to have both economic and social consequences. Whether a company wishes it or not, in the course of being a producer of goods or services, it generates a wide variety of social impacts. . . . Corporate social measurement is concerned primarily with the social consequences of business action; its end product—social information—is increasingly viewed as an important complement to the substantial amount of information that is available about the financial consequences of business actions. Together, they are thought to present a considerably better picture of a company's total performance than either can alone.

Although the President of the AICPA enters a specific disclaimer as to AICPA responsibility for this study, we may,

[14] Known as the Cohen Commission.

[15] This is quoted from AICPA (1977a), p. 8, File Ref. No. 2209, Draft 2/7/77, Sec. 6.

[16] See, for example, U.S. Comptroller General (1972, p. 1): "The interests of many users of reports on Government audits are broader than those that can be satisfied by audits performed to establish the credibility of financial reports. To provide for audits [and reports] that will fulfill these broader interests, the standards in this statement include those prescribed by the AICPA and [also] additional standards for audits of broader scope."

nevertheless, count it as one of the straws we are observing.[17] Nor is this kind of development confined to the United States or even to one country. Thus, in a recent report, the Accounting Standards Steering Committee of The Institute of Chartered Accountants in England and Wales [18] moves in the following direction. First, it broadens the viewpoint from the financial statements to the corporate report defined as "the comprehensive package of information of all kinds which most completely describes an organization's economic activity" (Institute of Chartered Accountants in England and Wales, 1975, p. 9). Second, it widens potential audiences, as in the following statement:

Users of corporate reports [are] those having a reasonable right to information concerning the reporting entity. We consider such rights arise from the public accountability of the entity whether or not supported by legally enforceable powers to demand information. A reasonable right to information exists where the activities of an organization may infringe on the interest of a user group.[19]

Then in the interest of servicing (routinely) the interests of specifically identified groups, they suggest extending the typical present form of corporate report to the provision of new kinds of information as well as the alteration of presently utilized types of reports. In the latter category, for instance, they suggest replacing the present income statement, directed only to investors and creditors, with a "value-added statement" that is directed to more general publics. In the former category (i.e., the addition of new kinds of information) they suggest a variety of new reports which extend from employee information of the usual kind to additional types that can cast light on career patterns, and so on, that must certainly be of interest to outside groups concerned with equal-employment opportunities as well as inside groups, such as company employees.

How these extensions will occur, if at all, and the form they may take will doubtless depend on the nature of future social pressures and the kinds of research and experimentation that we might presently undertake. We have very little control over the first of these forces. Hence, we have here concentrated on the second. Moreover, as we have already noted, the focus here has been on internal management processes. For purposes of perspective, however, we have tried to address the broader issues of identifying and servicing a complex of varying accountability relations in the opening section of this chapter as well as this one—with which we now close.

---

[17] As Martin Bronfenbrenner once remarked: "When better straws are made, a drowning man will grasp at them, too," and perhaps this is all we are presently doing.

[18] The report (Institute of Chartered Accountants in England and Wales, 1975) was issued in association with The Institute of Chartered Accountants of Scotland, The Institute of Chartered Accountants in Ireland, The Association of Certified Accountants, The Institute of Cost and Management Accountants, and The Chartered Institute of Public Finance and Accountancy.

[19] This is all subject to certain constraints that we do not reproduce here since we think they are either minor or self-evident, such as company size and cost of providing information relative to its benefits.

References

American Institute of Certified Public Accountants. 1977a. "The Boundaries of the Auditor's Role and Its Extension." New York: The American Institute of Certified Public Accountants, Inc.

——. 1977b. *The Measurement of Corporate Social Performance.* New York: The American Institute of Certified Public Accountants, Inc.

Borden, A. M. 1977. "The SEC Should Not Be Making Law." *The New York Times,* March 6, p. 12F.

Charnes, A., and W. W. Cooper. 1968. "Method and Substance in Change," a paper prepared for consideration by students of design in the College of Fine Arts, Carnegie-Mellon University, March 15.

Churchill, N. C., W. W. Cooper, J. San Miguel, V. Govindarajan, and J. Pond. 1977. "Development in Comprehensive Auditing and Suggestions for Research." *Symposium on Auditing Research, II.* Urbana Ill.: University of Illinois, Department of Accountancy.

Comptroller General of the United States. 1972. *Standards for Audit of Governmental Organizations, Programs, Activities, and Functions.* Washington, D.C.: Government Printing Office.

Cooper, W. W., and Y. Ijiri. 1976. "From Accounting to Accountability: Steps Toward a Corporate Social Report," in Norton Bedford, ed., *Accountancy in the 1980's—Some Issues.* Urbana, Ill.: University of Illinois Department of Accountancy.

Dewey, John. 1927. *The Public and Its Problems.* Chicago: Gateway Books.

Financial Accounting Standards Board. 1976. *Tentative Conclusions on Objectives of Financial Statements of Business Enterprises.* Stamford, Conn.: Financial Accounting Standards Board, December 2.

Institute of Chartered Accountants in England and Wales. 1975. *The Corporate Report—A Report of the Accounting Standards Steering Committee.* Chartered Accountants Hall, Moorgate Place, London.

Smith, Bruce L. R., and D. C. Hague, eds. 1971. *The Dilemma of Accountability in Modern Government—Independence vs. Control.* London: Macmillan & Co.

Toffler, Alvin. 1970. *Future Shock.* New York: Random House, Inc.

U.S. Congress. 1976. Subcommittee on Reports, Accounting and Management of the Committee on Government Operations. *The Accounting Establishment.* Washinton, D.C.: Government Printing Office.

Chapter 13

A Structure of Multisector Accounting and Its Applications to National Accounting*

Yuji Ijiri

Multisector Accounting

An accounting entity is often partitioned into multiple sectors and accounting is carried out simultaneously for each sector as well as for the entity as a whole. Such accounting is called multisector accounting. Corporate accounting is multisector accounting when divisions, regions, or product lines are treated as sectors. National accounting is multisector accounting in which enterprises, households, government, the rest of the world, and so on, are treated as sectors.

What makes multisector accounting different from ordinary accounting is the problem of *intersector transactions*.

Intersector transactions present interesting conceptual as well as practical problems which will be explored in this chapter.

Corporate accounting and national accounting took entirely different routes in handling intersector transactions. To illustrate the point, let us suppose that sector 1 buys 1 million bushels of wheat for $4 million in cash from sector 2. In corporate accounting, sector 1, say, a milling division of the corporation, enters the following entry:

$$\text{(Dr.) Wheat} \quad \$4 \text{ million} \qquad (1)$$

$$\text{(Cr.) Cash} \quad \$4 \text{ million}$$

On the other hand, sector 2, say, a

*This chapter was originally presented at the Summer Research Seminar at Stanford Graduate School of Business, August 2-5, 1976. The author gratefully acknowledges helpful comments by William W. Cooper and by participants of the seminar, in particular James M. Patell.

trading division of the corporation, enters the following entry:

$$\text{(Dr.) Cash} \quad \$4 \text{ million} \qquad (2)$$
$$\text{Wheat} \quad \$4 \text{ million}$$

assuming that wheat is transferred at cost.

In national accounting, the same transaction is recorded as

$$\text{(Dr.) Sector 1} \quad \$4 \text{ million} \qquad (3)$$
$$\text{(Cr.) Sector 2} \quad \$4 \text{ million}$$

Here, the journal entry is interpreted under a convention that goods and services flow from the credit sector to the debit sector while the corresponding financial claims (cash and claims on cash) flow from the debit sector to the credit sector. In this case, wheat flows from sector 2, say, the farm business sector, to sector 1, say, the government sector, while cash flows conversely.[1]

Here, we may note two fundamental differences between these two methods of recording intersector transactions. One is that entries in national accounting, as in (3), are recorded from the standpoint of the entity, the nation in this case, which contains sectors as its subunits, while entries in corporate accounting, as in (1) and (2), are recorded from the standpoint of a sector, a division in this case, and not from the standpoint of the entity, the corporation. It is through the process of consolidation that the orientation of the entries is changed from a sector to the entity. Therefore, until the time of consolidation, the ownership of the sector does not, in general, affect the way in which

records are kept for the sector. In other words, sectors in corporate accounting are generally the primary and independent units of accounting.

In national accounting, entries are made right from the beginning with a given entity in mind. The entity is the primary unit of accounting. Although there is a process of aggregation and consolidation in national accounting, the process refers to accumulation of a given type of transaction data and not to conversion of sector data into entity data.

The second difference between the two methods of recording intersector transactions is that entries in corporate accounting are oriented toward resources, while entries in national accounting are oriented toward sectors. In corporate accounting, wheat is wheat and cash is cash, regardless of where they came from or where they went to. What is important is which goods were received in exchange for which goods. The party with whom the transaction was made has only secondary importance in corporate accounting.

The opposite is true in national accounting. What is important here is which sector obtained a financial claim against which sector. Whether such a financial claim is obtained as a result of selling wheat, crude oil, or supplying services is only of secondary importance.

This difference between the resource orientation of corporate accounting and the sector orientation of national accounting suggests that perhaps it may be possible to combine both orientations in one journal entry. The following journal entry is one such possibility:

---

[1] See a comparison of "intra-entity transactions" versus "inter-entity transactions" in Mattessich (1964).

(Dr.) Sector 1—Wheat $4 million   (4)

(Cr.) Sector 2—Cash $4million

Here, the entry indicates a *receipt* of $4 million worth of wheat by sector 1 and at the same time a *receipt* of $4 million cash by sector 2. Implicit in this entry is the fact that sector 1 gave up $4 million in cash while sector 2 gave up $4 million worth of wheat in exchange. The entry may also be read to mean that sector 1 debits wheat and credits cash, while sector 2 debits cash and credits wheat.

Entries such as (4) differ from ordinary journal entries because reversing debit and credit has no effect on their meaning. The following entry,

(Dr.) Sector 2—Cash $4 million   (5)

(Cr.) Sector 1—Wheat $4million

has exactly the same meaning as entry (4) under the convention stated earlier. We may call entries (4) and (5) "dual-double entry," since they do represent two ordinary double entries merged together. When two double entries are combined together with sector identification, the need to identify debits and credits disappears. The important point is that [Sector 1—Wheat] is matched with [Sector 2—Cash].

It is possible to take advantage of debits and credits and adopt a convention under which a debit entry means the initiator of a transaction, or a convention under which a debit entry means a recipient of goods and services and a credit entry a recipient of financial claims.[2]

While entries such as (4) and (5) capture the basic information on an intersector transaction, there is a difficulty that can occur. That is, in the example above, the value of wheat carried on the books of sector 1 may be different from the one used by sector 2. This raises a fundamental question. What were traded in the example above are *not* [$4 million worth of wheat] and [$4 million cash] but rather [1 million bushels of wheat] and [$4 million cash]. Sector 1 bought wheat because to them these purchases are worth more than $4 million cash, and sector 2 sold because to them $4 million cash is worth more than 1 million bushels of wheat. Yet, one thing that both sectors agree upon is an exchange of [1 million bushels of wheat] and [4$ million cash]. Therefore, a journal entry, which is the most fundamental building block for multisector accounting, should take a form such as

(Dr.) Sector 1—Wheat   1 million bushels   (6)

(Cr.) Sector 2—Cash $4 million

Sector 1 may "translate" entry (6) in their own terms and record the transaction by debiting materials for $4 million and crediting cash for $4 million. Sector 2, on the other hand, may translate (6) in their own terms and debit cash $4 million and credit sales $4 million, recognizing profit or loss at the same time. In any case, it should be clear that (6) contains the basic data that

---

[2] It may be noted that if the latter convention is adopted, the sector entries under the dual-double entry conforms to the sector entries in national accounting under ordinary double entry.

come directly out of an objective agreement and performance of the agreement by each of the two parties.

Let us, therefore, consider a set of judgments that are needed in order to carry out journal entries such as (6) in multisector accounting.

The fundamental judgments that must be exercised in carrying out accounting measurement in general were stated in three axioms in Ijiri (1965). (See also Ijiri, 1967 and 1975, for later refinements.) A minor modification of these axioms seems to be sufficient for adapting them to multisector accounting.[3]

The three axioms are: axioms of control, quantities, and exchanges. Briefly speaking, the axiom of control states the need to determine a set of economic resources under the control of a given entity at a given point in time. The axiom of quantities states the need to classify resources based on their homogeneity and describe them by a set of physical quantities. The axiom of exchanges states the need to identify which resources were exchanged with which resources. These three judgments seem to be necessary for any kinds of accounting measurement systems that involve monetary valuation.[4]

In the next section, it will be shown that these axioms are also applicable to multisector accounting. It will then be shown that when these axioms are applied to national accounting, they highlight some interesting aspects of national accounting that have not heretofore been well explored.

Three Axioms for Multisector Accounting

What are the necessary ingredients for multisector accounting? Obviously, we must have economic sectors as subjects capable of engaging in economic activities. In addition to economic sectors, we must have economic resources toward which the sectors' economic activities are directed. We shall drop the adjective "economic" for the simpler "sectors," "resources," and "activities" in the interest of brevity. These three represent key concepts for our accounting structure.

Sectors are capable of controlling resources. This control capability may come from legal ownership, organizational authority given to the sector, geographical location of resources, and so on. In any event, sector activities are aimed at changing the resources under their control. The need for identifying which resource is under the control of each sector at a given point in time is, therefore, essential to multisector accounting.

While this is a straightforward extension of the axiom of control from unisector accounting to multisector accounting, the latter presents an additional problem that must be resolved,

---

[3]See the definition and the set of axioms in Kohler (1952), which seems to have been the first attempt to axiomatize accounting in the published literature.

[4]The three judgments are shown to be also sufficient for conventional accounting measurement based on the historical-cost principle, except for situations where market values are used as a supplemental means of measurement.

the problem of double counting upon consolidation of sectors if a resource is allowed to be put under the control of more than one sector. For example, joint ownership by subsidiaries, overlapping divisional authorities and responsibilities, or activities of a governmental agency ranging over the enterprise sector and the government sector are not uncommon. However, they are usually resolved in practice by some natural or artificial partitions of the resource in question. The axiom of control must, therefore, be strengthened by the requirement that no resources can be considered under the control of more than one sector simultaneously. (A formal statement of the revised three axioms will be provided shortly.)

The axiom of quantities states the need to classify resources in such a way that a quantity measure can be defined for each class of resources, such as barrels (for crude oil), bushels (for wheat), dollars (for money). The quantity measure must satisfy the following two conditions: additivity and indifference. The additivity condition requires that the quantity of a whole must be equal to the sum of the quantities of its parts. The indifference condition requires that for the purpose of economic activities, people are indifferent to the choice among sets of resources in a given class if and only if their quantities are the same. The indifference condition assures that resources in a given class are all homogeneous. Clearly, the axiom of quantities is not influenced by introduction of multiple sectors. We shall, therefore, use the one prepared for unisector accounting.

With the axioms of control and quantities, the set of each class r of resources

controlled by each sector s at a given point of time t can be presented by a matrix B^t of physical measures b_{sr}^t (b for balance) as in

$$B^t = \begin{bmatrix} b_{11}^t & b_{12}^t & \cdots & b_{1n}^t \\ b_{21}^t & b_{22}^t & \cdots & b_{2n}^t \\ \cdots\cdots\cdots\cdots\cdots\cdots\cdots \\ b_{m1}^t & l_{m2}^t & \cdots & b_{mn}^t \end{bmatrix} \quad (7)$$

where rows represent sectors and columns the types of resources. Note that the elements in B^t are commensurable columnwise, since they are measured by the same quantity measure, but not rowwise, since they are in different units.

We next consider changes in the matrix B over time. Changes in sector resources are not all independent. Some resource changes can be grouped together because they form an integral part of the consequence originated by an activity. For example, a sector gives up a resource with a definite intent to obtain another resource in exchange. This cause-and-effect relationship between resources foregone and resources obtained is essential in making accounting data more useful than data that merely express isolated changes in resources under the sector's control.

While an integrity of resource changes does not always take place in the form of an exchange, the concept of exchanges is so fundamental to accounting that we shall use the term to cover not only exchanges in the market but also transformations that resources go through in a production process as well as degenerate exchanges in which either resources obtained or resources foregone are missing. In this way, all changes in the sector-resource matrix are explained by a set of exchanges (market or non-market, complete or degenerate).

It may sound awkward to call it an exchange when resources are given away without any return, as in the case of contributions or transfer payments. But whether an act is an exchange or a non-reciprocal transfer is often difficult to determine, particularly when long-run potential benefits are taken into account. Broadening the concept of exchanges to cover nonreciprocal transfers, gains, or losses is, therefore, not without justification.

The axiom of exchanges for unisector accounting expresses the need for determining which resources of a sector were given up to obtain which other resources for the sector. It does not express the need to identify which sector, if any, was at the opposing end of the exchange. The axiom of exchanges must therefore be enriched to cover this point for multisector accounting.

Three axioms for multisector accounting will now be formally stated.

1. *Axiom of control.* For any sector, the set of all resources under its control at a given point of time can be uniquely identified at that point or later. In addition, no two sectors can control a given resource simultaneously.
2. *Axiom of quantities.* All resources under the control of any sector presently or in the past can be uniquely partitioned into a set of classes. Associated with each class is a unique quantity measure, satisfying the additivity and indifference conditions.
3. *Axiom of exchanges.* Changes in resources under any sector's control can be uniquely

partitioned into a set of exchanges, each of which identifies the resources exchanged and the sectors involved.

Earlier we introduced economic sectors, economic resources, and economic activities as three key concepts in multisector accounting. We now see a correspondence between these concepts and the three axioms above, since the latter deals with classifications of resources or their changes along the dimensions of sectors (the control axiom), resources (the quantities axiom), and activities (the exchange axiom).

It was stated earlier that the first two axioms together enable us to grasp the economic status of sectors at time t by means of an $m \times n$ matrix B with the sector and the resource dimensions as given in (7). Here, the superscript t indicates that the balance data are as of time t.

We now consider changes in the elements of B^t as t changes. We consider such changes to occur at a discrete point in time. In addition, we want to group changes in the elements of B^t that are mutually related as defined in the axiom of exchanges.

To be more precise, let us define "period t" to mean a time period that starts immediately after $t - 1$ and ends with t. We also define A^t as $B^t - B^{t-1}$, which represents a matrix of activities in period t (A for activities) that collectively caused the change from B^{t-1} to B^t.

Then, the axiom of exchanges implies that A^t may be decomposed into A_1^t, A_2^t, . . . , A_ℓ^t, in such a way that each activity matrix A_k^t ($k = 1, 2, . . , \ell$) represents changes in the resources under the control of the respective sector (an increase is positive and a decrease negative) that are united by the activity as determined by the axiom of exchanges.

Thus, we have

$$B^t - B^{t-1} \equiv A^t = A_1^t + A_2^t + \cdots + A_\ell^t \quad (8)$$

In this way, changes in the economic status of sectors from time $t - 1$ to time t are represented by means of $m \times n \times \ell$ arrays of physical quantities $[A_1^t, A_2^t, \ldots, A_\ell^t]$, where each A is a matrix with the sector and the resource dimensions and A's are arranged along the activity dimension.

Before we move to examination of national accounting from the viewpoint of these axioms, there is one additional concept that must be introduced—the concept of negative control, which is essential in describing liabilities of a sector.

There are three ways of introducing the negative notion into the relationship between a sector and a resource (see Ijiri, 1975). One is to classify resources into those with positive utility and those with negative utility such as garbage and pollutants. The second is to classify the mode of control into positive and negative so that resources can belong to a sector either positively or negatively.

Neither of these two methods is satisfactory in describing liabilities, as we see in corporate and national accounting. The object of liabilities (money in many cases) certainly has positive utility; hence, the first method is inappropriate. The second requires a complete change in the set-theoretic notions that underlie the axiomatic structure since set theory is built upon the simple notion of an element belonging to a set or not belonging to a set. Although it is possible to

devise a new concept, say, bisets (see Ijiri, 1967), to which elements can belong positively or negatively and define operations on bisets such as unions, intersections, and power sets, we have a much simpler and conceptually more appealing method of dealing with liabilities. This will be described below as a third method.

We follow the conventional concept of sets—an element either belongs to or does not belong to a set. However, we introduce the time dimension and recognize the fact that the contents of a set may change over time while the identity of the set remains the same. (This is a departure from ordinary set theory, in which a set is identified solely by its elements.) Then, if certain conditions are met, we allow, as a part of resources controlled by a sector, (1) resources that the sector expects to receive in the future (called future positive resources) and (2) resources that the sector expects to forgo in the future (called future negative resources), in addition to resources that are presently under the sector's control (called present resources). Thus, the negativity notion is introduced not in the static aspect of sets but in its dynamic aspect of changes over time. Therefore, present resources can only belong to a sector positively, while future resources can belong to a sector (1) positively when they are expected to be brought under its control or (2) negatively when they are expected to be released from its control.

The conditions for recognizing future resources, called recognition criteria, can be stated in a variety of ways. Resources involved in all exchanges that are forecast to occur during a given period in the future may be recognized if forecasted (or pro forma) statements are desired. Recognition may be limited to only those resources involved in exchanges that have been committed by the sector by means of a contract, a legal requirement, or a pledge by the sector. Recognition may further be limited, as in the case of present corporate accounting, to those resources in an exchange which has been partially performed.

Whatever the recognition criteria may be, we can now go back to the axiom of control and interpret the term "control" to mean in its extended form to include (positive or negative) control over future resources under the recognition criteria.

Similarly, we can also go back to the axiom of quantities and extend the notion of resources to include resources to be delivered or received at a certain point of time in the future, which will generally form a class separate from the same resources available at present time. It is then possible to adopt a convention that a sector's obligation to deliver such resources is represented by the negative of the quantity of resources involved, while a sector's right to receive them is represented by a positive quantity. Elements in the B matrices can thus be positive, zero, or negative.

Finally, we can interpret the term "resources" in the axiom of exchanges in an extended way to include future positive and negative resources. The meaning of elements in the A matrices can now be extended so that a positive entry means a present receipt, an expected receipt, or a cancellation of an expected delivery of resources, while a negative entry means a present delivery, an expected delivery, or a cancellation of an expected receipt.

It is important to incorporate this form of negative control into the most atomistic part of the axiomatic structure, since we can then deal freely with rights to receive and obligations to deliver resources in the future without first converting them artifically into equivalent monetary rights and obligations. A right to receive 1 million bushels of wheat a year from now is not the same thing as a right to receive $4 million in cash a year from now even if the present price of wheat is $4 a bushel, because of differences in the risk of future price fluctuations. Yet in corporate accounting as well as national accounting, such a conversion into monetary rights and obligations is built into the very heart of the system.

Of course, in order to limit the size of the sector-resource matrices to a reasonable level, resources in a given class may have to be aggregated considerably by means of a convenient quantity measure, such as units of standard resources in the resource class. A monetary measure is often used for such aggregation purposes. However, the resulting expression is clearly quite different from monetary rights and obligations, even if they are all stated in monetary units.

In fact, it should be noticed that the distinction between monetary and nonmonetary resources has not been introduced in the three axioms. This is because the axioms provide a structure upon which any valuation system can be built to suit particular information needs. Although monetary valuation is the most common form, valuation may be made in terms of a specific nonmonetary class of resources or in terms of a bundle of nonmonetary classes of resources.

Analysis of Activity Matrices

Let us next analyze one of the activity matrices A to see how they may be related to transactions in national accounting. In order to simplify notation, let us suppress the subscript k and the superscript t and simply express A_k^t by A. In general, A is an $m \times n$ matrix of a_{ij}, as in

$$A = \begin{bmatrix} a_{11} & a_{12} & \cdots & a_{1n} \\ a_{21} & a_{22} & \cdots & a_{2n} \\ \cdots\cdots\cdots\cdots\cdots\cdots \\ a_{m1} & a_{m2} & \cdots & a_{mn} \end{bmatrix} \quad (9)$$

where rows are sectors and columns are classes of resources. The a_{ij}'s in each column are all expressed in the units of measure defined for each column j.

We may consider five types of entries as the basic form of activities from which various combinations can arise. The first case, trading, involves two resource classes and two sectors. Suppose that sector 1 receives q_1 tons of resource 1 from sector 2 in exchange for q_2 bushels of resource 2 that are delivered to sector 2 from sector 1. Then, the northwest corner of A shows

$$\begin{bmatrix} +q_1 & -q_2 \\ -q_1 & +q_2 \end{bmatrix}$$

with zero in its remaining cells.

The second type is production activities, which are represented by an intrasector conversion of resources from one class to another. For example, sector 1 may obtain q_1 tons of flour as a result of consuming q_2 bushels of wheat in a production process. Then, the activity matrix A shows $[+q_1, -q_2]$ at its northwest corner and zeros in its remaining cells. While it is possible to establish a dummy sector representing "nature" and then treat the production activity above

as "trading with the nature," it is more convenient to allow an activity that is strictly internal to the sector and we shall follow this approach to handling production activities.

Transfers between sectors are characterized by an activity matrix that has nonzero elements only in a single column that sums to zero. For example, sector 2 transfers q_1 tons of flour to sector 1. In this case, A has

$$\begin{bmatrix} +q_1 \\ -q_1 \end{bmatrix}$$

and zeros in its remaining cells.

Final consumption (or simply consumption, unless otherwise noted) is represented by an activity matrix that has one negative element and no positive elements.

Activities that are diametrically opposite to consumption are what may be termed "generation," which means an increase in resources without any sacrifices (i.e., without decreases in other resources). Windfalls, natural products, discovery of mineral resources, and so on, are examples of generation when they are not accompanied by sacrifices. These types of "activities" are obviously characterized by an activity matrix A that has one positive element and no negative elements.

An activity matrix may thus be categorized by:

1. Trading: $\begin{bmatrix} +q_1 & -q_2 \\ -q_1 & +q_2 \end{bmatrix}$

2. Production: $[+q_1, -q_2]$

3. Transfers:
$$\begin{bmatrix} +q_1 \\ -q_1 \end{bmatrix}$$

4. Consumption:
$$[-q_1]$$

5. Generation:
$$[+q_1]$$

Actual activity matrices may, however, be much more complicated, consisting of a mixture of many such atomistic forms.

While these five steps of activities can be represented by the corresponding form of the activity matrix in (1)–(5), the converse need not be true. For example, not all activity matrices of the form $[+q_1, -q_2]$ with zeros in the remaining cells mean production, since it may represent a trading with a sector not included in the basic formulation of the sector-resource matrices. However, the correspondence can be made reasonably close to one-to-one, if, as in the case of national accounting, the rest of the world is included as a sector.[5] Then, any trading is represented by a matrix of the form

$$\begin{bmatrix} +q_1 & -q_2 \\ -q_1 & +q_2 \end{bmatrix}$$

while any production activities are represented by a matrix of the form $[+q_1, -q_2]$.[6] The same applies to the remaining three types of activities.

National Income Accounts

Let us now apply the preceding concept of activity matrices to an example of flows among national accounts. In 1968, the United Nations Statistical Office published a monograph called *A System of National Accounts,* suggesting a new, more detailed form of national accounts structure. In this publication, the matrix approach to national accounts is used extensively. In the most disaggregated form, an 88 × 88 matrix is presented. However, the principles involved are the same whether the matrix is aggregated or not. Therefore, for our illustration we shall use the matrix that is most highly aggregated from the 88 × 88 matrix. Such a matrix is given by a 4 × 4 matrix (see United Nations, 1968, p. 7), consisting of four sectors named "production," "consumption," "accumulation," and "the rest of the world."[7]

The 4 × 4 matrix is given in Table 13–1. Each element in this 4 × 4 matrix is an aggregation of elements in the most disaggregated 88 × 88 matrix.

Before we attempt to apply our activity matrix approach, we must first understand the meaning of the ten numbers in the matrix in Table 13–1. The matrix is prepared under the following convention. Each row represents credit entries to the sector, indicating receipts (of money or other financial claims) by the sector. Each column represents debit

---

[5] Sectors that are included in the sector-resource matrix can be divided into internal sectors and external sectors. External sectors can be grouped in one as in the case of the rest-of-the-world sector in national accounting or may be disaggregated into several sectors, representing different countries, for example.

[6] Of course, these signs may be reversed when the exchange or production activities are in the reverse direction.

[7] This matrix is presented as a submatrix of a 7 × 7 matrix which includes, in addition to the four accounts above, three additional accounts called "opening assets," "revaluations," and "closing assets." However, since the data in the 4 × 4 submatrix are sufficient to illustrate our approach, the rest is omitted.

TABLE 13-1

National Account Matrix

		Dr.		
	P	C	A	R
P: Production		210	47	52
C: Consumption	255		–19	5
A: Accumulation		27		
R: Rest of the World	54	4	–1	

Cr. (label at left of rows)

entries to the sector, indicating disbursements by the sector.

The first row shows money (or other financial claims) received by the Production Sector from the Consumption Sector (210 units), from the Accumulation Sector (47 units), and from the Rest-of-the-World Sector (52 units). Interpreting these figures in terms of the corresponding flows of goods, they may be stated as sales of consumption goods (210 units), sales of capital goods (47 units), and exports (52 units). The first column shows disbursements by the Production Sector to the Consumption Sector (255 units) and to the Rest-of-the-World Sector (54 units). They show corresponding flows of factor services from households (255 units) and factor services imported (54 units).

The second row shows income to the Consumption Sector. Out of 255 units received from the Production Sector, 19 units must be deducted for depreciation, leaving 236 units as domestic income. In addition, 5 units are earned abroad. Out of the total income of 241 units, 210 units are used for purchases of consumption goods and 4 units are given to the Rest-of-the-World Sector as transfers, leaving 27 units as savings.

The Accumulation Sector takes this savings as input and disburses 28 units

(net) on capital goods, which is 47 units in gross less depreciation of 19 units. In addition, there is a disinvestment of 1 unit by the nation in its account with the Rest-of-the-World Sector. Thus, net investment of 27 units matches with savings of 27 units.

The Rest-of-the-World Sector received 54 units from the Production Sector in return for goods imported to the nation and 4 units from the Consumption Sector given to the Rest-of-the-World Sector as transfers. The Rest-of-the-World Sector spent 52 units for goods exported by the nation and 5 units for income accruing to the residents of the nation. In net, the Rest-of-the-World Sector increased its claim on the nation by 1 unit, which is shown as a negative investment by the nation to the Rest-of-the-World sector.

Let us now consider how the picture of national account flows may be made complete by introducing resource classifications explicitly into the picture in addition to the sector classifications upon which Table 13-1 was prepared. In order to simplify the example, resources will be classified into only three classes: factor services (FS), finished goods (FG), and financial claims (FC). More detailed classifications may be introduced as needed.

TABLE 13-2

Sector-Resource Matrix

	FS *Factor Services*	FG *Finished Goods*	FC *Financial Claims*
P: Production			
C: Consumption			
A: Accumulation			
R: Rest of the World			

We then have a 4 × 3 matrix of sectors and resources as shown in Table 13-2: This matrix corresponds to the *B* and *A* matrices in (7) and (9) in terms of the row and column dimensions. However, for ease of presentation, we shall splice the matrix in Table 13-2 rowwise and adjoin each piece one after another in a long row. We then obtain headings as shown in Table 13-3. Activities are now expressed in rows and sector-resources in columns.

The first row of Table 13-3 indicates purchases of factor services. A slight modification is made for an easier presentation—that is, factor services purchased from the Consumption Sector are reduced by the amount of depreciation that is stated as factor services purchased from the Accumulation Sector. Generation of factor services (row 6) and consumption of finished goods (row 7) are estimates plugged in to balance the figures, since data on net changes in the stock of factor services and finished goods are not available except for capital goods. Production (row 2) is shown as a process of converting factor services into finished goods, while depreciation (row 8) is recognized as a reverse process. Saving and investment (row 9) is shown as a residual, although they can

certainly be presented in the same way as all other activities so that each column sums to zero.

Note that each of the three types of resources may be measured in different units: for example, factor services in manhours, finished goods in dollars of a base year, and financial claims in current dollars. We may, therefore, have an entry like (6), where one side of the double entry is in bushels of wheat and the other side is in dollars, if wheat is selected as a class of resources and bushels are chosen as a measuring unit.

Also note that even when entry is stated in dollars, each row does not necessarily balance for each sector, as shown in entries for generation (row 6) and consumption (row 7). A balancing column can be provided for the sake of completing the double-entry convention, but this is not essential from the standpoint of obtaining key data on national account flows.

Finally, note how easy it is to understand flows among national accounts if physical and financial flows are presented together. A table such as Table 13-3 is far easier to understand than the matrix in Table 13-1, which shows only an amount for each pair of sectors and conceals, by prior adjustment, a great

TABLE 13-3
Activity Matrix

	Production			Consumption			Accumulation			Rest of the World		
	FS	FG	FC	FS	FG	FC	FS	FG	FC	FS	FG	FC
1. Purchases of factor services	309		-309	-236		236	-19		19	-54		54
2. Production	-309	309										
3. Sales of finished goods		-309	309		210	-210		47	-47		52	-52
4. Income from abroad				-5		5				5		-5
5. Transfers to abroad						-4						4
6. Generation				241						49		
7. Consumption					-210		19	-19			-52	
8. Depreciation								28	-28			
9. Saving–investment	—	—	—	—	—	27	19	—	—	—	—	1
	═	═	═	═	═	═	═	═	═	═	═	═

deal of information that may be important to understanding these results. Even more serious, in fact, is that a matrix of sectors such as the one in Table 13–1 is not capable of presenting even an outline of activities giving rise to the indicated financial effect. In this sense, the format used in Table 13–3 is the basic one that should be adopted instead of the one in Table 13–1, which is heavily utilized in United Nations (1968).

Comparison with Other Approaches

In order to highlight the advantages of the preceding approach using activity matrices, let us compare it with other approaches that have been used or suggested in national accounting.

Most books on national accounting treat transactions only as flows of financial claims, neglecting corresponding flows of physical resources. For example, Stuvel (1965) states "it should be realized that what gets recorded in the national accounts, say in the case of a commodity transaction, is the flow of the instantaneous claim of the seller on the purchaser, which moves from the latter to the former, and not the flow of the commodity, which moves in the opposite direction" (p. 12). One of the reasons for this one-sided emphasis on financial flows is heterogeneity of physical resources and the difficulties involved in measuring them in anything other than financial terms.

However, ease or difficulty in measuring flows should not dictate the way in which national account flows are conceptually structured. A flow of wheat that is worth $3 million is not the same thing as a flow of $3 million cash, as emphasized before. By regarding a flow of 1 million bushels of wheat as a $3 million flow, we are biasing our view away from physical flows and toward financial flows that move in the opposite direction. An axiomatic approach like the one discussed in this chapter allows us to avoid such a bias and makes it easy to identify what is essential and what is peripheral.

This present chapter, however, is not the first article that has emphasized the importance of physical flows in national accounting. A 1949 article by Odd Aukrust emphasized physical flows in national accounting nearly 30 years ago. Since then Aukrust has also written an axiomatic approach to national accounting in his doctoral dissertation in Norwegian (Aukrust, 1955), an outline of which was published in English (Aukrust, 1966).

Aukrust's approach, however, fell short of completely eliminating the traditional bias toward financial flows, mainly because (1) he did not recognize the significance of physical quantities, and (2) he did not recognize that a sector can be short on physical resources. As a result, he had to compromise considerably with the traditional view favoring financial flows when he stated his "20 axioms of national accounting."

Let us examine the significance of quantities and why an axiomatic structure without quantities cannot stand alone. Clearly, without quantities it becomes meaningless to talk about prices. Furthermore, without quantities it becomes impossible to carry out trades in modern markets. An order cannot be issued without stating product specifications and a quantity in a modern market—unless the order deals with a specifically identifiable object such as an antique.

Owing to his lack of recognition of quantities, Aukrust had to move from economic objects directly to "values," thus missing an opportunity to base his structure upon quantities that are far more objective measures than values. This necessitated, as in the traditional approach to national accounting, the postulate of "the preservation of values in exchange," which he had to put in as the twentieth and last postulate of his axiomatic system.

As we pointed out already, this last axiom of Aukrust's is unnecessary in our approach and is actually undesirable since it hides from view the reality of a trading between, say, 1 million bushels of wheat and $4 million of cash. Whether the wheat traded is "worth" $4 million or not depends upon many factors ("worth" to whom, when, or in what country), as well as the basic frame of reference for valuation.[8] It is all right to put a price tag of $4 million on the wheat insofar as we recognize it as a price tag. An illusion that somehow the price tag determines the value is, however, what we should definitely avoid.

Another critical difference between Aukrust's system and ours lies in his overly heavy reliance upon financial objects (as against physical objects or "real objects," in his term) as a basis of the system. A barter of two physical objects is ruled out; a transfer of physical objects is similarly ruled out. Financial objects appear at least on one side of each exchange, and only they can appear in transfers.[9] Rights to receive and obliga-tions to deliver physical objects are not recognized in his system. Only financial objects can be objects of such rights and obligations.

As stated in the second section of this chapter, any resources can be objects of rights and obligations in our system. But in order to develop such a system, the concept of control over future resources had to be laid out so that it could be applied to any resources. Moreover, a quantity measure had to be established before such an attempt was made, because exchanges involving future resources cannot occur without quantity measures. In addition, recognition criteria had to be introduced to limit the extent to which future resources are recognized.

While such a development may appear to be a purely conceptual exercise, it also has significant implications for practice. In corporate accounting, for example, rights to receive or obligations to deliver nonmonetary resources are generally not reported unless money has already been paid or received for the resources. Even in the case where money has been paid or received, it is reported as advance receipts or payments, not as rights to receive or obligations to deliver nonmonetary resources. An axiomatic study of corporate accounting indicated, however, that there is no reason for not recognizing nonmonetary resources to be received or delivered in the future when they meet the same conditions as those required for recognition of future monetary resources. This led to a pro-

---

[8]The trading may contain an element of subsidies. The duties differ from country to country. Transportation costs must be considered. And so on.

[9]See Postulates XVI and XVII in Aukrust (1966, p. 184).

posal for a full-scale application of commitment accounting in which recording of transactions start at the time a commitment is made by means of some legal actions instead of, as in accrual accounting, waiting until a transaction actually occurs (see Ijiri, 1975, Chap. 8).

Similarly, the axiomatic structure above leads us to believe that there are no conceptual reasons why financial objects and their flows must be treated differently from physical objects and their flows in national accounting. Once we ascertain where the foundations of national accounting lie, we can then proceed toward solving difficulties in measurement and other practical issues in the light of such foundations.

Conclusions

In this chapter, we started by expressing our belief that corporate accounting and national accounting must derive from the same foundations. We found, in fact, that we could state three axioms of multisector accounting that can be applied to both corporate accounting and national accounting. We believe that corporate accounting can learn from national accounting, and vice versa, by first reaching down to the foundations that are common to both of them. This paper was written with the aim of improving interactions between these two branches of accounting, which have had rather separate development so far.

References

Aukrust, Odd. 1949. "On the Theory of Social Accounting." *Review of Economic Studies*, 16(41).

——. 1955. *Nasjonalregnskap: Teoretiske prinsipper* (National Accounts: Theoretical Principles). Samfunnsøkonomiske Studier No. 4. Oslo, Norway.

——. 1966. "An Axiomatic Approach to National Accounting: An Outline." *Review of Income and Wealth*, 12, September.

Ijiri, Yuji. 1965. "Axioms and Structures of Conventional Accounting Measurement." *The Accounting Review*, January.

——. 1967. *The Foundations of Accounting Measurement*. Englewood Cliffs, N.J.: Prentice-Hall, Inc.

——. 1975. *Theory of Accounting Measurement*. Sarasota, Fla.: American Accounting Association.

Kohler, Eric L. 1952. *A Dictionary for Accountants*. New York: Prentice-Hall, Inc.

Mattessich, Richard. 1964. *Accounting and Analytical Methods*. Homewood, Ill.: Richard D. Irwin, Inc.

Stuvel, G. 1965. *System of Social Accounts*. Oxford: Clarendon Press.

United Nations. 1968. *A System of National Accounts* (Series F, no. 2, Rev. 3). New York: United Nations.

Chapter 14

Auditing and Accounting—
Past, Present, and Future

Neil C. Churchill and William W. Cooper

"Auditing is preventive accounting. It is also preventive management. It examines past events with an unjaundiced eye, measuring them against both conventional and prescribed standards of performance, but always with a critical overlook at the standards themselves. It prosecutes its aims not by command, not by persuasion but by reports that reveal, appraise, and recommend. It has become a powerful instrument for molding as well as testing and correcting management policies. Its opinions, when disclosed, following its explorations, are value judgments heavily weighted with the public interest" (Kohler, 1965, p. 226).

Introduction

Auditing has had a long and close association with accounting. Indeed, in the days of Pacioli, an audit was a "call and check procedure"—an *auditus* or hearing—to determine the correctness of account balances before their transfer from one ledger to another. As account-

ing developed to serve larger and more complex organizations, so did auditing. Together, the two evolved, with auditing becoming a check on both the accounting procedures and practices utilized and on the general "quality" of the results of the accounting process, the financial statements and reports. Continuing with this evolution, auditing became, internally, an essential part of the system of internal accounting control and externally, a major factor for assuring the financial accountability of the management of business enterprises and the fiscal accountability of government officials.

In the past few years, the public has begun to expand its demands for accountability from both business and government. This concern for accountability has extended to managerial conduct in other than the customary financial dimensions. In addition to a proper accounting for expenditures and receipts and the custody of assets, the dimensions of accountability have begun to extend to the effectiveness, efficiency, and propriety of managerial actions and their consequences—social as well as economic.

Not surprisingly, this increase in accountability is being accompanied by extensions in the scope and character of auditing. Within some corporations, the internal audit function has expanded to deal with operational and managerial audits that go considerably beyond accounting in the narrow sense of the word. Within the federal government—especially at the U.S. General Accounting Office (see the chapters by Brasfield, Pois, and Cooper and Frese)—audits have moved from examinations of primarily fiduciary concern to audits whose purpose is to evaluate the propriety, efficiency, and effectiveness of managerial actions. There is now considerable pressure for this broader, more comprehensive, type of audit to move into state and local governments, to nonprofit organizations, and into governmental organizations and activities in other parts of the world (Independent Review Committee, 1975, App. II) and into the private profit-oriented sector as well.

This change in orientation from financial to managerial performance involves a broadening in the *scope* of the audit, first in the subject matter or the actions under audit, and second in the purpose of the audit (a move away from an evaluation of compliance to an evaluation of the effectiveness and efficiency with which management does its job), and a reorientation of the audit report toward those groups to whom an accountability is due.

These broadened concepts of accountability will be discussed in later parts of this chapter, where some of their consequences and possible limitations will be examined. First, however, we shall examine the nature and concepts of auditing as presently practiced, at least in the United States. Then we shall turn to some aspects of the evolutionary process toward the expanded accountability that was noted in our opening paragraphs. Following this discussion, we shall then return to the significance of this evolution and some of the problems that are likely to be encountered in expanding the audit function beyond its customary financial and economic disclosure dimensions.

Nature and Concepts of Auditing

At its most basic level, an audit is an examination of actions (or evidence of actions), a comparison of these actions against a set of criteria, and a report to a third party of the correspondence between the actions and the criteria.

First, we might review this third-party orientation by considering the possibility of "an audit" by one person of the actions of another with no intent to report to anyone else. Such an examination, while useful, is *not* an audit in the sense that we are using the term here. If a supervisor, for example, is examining the conduct of some of his subordinates, we may regard this as a supervisory review. Such an examination may also occur in other ways. It might occur, for instance, in the course of a consulting engagement during which the actions of an examinee are reviewed in the course of seeing how improvements might be effected, but with no intent to disclose the findings to anyone other than the examinee. As long as the results of the examination are not intended primarily for third-party disclosure, the examination is not, in our view, an audit. What separates an audit from other examinations and reviews is a report of the findings to one or more third parties.

This third-party orientation for an audit quite naturally influences the choice of audit criteria and hence the scope and character of the audit examination. This is true whether an audit is of the internal variety or whether it involves a report to public constituencies which are far removed from involvement with internal management and direction. Third-party considerations also enter into the kind of report that is rendered and the way it is indited and distributed.

Consider, for instance, the highly structured financial statements that emerge from the annual financial audits by CPAs. Here the affairs of business and the common language of commerce and finance have been structured into a compressed report in the form of an operating statement and balance sheet by which management accounts to its creditors and stockholders. Couched in a standardized terminology that is widely understood by those concerned with economic aspects of private enterprise affairs, these statements are accompanied by a statement of opinion, or attestation, by the independent auditors, which, in itself, is intended to convey information to these "informed" persons concerning (1) the scope of the audit in terms of what was examined,

and (2) the resulting findings. The auditor's report expresses the correspondence, or lack thereof, between (1) the standard *audit criteria* with the scope of a particular audit, and (2) the standard *accounting criteria* with the financial statements and the accounting systems that produced them.

In many cases the financial-statement attestation is accompanied by a "management letter," a report directed to company management. These letters frequently contain recommendations for the improvement of company operations and summarize findings on management practices that may not be immediately pertinent to the financial-statement attest function but which the auditors believe warrant management attention. Although these findings on management practice and recommendations for their correction are a result of the audit process, and perhaps even a justification for it, recommendations are not central to an audit,[1] and the management findings, while disclosed to third parties internally, fail the test of outside, third-party accountability—the purpose of the annual financial audit—and hence also are not an essential part of the annual audit. Their existence, however, indicates a potential dimension of additional capability for auditing which is pertinent to the evaluation of the audit function. Before examining these extensions, it is well to consider more carefully the referent of third-party accountability as a part of the major feature of auditing which distinguishes it from other examinations.

---

[1] Many audit reports in governments and corporations include recommendations by the auditor for corrective action to increase the correspondence between the actions taken and the audit criteria used. Yet, it is the state of this correspondence that comprises the audit report, not the statements of how to improve them.

The Third-Party Recipient of an Audit Report

The effectiveness of an audit is closely related to reactions of recipients of the audit report. If the recipients have both authority, or influence on those with authority and an inclination to take corrective action, then an audit, through its report, is likely to produce results.[2] If, however, the report goes to a third party who has authority but who associates his or her own interest closely with, and in the same direction as those of the auditee, then little action can be expected to be taken. Indeed, it is as though the auditee were the sole recipient of the audit report.

Thus, generally speaking, to have an effective audit the report must go to a third party

1. Who is in an authoritative relationship to the auditee even if not a direct one.
2. Who will have the motivation to take action on the merits of the audit report and not on an identification with the best interest of the auditee.

The latter may be called "third-party objectivity." The need for associating the audit function with third-party objectivity has long been recognized in audit practice by reference to careful attention to the audit report and the way it is distributed. In the public sector, the audit report is normally distributed beyond the agency or organization audited. The report is often made public.

Where audit reports are distributed only within an agency, less inclination to act may be expected than when they are public.

In private corporations, this need for third-party objectivity is exemplified by the tendency for audit committees of outside directors to be formed and for the internal audit reports to go to this committee. The latter (i.e., the audit committee) can be viewed as an organizational and even a social response to increasing concerns as to whether management and even the board of directors represents an objective third-party recipient of audit reports. Even a committee of outside directors, however, has a weakness, in that the directors are usually appointed by management and thus cannot always be sufficiently objective to monitor the corporation's activities. Thus, some have argued that directors should be appointed by the public in some fashion to oversee corporate management's behavior. The latter thus represents a social concern that does not stem only from a desire to hold corporate management more closely accountable for its economic performance. It also stems from a desire to hold management more accountable for its social performance—for the socially relevant consequences of its economic activities—a subject we shall discuss later.

Directions of Auditing Today

In both governmental and internal audits of the financial accounting pro-

---

[2] Of course, if the auditee knows that the report will reach someone with the authority to take action and if the report contains issues that will likely produce an inclination to act, then the auditee may take the report and/or the auditor seriously, and worry not only about the consequences of this audit report but also about what the next audit will uncover. This anticipation of an audit is a powerful tool of managerial control. It can cause an auditee's behavior to be in conformance with what is desired or specified in the auditor's criteria and perhaps even more, besides. To this extent, an audit can produce the effect of guiding behavior along lines that conform to an organization's policies, plans, and procedures.

cess, the attest function, as exemplified in the annual financial audits by independent CPAs, is being replaced in some cases by reports prepared by auditors and commented upon by management. This reflects something more than changes in the nature of the report. It also involves changes in the nature of the audit examination and the client-auditor relationship. Concomitantly, the scope of the audit as well as the criteria and conduct of the audit examination has broadened from financial to operational and even to managerial performance and/or concerns with the direction and performance of entire programs. With this extension of audit activity has come a corresponding extension of the audit report to include even management responses to audit findings in the same report.

As the scope of internal audits expands to encompass managerial activities at ever higher levels, a question arises as to whom the results should be directed. There seems to be a tendency at present for such expanded-scope audit reports to go to the board of director audit committees, as do the management letters of "outside" CPAs. The convergence of these broadened internal reports and the management letter of the outside CPAs toward a report to committees of outside directors suggests that the next step may be a report to the public which, albeit abbreviated, is nevertheless of the same genre we have just been discussing.

Some idea of what is involved with such an extension of accountability can be seen in the activities of the U.S. General Accounting Office. As now constituted, this agency reports directly to

Congress and is not subordinate to any executive agency authority. In this capacity it is responsive to congressional mandate and direction and, indeed, is legally obliged to respond to the directions and requests of congressional committees and their chairman. It also carries out audits on its own initiative, however, and is fully responsible for the scope of these audits as well as the reports flowing from them—reviewed first with the auditees and then with responses from those audited, distributed to the auditees, their superiors, the Congress, and the *public*.

As these audits developed, GAO expanded its scope to include examinations not only of financial and appropriation accounting but of virtually *all* aspects of management. This includes audit and evaluation of propriety, effectiveness, and efficiency of management, where:

1. Propriety refers to choices of management methods as well as objectives.
2. Effectiveness refers to management's ability to (a) state and (b) attain its objectives.
3. Efficiency refers to the quantity and character of economic resources utilized and the returns secured thereon by agency and/or program activities.

Audits pointed toward these purposes range from the customary CPA attestation of financial statements through audits of compliance to organizational procedures up to the grander reaches of program and even multiple-program audits of efficiency, effectiveness, and propriety.[3]

As we previously observed, many internal audits and the management letter accompanying the CPA-attest-

---

[3] Compare Herbert (1979) for detailed developments and descriptions of these terms.

type audits already suggests the presence of at least some of the requisite capabilities for conducting audits along these "more comprehensive" lines in other governments units (e.g., in local governments) and possibly in private-sector activities in addition. As evidence of a possible need and opportunity for expansion along these lines, we quote from a recent "exposure draft" (AICPA, 1976) pertinent to CPA undertakings:

The additional audit objectives designated by the GAO may pose extensive challenges for the practitioner who chooses to conduct expanded governmental audits. He will be called upon to use not only his financial auditing and accounting skills, but a variety of management advisory services skills as well. He will, in fact, be conducting audits which will require judgements based on expertise which may not be available within his staff and which are normally associated with other professional disciplines, such as engineering, medicine, social sciences, and public administration. The CPA undertaking such engagements, therefore, should be aware of the potential problems associated with these additional requirements and should understand how existing AICPA standards apply to expanded scope audits.

With some $80 billion per year and more in federal grants in aid, and other subventions, already going from the federal government to some 35,000 local government units, there is a growing need for CPAs to expand their auditing activities for auditing state and local governmental units. Thus, as a recent report observes, "CPAs will . . . be engaged to perform audits *in accordance with GAO standards* [italics in the original]" (AICPA, 1976, p. 2). We would

argue that this must, on the one hand, increase auditor experience and augment his capability for conducting comprehensive audits, and, on the other hand, it must increase public awareness of this capability. This increased competence and increased public awareness will, we believe, sharpen the sense of a need for some such service in the private sector, too, particularly since the same type of audits are being conducted within private corporations. Indeed, a number of companies have already moved their audit activities from fiduciary audits, and assistance to outside CPAs, to a point where operational and management audits of the kind we have been discussing in the public sector occupy the major portions of their internal auditing activities (see Churchill et al., 1978).

In concluding this section, it should be noted that other organizations besides CPAs are beginning to respond to the needs for an expanded audit function. Firms with a background in management consulting such as Arthur D. Little, Inc., of Cambridge, and Theodore Barry, Inc., of Los Angeles, have performed expanded scope audits in the form of "management audits" requested by various regulatory commissions. Witness, for instance, the following quotations from the results of such an audit recently released by the Public Utility Commissioner of Oregon[4]:

One year ago, Public Utility Commissioner Charles Davis took office and immediately began to investigate whether the utilities under his jurisdiction were operating efficiently and

---

[4] From pages 1 and 2 of an announcement from the Office of the Public Utility Commissioner of Oregon dated April 21, 1976, releasing the response by the management of PGE to the Arthur D. Little Report. This form of audit report accompanied by management response is also employed by the GAO in the reports it releases.

properly using the money they collect from their customers. The management audit of Portland General Electric Company, released today, represents completion of a major phase of the Commissioner's investigation of one such company's operations. Similar investigations of other Oregon utilities are in progress.[5]

The nature of this management audit is then described as follows:

A "management audit" is one of many ways to evaluate a particular company's operations and efficiency. Management experts, technicians and business analysts closely observe a company's operations; interview its personnel, customers and public; review public and internal documents and analyze its organization and financial condition. The analysts review already recognized problems and, from their experience, recommend possible solutions. New problems uncovered by the audit also are reviewed and solutions suggested. The management auditor's broad experience permits comparisons with other companies similarly situated and makes available to the audited company suggestions for action which others previously have taken sucessfully.

Finally, the flavor of some of these audit findings may be gained from the following selected quotations from the same source:

The [ADL] report focuses on certain issues of major and immediate importance. ADL concludes PGE built the Trojan Nuclear Generating Plant efficiently, quickly, and, when compared to other similar plants nationwide, at relatively low cost. Similarly, ADL gives PGE high marks for its overall engineering and technical capability and for the operation of its distribution system. The PGE organization deserves credit for these faces to its operation.

On the other hand, the ADL audit raises serious questions as to some major projects which PGE presently has underway. . . . There is little record of whether PGE carefully or comprehensively justified these and other very expensive decisions, the cost of which it seeks to pass to its ratepayers. The Arthur D. Little report is very critical of this aspect of PGE's management and PUC team agrees with this criticism. PGE must realize that it will be required in the future to document rigorously the analysis which has led to its major decisions.

The elusive character of the third-party relation to persons who have had little experience with it is evidenced, however, by the following discussion of issues related to these reports (Rodgers and Smith, 1976, p. 5):

The A. D. Little report on PGE, like the consulting firms report on Con Edison, seems harsher than some audits ordered by utilities. William J. Kaffer, Vice President of Theodore Barry, says that his firm's utility audits involve close cooperation with management. "Before we give our findings to a commission, we want to get management thinking on the results," he says. He thinks Little takes more of an "adversary approach." Little Senior Vice President Hamilton R. James denies that, but he acknowledges that a management audit mandated by a utility commission—the results of which are to be made public—does not bring forth quite the same cooperation as an audit the company orders for itself. "We're not on a witch hunt," says James. "We're not trying to dwell on past mistakes except as they apply to conduct in the future. But it's a little more difficult with a commission-ordered study—there is more of an adversary relationship. We're viewed as tools of the commission."

This underscores our concern with a proper, third-party relationship.

[5] "At the Commissioner's direction, Theodore Barry, Inc., Los Angeles-based management consultants are reviewing Oregon's other large electric utility, Pacific Power & Light Company. Yankelovich, Skelley & White, Inc., a Connecticut opinion research firm, is concluding a major [opinion] survey of General Telephone Company of the Northwest's service quality. Similar studies and surveys of other utilities are planned."

Broadening Concepts of Accountability

It is not our purpose to discuss developments such as those described above in any great detail. We propose rather to use them only as a springboard for examining possible courses of future evolution in both auditing and accounting. Thus, having earlier observed the interrelatedness of accounting and auditing evolution, we turn next to some nascent developments in accounting and then return to auditing with the broadened perspective that an examination of these developments can allow.

Business enterprises have grown to a point where activities of some of the larger corporations involve economic magnitudes in the range of $40 to 50 billion of sales per year for each of them, a magnitude comparable to the gross national products of many nation states.[6] In potentially affected publics, this has produced the need for some sort of assurances, by means of expanded regulations, accountability, or both, that these enterprises will behave in a socially responsible way while pursuing their economic interests.

The topic of concern in this chapter naturally lends itself to the latter, that is, increased accountability as a possible alternative to regulation. The idea is to allow the fullest scope possible for business–economic conduct, while requiring management to justify any and all consequences of its acts—social as well as economic. Such a requirement must be accompanied by a correspondingly expanded system of accountability if this requirement is to be met. This will lead us back to the ideas of effectiveness and efficiency audits but in expanded dimensions for corporate social reporting in the private sector.[7]

Accounting and Corporate Social Reporting

Accounting (and hence auditing) has been organized around certain elementary concepts, sometimes taken as "primitives" in axiomatic approaches to accounting. In his monumental volume, *A Dictionary for Accountants* (1952), Eric Kohler introduced these kinds of ideas to accounting as part of his definition of "axioms":

> In an applied field, such as accounting, the axioms are identical with propositions which belong equally to other disciplines. Some of the axioms often employed in accounting reasoning are: (a) an economic unit has an identity apart from other economic units; (b) the life of a typical economic unit extends indefinitely into the future; (c) relations between economic units are carried on by means of identifiable,

---

[6]We do not deal with multinational firms as a separate issue since this raises a host of additional problems in both regulatory and accountability possibilities. See, for example, Kartte (1976). Of special interest here perhaps is the following quotation from Kartte (1976, p. 99), President of the Federal Cartel Office, Berlin: "A success [i.e., an advance in corporate accountability] was recorded with the decision of the Kammergericht (Superior Court of Justice) in proceedings against the British Petroleum oil group to the effect that in accordance with . . . GWB [Gesetz gegen Wettbewerbschränkungen = Act against Restraints of Competition], the cartel authority may demand information from a foreign group firm regarding any abuse on the domestic market, where necessary through the German subsidiary."

[7]This is not intended to deny the importance of audits for propriety, too, and, indeed, important steps in that direction are already being considered. See, for example, the discussions of auditor responsibilities for reporting illegal and questionable payments in AICPA (1978).

separable, and measurable transactions; (d) the transactions of an economic unit are expressed in terms of a common medium of exchange; (e) transactions, collectively, measure both economic wealth and economic activity.

In his book *Accounting for Management* (Kohler, 1965), Kohler came at the topic in a different way by explicitly delineating three elements "which are implicit in any scheme of accounting:

1. The entity—an independent fuctioning activity.
2. The transaction—an exchange between entities expressed in money terms.
3. The accounting period—the time period for which flows of transactions are measured, (pp. 10-11).

Although the fundamental "entity-transaction–accounting period" triad continues to be maintained, it is clear that Kohler's characterizations need to be modified if the purposes of corporate social reporting are to be served. In particular, the limitation of accounting to monetary and/or economic aspects of transactions needs to be augmented. If social impacts beyond the transacting entities are to be accommodated, for instance, then the requirements for accountability cannot be fulfilled without either (1) expanding the entity concept to cover all potentially affected segments of society or (2) expanding the nature of the reports to accommodate wider audiences than those who have heretofore been interested in an accounting in only monetary terms.

We here elect to follow the latter rather than the former course[8] since this choice (1) involves the least departure from past experience and (2) offers the most immediate prospect of successfully servicing the accountability requirements of various groups. Moreover, we propose to do this in a way that services a variety of new groups without in any way attenuating the considerable accomplishments that accounting has already attained in servicing the needs of such groups as investors and managers, whose interest is centered on accountability in the monetary units that Kohler uses in the definitions cited above. In brief, we propose to continue to regard these entities as being organized primarily for economic purposes but engaging in transactions on scales that have further social impacts of sufficient magnitude and importance so that an adequate accounting must then be concerned with "measuring and reporting the effects of economic activities of individual entities" (AICPA, 1978, p. xiii).

Thus, without denying that audited entities may be organized for the conduct of economic activities, this characterization extends accounting and hence auditing to measuring and reporting the additional effects of all such activities. Correspondingly, one may expect a variation in the kinds of reports that auditors may issue along with differences in the audiences to which they are rendered.

A Balanced Approach

The magnitude of the actions undertaken by many corporations, the innumerable effects they produce, and the

---

[8]Examples where the former course has been followed with consequent alterations in the entity concept are presented along with a variety of critical comments in Colantoni, Cooper, and Deitzer (1974).

large number of publics upon whom the effects fall make corporate social measurement an extraordinarily difficult task. One approach is to focus upon the social conditions that society views as important and to develop a "balanced picture" of a corporation's impact on these conditions. What are the positive effects if produced in this area; what are the negative ones; and what are the appropriate units of measurement and reporting? This is the approach put forth by the Committee on Social Measurement of the AICPA (AICPA, 1977). It involves:

1. The development of an agreed upon set of actions and impacts to be looked at.
2. The attributes of the impacts that must be commented upon or measured.
3. The measures that are appropriate to these attributes.
4. The possible attestation to these procedures by external auditors.

We would add to this a need for experiments with different kinds of auditor reports and auditor-management relations over time.

Some areas of interest for corporate social reporting lend themselves quite readily to such an approach. The results of equal employment opportunity policies in hiring and promotion can be recorded in terms of stocks (people of different categories in different jobs at the end of a period) and flows (hiring patterns in a period, promotion rates in a period) (see Churchill, 1977). Other areas are more difficult, as when the causal connection between corporate actions and their social impacts are remote or indirect or when desired evaluations involve abstruse concepts with vague and subjective meanings that are

difficult to interpret and apply. Examples of the former might involve the recruitment and training of employees (e.g., minority employees) by one entity whose skills are then exercised in another entity. Examples of the latter might involve concepts of quality of life in and out of the workplace which possess a subjective nature that varies from one entity and place to another. The consequences of other such corporate actions may well include inter-entity results that cannot readily be imputed to any one entity, as when, say, the simultaneous effects of pollution from several sources is harmful while the effects from any one of them alone is not.

As the AICPA's Committee on Social Measurement (AICPA, 1977) states:

1. Measurement of the important aspects of corporate social performance is difficult and anything that can be done in the near future is far from ideal.
2. In spite of the difficulties, a number of significant measurements can be made that can, from the outset, be used in reaching decisions within the corporation and communicating corporate actions to the outside world.
3. It is best to start measuring with a system that is less than ideal, but build in an informed way toward better future systems, and even toward attestation.

A Structured Approach

Another approach would begin with those aspects of corporate social performance which are relatively easy to identify and measure but which are, nonetheless, significant for developing a corporate social reporting format and its related audit and attest possibilities. This is not inconsistent with the approach suggested in the AICPA Committee on

TABLE 14-1

Economic Environment			Physical Environment			Social Environment					
Private		Public	Air	Water	Other	Employment					
Reve-nues and ex-penses ($)	Funds flow ($)	Value added to GNP ($)	Partic-ulate emis-sions (tons)	Acid dis-charge (gals.)	Soil removal and resto-ration (acre-feet)	Black		Women		Total	
						(% of total)	($)	(% of total)	($)	Man and woman years	($)

Social Measurement. It also need not be restricted to the kind of "laundry-list" reports (term from Churchill, 1974) that many corporations are now using for these purposes. In fact, a suitable systematization may be used as a basis for further revolution, as well as immediate use.

One such possibility for systematization may be depicted as shown in Table 14-1. This systematization, it should be observed, is intended to relate items to one another in a meaningful way. For instance, mathematical relations[9] that can be established between manufacturing volume and particulate emissions should be used to justify placing the latter on the same line as manufacturing cost in the statement of revenue and expense. Alternatively, if part of total employment is occasioned by sales activity—as distinguished from manufacturing—then these should also be aligned. The objective, in short, is to produce an *articulated* statement that can (1) add meaning to the various items

being reported as well as (2) provide a framework for future accounting evolution in these dimensions.

For the present we may observe that one reason for the way of proceeding suggested above is to ensure that accountability for corporate actions is being extended in significant and meaningfully accurate ways to audiences where an auditor deems that a relation of accountability needs to be served. Such relations of accountability are then to be accommodated within the *desiderata* noted above by restricting these reports to "auditable information" and then assigning to the auditor a duty of ensuring that the indicated relations of accountability are served in meaningful ways.

Note, for instance, that the component statements in Table 14-1 are not all stated in the same units, since each statement is to be couched in units that are naturally meaningful to the audiences being served. Thus, whereas the reports portrayed under "economic environ-

[9] See the discussion in the section entitled "Goal Programming Impact Analysis" in the chapter by Cooper and Ijiri.

ment" are, as usual, all stated in monetary units, this is not necessarily true for the other component statements. In any case, the statements are all intended to contain information of an auditable variety, starting with present capabilities but allowing for future extensions as progress in auditing and other technologies may admit.

These topics will be elaborated upon in the next section in terms of their auditing significance. In closing this section, however, we should perhaps underscore that the information above is all of a flow variety. We may, of course, allow for a variety of supporting exhibits in which stocks are also reported, such as, say, number of employees at a given grade or salary or in which an analysis of working-capital changes augments the flow of funds associated with current operations, and so on. We do not propose to go as far as to alter the balance sheet, however, since to do so will almost inevitably involve issues concerning the definition of the entity and the meaning of managerial and/or owner responsibility for its actions.

Auditing in the Future

Accountability for Past Actions

The increase in society's desire to hold organizations more accountable in broader ways for their performance will continue to have an impact on the way the audit function will evolve. The scope of audits will be broadened to new areas and made more comprehensive in their applications. The concerns for propriety, which have extended audits in the private sector to encompass "improper payments," is an example of such an expansion in scope. The experiments

with audits of "sensitive agencies," such as the GAO's audit of the FBI, is an example of extension to new areas.

The concern with corporate social accountability, which is more likely to increase than diminish with the growth of multi-billion-dollar corporations, will stimulate demands for the audit of social as well as financial reports by these entities. The fact that such reports may not be confined to ideal information may only mean that society will seek additional assurance. As the AICPA's Committee on Social Measurement stated (AICPA, 1977):

> The degree of credibility accorded a particular piece of information results primarily from what the reader knows about (1) the characteristics inherent in the information itself, (2) the availability of techniques for obtaining it, (3) its source, and (4) the extent of independent verification (p. 243).

Here we should extend these considerations to the possible effects on the auditee of the anticipation as well as the occurrence of an audit with respect to each of the four items we have just listed.

Besides accountability for the propriety of results achieved and actions taken, there is an increasing demand for accountability of the effectiveness and efficiency with which resources are used. This, as we have discussed in the first section, has taken place in the public sector at the federal level and is being extended to the state and local level as well. It is also becoming an important part of internal auditing within organizations in both the public and private sectors, and we believe this will continue to increase. The broadening of both the scope and purpose of audits will leave its impact on the methods and experience of auditors. The beginnings of a theory of audit quite separate from the theory of accounting is emerging and an increasing amount of research is being directed toward auditing in nonaccounting contexts. (See Churchill, *et al,* 1978.)

Accountability for Future Actions

Both the auditing and accounting, be it economic or social, discussed to this point have had as their base the historical record of past transactions. But the future need not be thus restricted. While initiating a search for audit criteria by reviewing company policies and board minutes or company manuals, the auditor (like the accountant) must look to the future to gauge the significance of the various criteria he or she might employ. Curiously, however, this has not usually included a review and audit of company budgets.

The budget is the instrument *par excellence* for what Eric Kohler referred to as "forward accounting" (Kohler, 1965):

Forward accounting is a device of modern management. It provides a major mechanism for planning, instituting, and controlling an organization's activities. Its function is to make possible two-way communication between levels of exercised authority by establishing operating standards against which performance is reported and critically reviewed. In the form of a skillfully devised budget it sharpens operating responsibilities, demands accountability from those operating under delegated authority, and assures planning that coordinates policy management competence, and technical skills (p. 186).

Together with its surrounding procedures, the company budget forms an important and convenient (almost ready-made) basis for the further expansion of auditing. Regardless of how management arrives at its decisions, the resulting bud-

get documents generally provide the best available evidence for proposed future courses of action. Moreover, since the budget serves as a control as well as a planning document, it also provides a basis for judging the "effectiveness" of company performance and evaluating the "efficiency" of its plans (these terms were defined on p. 229).

Many organizations have formulated a set of strategic plans or goals against which year-by-year plans or programs can be compared. In this comparison, the budget becomes the basis for evaluating an organization's ability to develop and make its strategic plans operational. The same budget then becomes the plan or set of "managerial expectations" that can serve as a basis against which to evaluate actual performance. This comparison of the budget with the record of subsequent events begins to provide a basis for determining a company's ability to attain its stated objectives—which, we may recall, constitutes one part of the definition of "effectiveness."

Of course, a marked deviation between "budget" and "actual" may occur as a result of developments in the external environment which are beyond the company's control. This, too, may enter into an evaluation of the effectiveness of the company's controls by reference to its ability to sense and adapt to such changes by duly revising pertinent parts of the budget within some reasonable interval of time. This is to say that this part of a company's planning system can also be audited and evaluated by reference to concrete events.

The ability to carry out its plans, as well as a company's ability to plan, thus constitutes auditable aspects of management effectiveness. There is, of course, a more difficult part of the effectiveness issue, at least as far as auditability is concerned, and that is management's ability to state its objectives, strategy, and goals.

This audit of the budget can be developed in the social area as well. Consider the formulation in Table 14–1 where economic and socially relevant "environments" are set forth. Plans for the future can be formulated in multiple dimensions utilizing models of a mathematical or computer variety which relate the economic, social, and environmental dimensions to one another. These models may also be subjected to audit and evaluation for third-party use. Properly formulated, these models should constitute an integral part of the planning process devised by management to guide its decisions so that, on the one hand, it can gauge the environmental and social consequences of its economic decisions and, on the other hand, it can reverse the process to determine the economic consequences of any program that might initially be considered for their social or environmental benefits.

Audit of this multidimensional budget, and the resulting statement of what occurred, must include an assessment as to whether the "correct" dimensions have been identified as well as the "correctness" of the magnitudes specified for the company's goals in them. In some dimensions (e.g., the economic dimension) there may be no problem, since long experience and a tradition common to almost all companies make it reasonably clear what is required.[10] In other dimensions, the situation is more ambiguous not only as to the kinds of evidence

to be considered but also with respect to the kinds of audiences to be serviced. Thus, a period of experimentation would seem to be required.

One possibility for such experiments is in the area of local government auditing, where, as observed earlier, an extension of GAO-type audits is already being considered (see the chapter by Brasfield). Another possibility is in the area of internal auditing, where companies are already moving (see Churchill et al., 1978). Although some have evolved very far in their audits of efficiency and effectiveness, none appear to have gone as far as we have suggested for audits in connection with an articulated system such as we have been describing. A development along these lines is much needed and should not be beyond the capacities of a profession which has evolved from the ancient concept of an auditus—a calling and hearing of ledger accounts—into the highly sophisticated GAO-type audits. For the business community as well as the public at large, this increased accountability may provide a new alternative to the "regulation versus nonregulation" discussions which seem to be almost the only form that considerations involving the control of business conduct is now taking. Not only is the profession of auditing involved in these developments, but so is the way business can be conducted. Disclosure, especially disclosure with the third-party orientation of the auditing profession, is an alternative with a promise that remains to be exploited in the future. It is a topic worthy of increased research.

---

[10] For further discussion of what is involved in the economic dimensions, see Cooper, Dopuch, and Keller (1968). See also Davidson et al. (1977).

References

American Institute of Certified Public Accountants. MAS Task Force on Evaluation of Efficiency and Program Results. 1976. *Guidelines for Participation in Government Audit Engagements to Evaluate Economy, Efficiency and Program Results,* Exposure Draft. New York: The American Institute of Certified Public Accountants, Inc.

——. Committee on Social Measurement. 1977. *The Measurement of Corporate Social Performance.* New York: The American Institute of Certified Public Accountants, Inc.

——. Commission on Auditor's Responsibilities. 1978. *Report, Conclusions, and Recommendations.* New York: The American Institute of Certified Public Accountants, Inc.

Churchill, Neil C. 1974. "Toward a Theory for Social Accounting." *Sloan Management Review,* Spring.

——. 1977. "Analyzing and Modelling Human Resource Flows," in *Conference Board, Monitoring the Human Resource System* (Conference Board Report No. 717). New York: The Conference Board, Inc.

Churchill, Neil C., W. W. Cooper, J. G. San Miguel, V. Govindarajan, and J. Pond. 1978. "Field Studies in Comprehensive Auditing and a Program for Research," in Symposium on Auditing Research, II. Urbana, Ill.: University of Illinois Department of Accountancy.

Colantoni, C. S., W. W. Cooper, and H. J. Deitzer. 1974. "Accounting and Social Reporting," in *Objectives of Financial Statements,* Vol. 2, Selected Papers. New York: The American Institute of Certified Public Accountants, Inc.

Cooper, W. W., N. Dopuch, and T. Keller. 1968. "Budgetary Disclosure and Other Suggestions for Improving Accounting Reports." *The Accounting Review,* October.

Davidson, S., D. O. Green, W. Hellerstein, A. Madansky, and R. Weil. 1977. *Financial Reporting by State and Local Government Units.* Chicago: The University of Chicago Center for the Management of Nonprofit Enterprise.

Herbert, Leo. 1979. *Performance Auditing.* Belmont, California: Lifetime Learning Publications.

Independent Review Committee. 1975. "Government Auditing in Other Countries." Appendix II in *Report of the Independent Review Committee on the Office of the Auditor General of Canada.* Ottawa.

Kartte, Wolfgang. 1976. "Are New Instruments Needed for Government Control of the Decision-Making Process in Multi-national Firms?" *The German Economic Review,* 14(2).

Kohler, Eric L. 1952. *A Dictionary for Accountants.* Englewood Cliffs, N.J.: Prentice-Hall, Inc.

——. 1965. *Accounting for Management.* Englewood Cliffs, N.J.: Prentice-Hall, Inc.

Rodgers, Paul, and J. Edward Smith, Jr. 1976. "A Survey of Management Audits of Utility Operation and Efficiency." Washington, D.C.: National Association of Regulation Commissioners.

Contributors

William W. Cooper

Dr. Cooper received his B.A. at the University of Chicago, his M.A. at Harvard, and his D.Sc. at Ohio State University, the last two being honorary degrees.

He is the Arthur Lowes Dickinson Professor of Accounting at Harvard University's Graduate School of Business Administration, where he also serves as the Special Field Coordinator for the DBA program in Planning, Accounting and Accountability Systems. Dr. Cooper is also Research Professor (on leave) at the School of Urban and Public Affairs at Carnegie-Mellon University, where he has also been the University Professor of Management Science and Public Policy, Dean of the School of Urban and Public Affairs, and one of the founding faculty of the Graduate School of Industrial Administration. He served as assistant to Eric Kohler at Arthur Andersen & Company, the Tennessee Valley Authority, and the Economic Cooperation Administration (Marshall Plan), and was Kohler's research assistant for *A Dictionary for Accountants* and on terminological and conceptual problems in the development of accounting principles.

Dr. Cooper was U.S. Bureau of the Budget Coordinator for the Federal Government's accounting statistics programs during World War II. He served as chairman of the interagency committee for the post-World War II program in accounting and financial statistics. While serving in the above government capacities, Dr. Cooper made extensive use of help from Eric Kohler and also used Kohler's services as consultant in developing the innovative quantitative control courses, combining accounting statistics and other quantitative approaches to management, for the new Graduate School of Industrial Administration at Carnegie Institute of Technology (now Carnegie-Mellon University).

He has been author or co-author and editor or co-editor of ten books and more than 200 scientific professional articles. The article "Costs, Prices and Profits—Accounting in the War Program," which Cooper co-authored with Eric Kohler in the 1945 *Accounting Review,* received the first American Institute of Accountants (now AICPA) award as the most valuable article on an accounting subject during that year.

Yuji Ijiri

Dr. Ijiri holds his bachelor of law degree from Ritsumeikan University, Japan, his Master of science in business from the University of Minnesota, and his Ph.D. in Industrial Administration from Carnegie-Mellon University.

He is Robert M. Trueblood Professor of Accounting and Economics at Carnegie-Mellon University's Graduate School of Industrial Administration. He received a CPA certificate in Japan, and worked in the Tokyo Office of Price Waterhouse & Co. Dr. Ijiri taught at the Stanford Graduate School of Business before accepting a faculty position at Carnegie-Mellon University in 1967 as Professor of Industrial Administration.

He is a member and former Vice President (1974–1975) of the American Accounting Association. He is also a member of the American Economic Association, the Econometric Society, the Financial Executives Institute, and

the International Association for Research in Income and Wealth.

A four-time winner of the Accounting Literature Award given annually by the American Institute of Certified Public Accountants, he has published five books and over sixty articles in professional journals on accounting, business, economics, management science, and statistics.

Andrew Barr

Mr. Barr holds his B.S. and M.S. from the University of Illinois, and a CPA certificate (Illinois).

After two years in public accounting, he taught accounting at Yale University for twelve years. He joined the staff of the Chief Accountant of the Securities and Exchange Commission (1938) and served in various capacities with increasing responsibilities, except for five years in the Army (1941–1946), retiring in January 1972 as Chief Accountant with over fifteen years in that position. Upon retirement, he was a visiting professor of accountancy at the University of Illinois and thereafter was a consultant on SEC accounting practice in the Washington Office of the American Institute of Certified Public Accountants.

Mr. Barr is a founding member of the Association of Government Accountants (formerly the Federal Government Accountants Association) of which he was President. He served as President of the Washington Chapter of the National Association of Accountants, Member-at-large of the Council, American Institute of Certified Public Accountants, and a member of the Financial Accounting

Standards Board Advisory Council from its inception to September 1976.

Carman George Blough

Carman Blough received his A.B. and LL.D. degrees from Manchester College, his M.A. from the University of Wisconsin, and his D.B.A. from Bridgewater College.

As the first Chief Accountant of the Securities and Exchange Commission, he had a major part in establishing the Commission's accounting policies and its administration of the acts under its jurisdiction. It was largely due to his early influence that the SEC has always recognized the importance of working with the leaders of the accounting profession, which in turn has brought pressure on the profession to take major responsibility for the elimination of many areas of differences in accounting practices. As a member of the Committee on Accounting Procedures and later of its successor, the Accounting Principles Board, Mr. Blough played an important part in helping to guide the profession into sounder practices.

After completion of his World War II service as Director of the Procurement Policy Division of the War Production Board, for which he had resigned his partnership in Arthur Anderson & Co., he became the first Director of Research of the American Institute of Certified Public Accountants on a full-time basis. In that capacity he worked with all the technical committees of the Institute, particularly with the committees of accounting and auditing procedures.

In addition to working with the committees, he addressed hundreds of meetings of accountants, bankers, and security analysts, reporting and explaining current accounting problems and the views of leaders in the profession regarding them. His monthly column, "Accounting and Auditing Problems" in the *Journal of Accountancy,* and his numerous other publications, along with his adjunct or visiting professorships at various universities, did much to promote the progress of accounting and to impress their importance both on those who prepare and those who use financial statements.

Karney A. Brasfield

Mr. Brasfield received his B.S. from Washington University, St. Louis, Missouri and later his CPA certificate (Arkansas). He is a senior partner (retired) of Touche Ross & Company and earlier served as Assistant to the U.S. Comptroller General, Controller of the Commodity Credit Corporation (USDA) and Comptroller of the Farm Credit Administration.

He has served as chairman of committees on Relations with Federal Government and Auditing for Federal Agencies, and was a member-at-large on the Council, all of the above with the American Institute of Certified Public Accountants. He is a founding member and past national President of the Association of Government Accountants, and a member of the American Accounting Association, the National Association of Accountants, and the District of Columbia Institute of Certified Public Accountants.

Neil Center Churchill

Dr. Churchill received his B.S. and MBA at the University of California, and hia Ph.D. at the University of Michigan.

He holds the Royal Little Professor of Business Administration at the Graduate School of Business Administration of Harvard University. Dr. Churchill holds a CPA certificate (California) and practiced public accounting with Haskins & Sells (1951-1953). He served as an instructor at San Diego State College (1954-1956), joined the faculty of the Carnegie Institute of Technology (1958), and was appointed to the faculty of Harvard University in 1967.

He is active in such professional societies as the American Institute of Certified Public Accountants.

His publications include frequent contributions to professional journals. He co-authored with M. Miller and R. Trueblood *Auditing, Accounting and Management Games;* with J. Kempster and M. Uretsky *Computer-Based Information Systems for Management: A Survey;* and with several other authors *The Measurement of Corporate Social Performance.*

Walter F. Frese

Professor Frese studied for his B.A. at the University of Iowa where he was elected to Phi Beta Kappa, and for his M.A. at the University of Illinois. He was awarded an honorary LL.D. from Southeastern University and an honorary M.A. from Harvard University.

He is the Arthur Lowes Dickinson Professor of Accounting Emeritus at the Harvard Business School. He joined the Harvard Business School faculty in 1956 after twenty years of federal government service. He was the first appointee to the Arthur Lowes Dickinson Professorship when it was established in 1969 and became Emeritus in 1972. He previously taught accounting at the University of Illinois (1928-1935 and 1937-1938) and served as Visiting Professor of Accounting in the Carman G. Blough Chair at the University of Virginia (1974-1975). He has also taught in numerous executive development programs in the United States and Europe. He served as Director of the Accounting Systems Division (1948-1956), U.S. General Accounting Office, and in 1956 he was appointed Director of the GAO's Accounting and Auditing Policy Staff. Professor Frese was with the U.S. Treasury Department (1935-1948), serving in a wide variety of assignments on the staff of the Commissioner of Accounts and the Fiscal Assistant Secretary of the Treasury. He was the head of the Fiscal Service Operations and Methods Staff (1944-1948).

He has served as consultant to many organizations and government agencies and for a number of years was a member of the Consultant Advisory Panel to the U.S. Comptroller General. He has received many awards for his contributions to improvements in financial management in the federal government, including the 1974 GAO Award for Public Service from the U.S. Comptroller General.

One of the founders and a Past President of the Federal Government Accountants Association (now Association of Government Accountants), Professor Frese has also served as a member of the Accounting Principles Board of the American Institute of Certified Public Accountants (1961-1967). He holds his CPA certificate from the State of Illinois.

Myron J. Gordon

Dr. Gordon received his B.A. at Wisconsin and his Ph.D. at Harvard University.

He is Professor of Finance at the University of Toronto, and previously held positions at Carnegie-Mellon University, Massachusetts Institute of Technology, and Rochester. He has held visiting appointments at University of California, Los Angeles, University of California, Berkeley, Hebrew University, and The Wharton School. Dr. Gordon has held various positions in the American Accounting Association and served as President of the American Finance Association.

Dr. Gordon has published over 50 articles on accounting, finance, and the economics of industrial organization, and was co-author with Gordon Shillinglaw of *Accounting: A Management Approach,* and author of *The Cost of Capital to a Public Utility* and *The Investment, Financing and Valuation of the Corporation.*

Robert K. Mautz

Robert Mautz received his B.S. from the University of North Dakota and his M.S. and Ph.D. from the University of Illinois. Dr. Mautz has been a partner in the National Office of Ernst & Ernst since 1972.

He was on the accounting faculty of the University of Illinois where he held the second Weldon Powell Memorial Professorship in Accounting (1969–1971).

He served as the President of the American Accounting Association and Editor of its *Accounting Review.* He was one of the original members of the Cost Accounting Standards Board.

Dr. Mautz has been a member of Council, member of the Board of Directors, Distinguished Visiting Professor, and member of several committees for the American Institute of Certified Public Accountants, as well as consultant for the General Accounting Office on several matters.

His publications include textbooks, research monographs, and articles in various professional periodicals.

Samuel Nakasian

Mr. Nakasian received his B.A. in Economics at New York University. He received his M.A. in Economics and Finance and completed his Ph. D. residency requirements in Economics at Columbia University, and received his LL.B. at Georgetown University Law School.

He is currently a negotiator, lawyer, and economist, and lectures at various universities while maintaining a private practice. He is consultant and negotiator with principal responsibility for negotiating oil and mineral concessions and supply contracts for American companies in Libya, Iraq, Pakistan, Algeria, Venezuela, Argentina, and Korea.

He holds memberships in the New York State Bar Association, the American Arbitration Association, the District of Columbia Bar, and is admitted to practice before the Supreme Court of the United States.

Mr. Nakasian's publications include "The Security of Foreign Petroleum

Resources," *Political Science Quarterly;* "The Anglo-Iranian Oil Case, A Problem in International Judicial Processes," *Georgetown Law Journal:* "Prices via Costs," *Chemical Week:* "Manufacturers' Problems Under Price Controls," *Harvard Business Review;* and has contributed to various other publications, including Eric Kohler's *A Dictionary for Accountants.*

Joseph Pois

Dr. Pois holds his A.B. from the University of Wisconsin, his M.A. and Ph.D. from the University of Chicago, and his J.D. from the Chicago Kent College of Law.

He is Professor Emeritus of Public Administration in the Graduate School of Public and International Affairs at the University of Pittsburgh, where he has served as Chairman of the Public Administration Department and as Associate Dean of the School. He served formerly as a staff member with the J. L. Jacobs and Company and with the Public Administration Service, as Chief, Administrative and Fiscal Reorganization Section, U.S. Bureau of the Budget, as Company Counsel and subsequently Vice President, Treasurer, and Director of the Signode Corporation, and as Director of Finance of the State of Illinois.

He has been a member of the Chicago and Pittsburgh Boards of Education and a member of the Consultant Panel of the U.S. Comptroller General. Dr. Pois holds membership in the Allegheny County (Pennsylvania) Bar Association, the American Academy of Political and Social Science, the American Accounting Association, the American Society for Public Administration, the Chicago Bar Association, the Federal Bar Association, the Financial Executives Institute, the National Association of Accountants, and the Royal Institute of Public Administration (Great Britain).

Among Dr. Pois' publications are "Trends in General Accounting Office Audits" (Chapter Three in *The New Political Economy* by Bruce L. R. Smith); "The General Accounting Office as a Congressional Resource" (included in *Congressional Support Agencies* published by The Commission on the Operation of the Senate); *The School Board Crisis: A Chicago Case Study;* "Personnel Implications of New York City's Budget Process" (included as an appendix in *Professional Personnel for the City of New York* by David T. Stanley); *Financial Administration in the* Michigan State Government; *Kentucky Handbook of Financial Administration; Public Personnel Administration in the City of Cincinnati;* and (with Edward M. Martin and Lyman S. Moore) *The Merit System in Illinois.*

His long-standing friendship with Eric Kohler began early in Pois' career when Kohler became interested in the work which the Jacobs Company was doing during the 1930's to improve the City of Chicago's financial practices and procedures. Later, both served as fellow officers of the City Club of Chicago.

Gary John Previts

Dr. Previts holds a bachelor's degree in business administration Magna Cum Laude, from John Carroll University, a Master's Degree in Accounting from The Ohio State University, and a Ph.D. in Economics and Accounting from the University of Florida.

He is presently a Professor of Accounting at the University of Alabama, and has been a visiting faculty member at Northwestern University as well as a staff member and consultant to various accounting firms.

A past president of The Academy of Accounting Historians, Dr. Previts has written extensively on the subject of accounting history. Among his publications are *Early 20th Century Developments in American Accounting Thought: A Pre-Classical School* and *A History of Accounting in America,* with Barbara Merino. He is also co-editor of *The Accounting Historians Journal.*

Jerry F. Stone

Mr. Stone attended Washington & Lee University, and the University of Tennessee.

After seven years of public accounting, Mr. Stone became one of the first members of the accounting staff of the Tennessee Valley Authority, and was engaged in systems development. He later served as head of a procedural audit section examining payroll, inventory, cash receipts, and general accounting procedures in all TVA offices, thereby gaining an intimate knowledge of the operations and strengths and weaknesses of the organization. This proved valuable to Eric Kohler when he arrived as Comptroller. Subsequently, Stone became Kohler's principal assistant in all phases of the development of the accounting system and the reporting methods, from internal accounting and reporting design to the synthesis of external financial statements.

During his early years with the TVA, Mr. Stone was assigned temporarily to the Electric Home and Farm Authority to assist in the organization and operation of this sales finance company which purchased dealer paper arising from consumers of major electric appliances, all to promote the use of electricity.

Upon Eric Kohler's recommendation, Stone became Special Assistant for Finance in the War Shipping Administration and was responsible for budgets and accounting, reporting directly to the Administrator of the WSA.

After service with the TVA and the WSA, Mr. Stone developed his own mortgage banking and consumer finance business and also served as a consultant to other finance companies.

He is currently with Fitch Investors Service where, as vice president in charge of rating commercial paper, he developed this service for rating the commercial paper of all types of enterprises, including bank holding companies, finance companies, public utilities, industrial, and mercantile organizations. This business has been extended to international activities with involvements in Swiss bank holding companies and foreign automobile manufacturers.

Herbert F. Taggart

Dr. Taggart received his A.B., M.A., and Ph.D. from the University of Michigan and holds his CPA certificate in the state of Michigan.

He is presently Emeritus Professor of Accounting, Graduate School of Business Administration, University of Michigan. Previously Dr. Taggart was a faculty member of the University of Michigan (1920-1967), the University of Kansas, Arizona State University, Emory University, and Eastern Michigan University. His government service includes positions as Chief, Cost Accounting Unit of the National Recovery Administration (1933-1935); Consultant on Distribution Costs for the U.S. Department of Commerce (1938); Director of Accounting and Assistant Administrator, Office of Price Administration (1940-1943); Major and Lt. Col., Finance Department, U.S. Army (1943-1946); Member, Advisory Board on Contract Appeals, Atomic Energy Commission (1949-1959); and Chairman, Advisory Committee on Cost Justification, Federal Trade Commission (1953-1956). In his private practice, Dr. Taggart has served as advisor to and expert witness for many industrial companies and departments of the federal government on matters concerning the relation of costs to prices, including commodities, airmail rates, and income tax problems.

His professional affiliations include service as President of the Washington Chapter (1945) and National Director (1947-1948) of the National Association of Cost Accounts, and President (1942) of the American Accounting Association, preceded by service as Director of Research.

Dr. Taggart was a longtime friend of Eric Kohler. His professional contacts with Kohler came principally while he was Director of Research for the American Accounting Association.